GUILTY ADMISSIONS

ALSO BY NICOLE LAPORTE

The Men Who Would Be King:
Movies, Moguls, and a Company Called DreamWorks

GUILTY ADMISSIONS

THE BRIBES, FAVORS, AND PHONIES BEHIND
THE COLLEGE CHEATING SCANDAL

NICOLE LaPORTE

TWELVE

New York Boston

Twelve
Hachette Book Group
1290 Avenue of the Americas, New York, NY 10104
twelvebooks.com
twitter.com/twelvebooks

First Edition: February 2021

Twelve is an imprint of Grand Central Publishing. The Twelve name and logo are trademarks of Hachette Book Group, Inc.

The publisher is not responsible for websites (or their content) that are not owned by the publisher.

The Hachette Speakers Bureau provides a wide range of authors for speaking events. To find out more, go to www.hachettespeakersbureau.com or call (866) 376-6591.

Photos from the *Sacramento Bee* © 2020 McClatchy. All rights reserved. Used under license.

Library of Congress Control Number: 2020938839

ISBNs: 978-1-5387-1709-7 (hardcover), 978-1-5387-1708-0 (ebook)

Printed in the United States of America

LSC-C

Printing 1, 2021

For Alexei & Katrina

Contents

Those who have power ought not exercise it wrongfully. Nor when they are fortunate should they imagine that they will be so forever.

—Euripedes (engraved on a statue of Hecuba at the University of Southern California)

CHAPTER 1

College Night Terror

One fall evening in 2016, Frank Bruni, the author and *New York Times* op-ed columnist, took to the stage of the auditorium at Harvard-Westlake School in Los Angeles. Bruni had come to the elite institution, whose forebears proudly proclaimed it "the leading prep school west of the Charles River," to talk about his book *Where You Go Is Not Who You'll Be*. The presentation was part of the school's annual Senior College Night, when parents of students in the senior class gather to have the mysterious and often infuriating process of applying to college demystified.

Harvard-Westlake's upper-school campus sits in the craggy foothills of Coldwater Canyon, a sylvan corner of the city where luxury SUVs careen down winding, wooded roads that splinter off into cul-de-sacs dotted with midcentury architectural masterpieces wedged into the mountainside—or leaning against it on terrifying one-hundred-foot stilts. Here, nature and wealth seamlessly coexist in a kind of stubborn harmony. If you can dream it, you can build it, mudslides and gravity be damned. Situated less precariously, at the foot of the canyon, Harvard-Westlake brings an old-world vibe to these distinctly LA environs. The school—which was originally the all-boys Harvard School—moved to the site in 1937, marking the territory with a Tudor-style chapel that was a replica of a chapel at Rugby School in England. Harvard's founders built its version in 1914, and when the school made the move from another area in the city to Coldwater Canyon, the sanctuary was dragged across town in sixteen pieces. The chapel still stands proudly as a reminder of Harvard-Westlake's aspirational ties to blue-blooded prep schools farther east.

But if Harvard-Westlake originally functioned as a finishing school for young white Protestant males—who dined on lobster Newburg and caught glimpses of Clark Gable trotting across campus on horseback—today the school, which is much more ethnically if not economically diverse, is considered a rocket launcher to twenty-first-century success. "It's the ultimate bumper-sticker school," declared one LA parent. Gettys, Fairbankses, and Gyllenhaals have all received diplomas from Harvard-Westlake, whose handsome red-roofed campus has led some to dub it a "mini Stanford."

The comparison goes beyond physical attributes. More so than any other school in LA, Harvard-Westlake is proudly steeped in the religions of rigor and working your ass off. Some view it more as a corporation than a place of higher learning. The school's top administrator carries the title of president, along with the more folksy "head of school" moniker adopted by other private schools in the area. Students slog through hours of homework a night in their college-level literary theory and microeconomics courses, and scoff at more progressive institutions across town, like Crossroads School, where there are no AP offerings and academia is considered just one part of a holistic journey. Until recently, a lunch break wasn't mandatory at Harvard-Westlake, meaning many kids would eat on the run, in order to keep grinding. "Type A on steroids" is how one Harvard-Westlake parent described

2

the school's ethos. "Everyone is competing with each other, and people are determined to win."

Bruni's talk was part of the school's effort to calm nerves and send the message that life isn't, in fact, all about winning—specifically when it comes to getting into college. His book, after all, was a rebuke of the notion that success in life is dependent on an Ivy League degree. So what if your kid didn't get into Princeton? His research had proven that reams of highly successful people—former US secretary of state Condoleezza Rice; former Starbucks CEO Howard Schultz; and Doug McMillon, CEO of Walmart—were doing just fine without an Ivy League diploma. What mattered, he told the crowd that evening, is the experience kids have wherever they wind up, not to mention their family and personal relationships and the communities they involve themselves in; all of this is far more important when it comes to crafting an identity and sense of self than a sweatshirt bearing the name of a prestigious college.

There are places where this message might be embraced and celebrated, where the idea of sending a child off to one of the "Colleges That Change Lives"—as former *New York Times* education editor Loren Pope dubbed intellectually stimulating but obscure colleges such as Goucher and Hope—would be considered sound advice. But Harvard-Westlake, which has an annual tuition of $39,700 and is populated by the offspring of the city's top entertainment executives, attorneys, and business titans, is not one of them.

As one parent who was in attendance that night put it: "Everyone's sitting there like, 'I pay forty thousand a year, and my kid kills himself doing the work.' Nobody wants to hear that Wash U is a fantastic place. It's Harvard, Harvard, Harvard. *Maybe* Princeton."

This mind-set, which dominates the elite world of LA education, explains why the city was the epicenter of the Varsity Blues scandal, which broke in March of 2019, and why parents here were so easily swindled by a con man. Dubbed "the biggest college admissions fraud of all time," the scandal was masterminded by William "Rick" Singer, an independent college counselor based just south of Los Angeles, in Newport Beach, California, who used bribery and fake athletic profiles to get students admitted to such universities as Yale, Georgetown, and the University of Southern California. Criminal charges so far have been brought against forty parents, including actresses Felicity Huffman and Lori Loughlin— the latter paid $500,000 to get her two daughters into USC as fake crew recruits—and has reverberated nationwide ever since.

Harvard-Westlake has not been implicated as part of Varsity Blues, but prominent parents at the school hired Singer for his (legitimate) services and recommended him to others. Indeed, the school, along with a handful of other top private academies in Southern California—where more than a dozen of the charged parents reside—provides a lens through which to examine the culture that exists surrounding college admissions in the wealthiest, most privileged pockets of the country. By peeling back the layers of this culture, one begins to grasp why many of these parents went to the lengths they did, and why they risked so much—including jail terms—in order to get their children into the right college.

Los Angeles, specifically, is a microcosm where extreme wealth and ambition collide, undercut by a shamelessly transactional attitude toward business—including the business of education. This is a place, after all, where money is freely dispensed to procure yet another upgrade or VIP experience and where there's always a way to grind out more favorable deal points. Indeed, "pay or play" is a widely accepted contract stipulation. "LA appreciates the game of it," said one former private-school administrator. "Their whole take on it is, 'Let's just try to best the game. Let's try to figure out where the pressure is.' Because they do this on everything. They do this when they negotiate film contracts. They do it when they're trying to add on to their house that they're trying to show off. Everything is a deal."

In top LA private high schools, the game for parents is getting their kids into a top college. Parents tackle it the way they do everything else in their lives: by winning favor with Important People—like the head of school and the members of a school's board. They throw around their checkbooks to gain influence. A big enough donation, many believe, will put a child on the radar of the board, whose high-profile members will scour their contacts when it comes time to apply to college and make calls on the child's behalf. Even a reasonable gift will procure an invitation to a private cocktail party at the head of school's house, an evening that will not be forgotten when college applications are due. Expensive gifts are lavished on teachers (iPads, trips to Paris), and private pitching coaches are hired to work with the school's baseball team—all to make it clear which parents have VIP status and which offspring need special care come college application time.

The elite schools, meanwhile, play into this, all but demanding "donations" and other acts of "giving" as soon as a child is accepted. At Harvard-Westlake (as at most private schools in LA), the letter each family receives requesting an annual donation, which the school stipulates is necessary to provide all of its outstanding services and resources (as well as to provide financial aid for students), often specifies an amount that's expected. This systemic fundraising has helped Harvard-Westlake become a leader in annual giving— just shy of $10 million a year. According to IRS filings, the school's assets are worth $419 million. Its revenue in 2019 was $116 million.

The practice of donating money to schools is a key factor in the Varsity Blues case. In some cases Rick Singer told parents to write checks to universities their children were applying to as part of his scheme; the money went to funds overseen by coaches and administrators who have been charged in the crime. Parents who are fighting the charges claim that their payments were just that— a donation, not a bribe. One parent told me that when Singer brought up the idea of making a donation, it didn't seem strange. "We've been writing checks to schools since our kids were in elementary school," this person said.

Schools like Harvard-Westlake do "not conceal the fact that they want to raise as much money as possible from as many people as possible," said a Harvard-Westlake parent. "Like any other organization, they're constantly saying that tuition isn't enough to provide everything that you guys want, so we need annual donations. And it starts right away. Like, literally right after you get your admissions letter.

"A lot of people try to put in their annual donations before they receive that letter," the parent added. Otherwise, they run the risk of looking like they're not doing what's expected if they give lower than the requested amount.

Public accolades for these acts of "generosity" come in the form of the school's annual report, which is sent out to the community and which groups families into elite circles based on how generous they've been. Members of the Dean's Circle contributed between $3,500 and $7,499; Leadership Circle members ponied up between $25,000 and $49,999; and those who are part of the vaunted Heritage Circle gave over $100,000. Important note: Anyone who gives at least $7,500 scores an invite to the annual President's Reception.

Less overt fundraising comes in the form of so-called Party Books. Organized and paid for by parents, who serve as hosts, Party Book events are thrown throughout the year, typically at the homes of wealthy parents who can afford to shell out for a fully catered meal or private whiskey tasting, not to mention valet parking services, for dozens of fellow parents. The money raised by selling tickets to the event all goes to the school, making Party Books a painless and efficient fundraising tool. "They provide a nice little chunk of change for the school, which basically has to do nothing," said Christina Simon, the coauthor of *Beyond the Brochure: An Insider's Guide to Private Elementary Schools in Los Angeles*.

Party Books are a way to flaunt wealth and influence, as well as make inroads at a school, which often approaches its A-list parents about opening up their lavish pads. A recent list of Harvard-Westlake's Party Book lineup reads like a Hollywood red carpet calendar: a dinner catered by hip, LA chef-restauranteurs Jon Shook and Vinny Dotolo—the owners of Animal and Trois Mec—at the home of Will Ferrell and his wife, Viveca Paulin-Ferrell ($300 a ticket); a private dinner at Spago hosted by Wolfgang Puck ($500); a movie screening and meal at the home of Jeff Shell, the CEO of NBCUniversal ($500); and a truffle dinner at Il Pastaio hosted by its chef and co-owner Giacomino Drago ($500).

When Party Book listings go up, parents scramble to sign up, lest they be relegated to the dreaded wait list, while at the same time fretting about how many people they'll actually know at the A-list soirees. They can be stressful for hosts, too. There was the studio executive parent who planned a Party Book screening of an upcoming movie from her studio. Only word got out that the movie was a dud, and no one signed up—which was glaringly evident on the Party Book website—so the executive canceled the event.

Party Books fuel the keeping-up-with-the-Joneses culture at private schools in Los Angeles, including the pressure to be able to say that a child will be attending a prestigious college. Some kids cringe at the very mention of a Party Book, knowing that their futures will be discussed over passed crudités, and beg their parents not to attend. Their parents, meanwhile, know exactly what they're getting into. One dad called them "a cesspool of insecurity. It's where parents mingle and talk about colleges—where their kid is going. On the drive home, there's a lot of 'Can you believe that idiot got into wherever.'"

Then there are the gala fundraisers, where items and experiences, such as a weekend getaway to another parent's private island off Fiji for $50,000, are auctioned off. A VIP parking spot for pickup and drop-off might be worth $30,000. "We just bought a ticket to the gala. I don't know if we're going to go," said one parent with children at the Buckley School. "It truly is an endless series of checks that you write. I feel like this is a racket on some level, and I don't know what I'm going to get out of it. Will they pay extra close attention to [my child]? Will they make the call for him?" She hasn't asked. Yet she continues to write checks, assuming, praying, there is a causal relationship at work.

Things work smoothly . . . until they don't. When the child gets a wait-list letter, or is flat-out denied admission to his or her school of choice, the shit hits the fan (as is customary in the see-and-be-seen, scream-and-be-heard culture of the entertainment business). Or even before that, if a student receives a B in a class—which in today's unforgiving college admissions environment means you can forget the Ivy League—parents will call in the teacher and even the headmaster and cry foul, and then do what they can to have the grade changed. Tales of unhappy parents (i.e., the school's clients) are endless. There was the dad who threatened to sue a private high school when his child didn't get into their college of choice. There were the parents who campaigned to have a guidance counselor fired because the counselor wasn't getting what the parents deemed were good enough college results. And then there was the director who was called over Christmas break and told to do something about the boy who wouldn't come out of his room because he didn't get in early admission to his school of choice. In other words, the director should make some calls—now.

"People think it's a service," said Caitlin Flanagan, the *Atlantic* writer who worked as a guidance counselor at Harvard-Westlake in the 1990s. "It's like they're flying in the first-class [cabin] of the plane now. Not business. Not economy. They're in first class. They want the best coffee, the best cocktail, the best sweet. But the thing is, when college counseling comes, your kid might get sent back to the back row by the lavatories. And they're outraged! 'I paid for first class! Why is my kid sitting by the overflowing lavatory?'"

Flanagan recalled the time that a father showed up in her office after his son was denied admission to Yale. The father was a Yale alum, and his older son had gotten into the school. He was fuming that the trend hadn't continued with his second son. "The father was screaming, 'It's his turn to go to Yale!'" Flanagan said, chuckling. "It's like, well, I don't think Yale has turns."

Flanagan quickly learned, as she wrote pithily in the *Atlantic*, that Harvard-Westlake's "impressive matriculation list was not the simple by-product of excellent teaching, but was in fact the end result of parental campaigns undertaken with the same level of whimsy with which the Japanese Navy bombed Pearl Harbor."

Until recently, these campaigns were surefire strategies. With enough meticulous planning and access to artillery—in the form of connections and money—entree into a top college was all but guaranteed for the privileged class (unhappy Yale dads notwithstanding). Legacies and kids whose parents could write fat checks toward a college's endowment or a new library wing were all but escorted through the gates of these higher learning institutions. One former admissions officer at an Ivy League school said that the acceptance rate for "tagged" applicants could rise as high as 60 percent (in comparison to the school's single-digit acceptance rate for regular applicants). Tagged students include development cases (students of parents with a prior donation or the potential to donate), political cases (where a politician or highly influential community member is advocating for a student), VIP cases (the child of a celebrity), and trustee cases (a member of the board of trustees is advocating for a child), as well as legacies and children of staff, to a lesser extent. As for recruited athletes, this person said that the acceptance rate can rise as high as 100 percent.

Tagged kids generally have access to endless forms of preparatory services and tutors to help burnish their applications and transcripts, setting them yet further apart from less monied applicants. This favoring system is far from dead. Yet in speaking to dozens of parents at the most elite schools in LA, some of which—such as Buckley School, Marymount High School, Loyola High School, Marlborough School, Campbell Hall, and Brentwood School—have had students whose parents were charged in the Varsity Blues scandal, it's clear that a distinct anxiety has settled on the upper classes when it comes to getting their kids into college. There is a gnawing frustration that a system that was previously unfair but ultimately possible to manipulate—no one ever believed that college admissions was the meritocracy it's proclaimed itself to be—has become both opaque and unknowable.

The reasons why are fairly clear: With more and more students applying to schools whose freshman classes aren't getting any bigger, college acceptance numbers are plummeting. Stanford's admission percentage is now so low—4 percent—that it no longer bothers announcing it. Meanwhile, colleges have made it a priority to enroll more first-generation and underrepresented minority students in order to better reflect the country's demographics. Multicultural "fly-in" programs, where high-achieving seniors from low-income and minority households are flown in for a campus tour, are now de rigueur. This shift has sent privileged parents into a tailspin, worrying that their accolade-drenched white kid from an academically rigorous school has become a tad, well, boring, in the eyes of an admissions officer. As the former private-school administrator said, "We started to hear that our students weren't that interesting. And that if you're going to be a white girl from Beverly Hills who has a 4.0 and did horseback riding, you better have something to say. It better be a really fresh, original voice. Because Stanford doesn't need another white girl who rides equestrian *okay*."

"That's a bitter, bitter thing for a child to realize," this person continued. "But the parents' reaction was always more severe: '*How dare they?*'"

One student at Harvard-Westlake admitted to being embarrassed to list horseback riding on her application due to this very fear.

With the sense that the drawbridge is closing, suddenly things like legacy status or the ability to donate a library wing no longer feel like guarantees for the privileged class. As for kids who are simply working their butts off? It seems no one cares. A constant refrain among some private-school parents is how good old-fashioned hard work, monitored in the perfectly calibrated setting of a place like Harvard-Westlake, now gets you nowhere.

The feeling, in short, is that nothing is enough.

"To be a white kid from a private high school in LA—my daughter would come home and say, 'We have nothing. We're not diverse. We've never had a parent die. We don't have to support

11

ourselves,'" said a parent at Campbell Hall, a tony school in the San Fernando Valley. (The son of one of the indicted parents in the Varsity Blues scandal, Adam Semprevivo, graduated from the school and went on to Georgetown, thanks to Rick Singer, who sold him as a tennis recruit.)

One former Harvard-Westlake parent told me that when her daughter was a senior and applying to an Ivy League school where her father had gone, her dean told her that she had no shot. "She came home and said, 'Why would they want another little Jewish girl?' She wasn't particularly resentful. She was just sort of honest."

Asian Americans at top private schools feel a similar sense of despair, as came to light in a federal lawsuit against Harvard by a group of students who were rejected by the university. The suit accused the university of discriminating against Asian American applicants. Although the judge ruled against the case in 2019, filings in the lawsuit revealed that while Asian Americans often had higher test scores than other minority students and white students, they were penalized for coming up shorter on soft skills, like leadership and grit. The feeling that lingers among Asian American parents is that their kids get lumped into a bucket—smart, hardworking students who are stereotypical grinders—and therefore have to do more to distinguish themselves to admissions officers. "Parents feel that everything is negatively prejudiced against Asian kids," said one parent. "It's like Jews in the fifties. 'They won't let us in.' There's a lot of anger there." There are also simply larger percentages of Asian Americans at elite private schools in comparison to other minorities, creating a numbers crunch. How many from each school will, say, Stanford, accept? (In the Varsity Blues case, one indicted parent is Asian American, I-Hsin "Joey" Chen, who has pled not guilty. Three parents are Chinese nationals—one has been sentenced and two have not been charged.)

This pinpoints the real issue that's underway: Families at schools like Harvard-Westlake aren't bemoaning how hard it is to get into college; they're bemoaning how hard it is to get into certain colleges, i.e., status schools that they themselves in many cases attended. "These parents are stressing because they have their ambition set on only a handful of colleges," said one former Ivy League admissions officer. "So if their kid doesn't get into an Ivy or a Stanford or a Duke or a Georgetown…They're just focused on that small number of schools. But less prestigious schools would do anything to get those students."

The question is, how much of this agita is valid? Harvard-Westlake's track record for placing kids in top institutions remains intact. Between 2014 and 2019, the school sent fifty-one students to Harvard, forty-four to the University of Pennsylvania, thirty-six to Stanford, and twenty-four to Yale. These stats underscore a reality that parents don't generally mention: For all of universities' interest in diversifying their ranks, the great majority of them need families who can pay full tuition in order to support that mission. Private high schools are a reliable supplier of such families. Data backs up the notion that things have not changed all that dramatically. In Paul Tough's book *The Years That Matter Most: How College Makes or Breaks Us*, he describes how in 2017 a group of economists at Stanford studied data proving that the most selective colleges in the United States were the least socioeconomically diverse. At Yale, for instance, only 2.1 percent of the student body came from the bottom fifth of the income distribution ladder. For a broader statistic, and to look at it from the other side, consider that more than two-thirds of Ivy League students come from the top 20 percent of the income scale. At Dartmouth, Princeton, Yale, Penn, and Brown, more kids come from the top 1 percent than from the entire bottom 60 percent of the country.

Most of the parents I have interviewed—most preferred to speak off the record for fear of facing retribution from the schools where their children were enrolled—are self-aware about their woe-is-me railing against what they ultimately feel is a form of reverse discrimination. Indeed, most of these parents, who are overwhelmingly liberal Democrats with a strong social-justice bent, outwardly applaud schools' efforts to admit a more diverse student body, genuinely believing it is for the greater good of the campus and society overall. They are completely down with it, in fact—until they feel it affects their own child's chances of getting in.

Julie Lythcott-Haims, a former Stanford dean and the author of *How to Raise an Adult: Break Free of the Overparenting Trap and Prepare Your Kid for Success*, said that the panic of these parents comes down to their fear of losing a privilege that they have long taken for granted. "As America becomes more diverse, I think white parents are losing their toehold on exclusive experiences," Lythcott-Haims, who is Black, told me. She noted that as private prep schools and colleges have evolved over the years from elite bastions for white Protestants into campuses that now are striving to "reflect the diversity of America," it's coming as a shock to people who have always assumed that a degree from a top college was a given. "Colleges have been saying for some time now, 'Hey, we want Black and Brown kids, too. And we want Asians, too.' And I think that's making white people terrified, because they're losing a privilege that they never realized was a privilege."

Ned Johnson, the go-to independent college counselor among hypercompetitive families in the Washington, D.C., area, and the president of the tutoring company PrepMatters, said parents of kids at elite high schools feel "a lower sense of control because it used to be that if you went to Andover or Exeter or whatever, two generations ago, the director could call up Harvard or Columbia and say, 'Here are the boys that you want.' There were these relationships between the best independent schools, or even the best public schools, with this or that university. And that is so, so, so far gone. So a lot of the perceived power or control of the very well-to-do has been diminished.

"It's been diminished because in many ways colleges are trying to create greater access for women, for lower-income people, and for people of color—not just for WASPy people from Connecticut. And I'm one of those so I can say these things. So it's become much more diverse socioeconomically, ethnically, and so on. But in many ways a lot of this has come at the 'expense' of white, rich people. And they don't like it and it stresses them out."

On a more micro level, wealthy parents' sense of injustice stems from the feeling that schools like Harvard-Westlake are failing them simply because they are so excellent. Several parents said that because there were so many high academic achievers at the school—most of whom were from similar backgrounds and were applying to the same ten schools—their child had a tougher case to make to colleges. The sense is that all of these type A kids are battling it out for a certain number of slots, and so some will, inevitably, not make the cut, whereas if their child were at a less demanding private school, or even—God forbid—a public school, they'd be the standout valedictorian and would have their choice of top schools. Furthermore, they believe that college admissions officers assume that kids from Harvard-Westlake had all the help they could get in the form of private tutors, test-prep courses, and access to a wide range of activities and experiences—internships at Hollywood movie studios, character-building summer camps in Costa Rica, building houses for the poor, not to mention the freedom to be able to study and not hold down a part-time job—

so they would ultimately be held to a higher standard than kids who didn't have these luxuries.

"If you get a fifteen hundred on the SAT and went to Harvard-Westlake, and some kid from LA High got the same score, the assumption is the Harvard-Westlake kid spent tens of thousands of dollars for tutors, extra time, whatever, so it's a threshold issue," said one parent. "If you don't have a great score, [admissions officers] are like, 'What the fuck happened?'"

When one kid suddenly transferred from Harvard-Westlake to a less competitive school their sophomore or junior year, there was immediately chatter that the family was trying to game the system, this parent said. "There aren't that many idiots at Harvard-Westlake," the parent told me. "All of the kids there work really hard and are really academic. Every kid is doing hours and hours of homework. They have to be really disciplined. I would say there are definitely more kids at Harvard-Westlake that are capable of doing college-level work. But the fact is, you have a really smart kid with a four-point-three GPA [a 'weighted' GPA, taking into account the difficulty of AP and honors classes, which goes up to five] and that kid is still trying to get into Emory. The conversation at Harvard-Westlake is not 'Should my kid be working harder?' It's 'Would my kid be better off going to Crossroads?'"

❧

This anxiety isn't limited to wealthy parents living in Bel-Air or Beverly Hills. It's an endemic that's become a universal among almost all parents who plan to send their child off to a four-year institution in the hopes of launching them successfully into the world. Indeed, for middle-class families, who don't have a cushion of wealth and resources to fall back on, one of the most significant rites of passage for an American teen has become fraught with fear. The fear stems from the extreme wealth divide in our country, and the belief that simply getting a college degree—any college degree—no longer implies upward mobility the way it once did. Given the current state of affairs in the United States—the endless headlines about burdensome student debt, the high cost of living, and the growing unemployment rate for college graduates—the desire for an impressive college degree is not just a lofty wish; it's a do-or-die imperative.

As Frank Bruni told me, "You can't divorce this from a climate in which income inequality is so severe and the stakes of landing on the right or wrong [side of that] are higher than ever. You can't divorce this from the economic landscape.

"This is no longer an America where the assumption is that the pie will keep getting bigger. In this climate of pessimism and anxiety, the feeling amongst parents is, 'Shit, I've gotta give my kid every single advantage there is, or every possible or likely advantage. If that means the University of Chicago, Duke, or Princeton, damn it, I've gotta make that happen. That's my job as a parent.'"

Even though following his Harvard-Westlake talk, some parents came up to him and said, "I don't believe a word of what you're saying," Bruni sympathizes with them. "It must be said that parents aren't just doing this because they want the educational equivalent of a Birkin bag to carry around. Yes, they want the sticker on the back window, and they want to be able to walk around in the T-shirt or sweatshirt of a very impressive school," he said. "But at the end of the day, even before that stuff, most parents just want to usher their kids into adulthood with the best chances of thriving, and they've convinced themselves—and been convinced with some reason, not nearly enough reason—that a brand-name, elite, coveted school is going to be one of those things that greatly maximizes the chance of their kids having the life he or she wants."

In certain pockets of LA, where obsession with status is omnipresent and where the population is relatively new to the elite educational system—this is not a land of Cabots and Morgans who have centuries-old ties to the Ivy League—the desire to "win" at the college game is all the more intense. The Hollywood elite live in a constant fear of being kicked out or fired—from the movie or TV show, from the studio head's office, from the VIP list—which makes the desire for a name-brand school, and the validation that it provides, all the more crucial, and makes people all the more desperate for it. There is also less familiarity in LA with the smaller liberal arts schools on the East Coast that have programs as competitive as Ivy League schools—Bowdoin, Bates, Williams, to name a few—making families set their sights aggressively on only a handful of schools with sweatshirt cred. "I think, being on the West Coast, people only know of the colleges that have names," said Priscilla Sands, head of Marlborough School, considered the top all-girls private school in LA. "So Georgetown is big, as are all the Ivies, as is Stanford."

All of this makes Los Angeles the perfect place to witness the breakdown of the college admissions system. By putting a spotlight on the most extreme components of the ecosystem—the ultraelite schools, the ultradriven parents, and the exorbitant levels of money that are tossed around—one can glean how badly things have gone off the rails and begin to try to understand why.

This book is not only an attempt to show the inanity of what college admissions has become, but also to show the absurdity of how early the process now begins in a child's life. While the Varsity Blues scandal highlights the scheming that can go on during the high school years when trying to manipulate a child's acceptance into college, the game begins much earlier for some parents. It can start as early, in fact, as infancy, when a spot is secured in a select "mommy group," led by a child development guru who doubles as a preschool whisperer and who can pick up the phone and help ease a family's acceptance into a "competitive" nursery school. The boutique preschool with the organic garden out back and the indoor waterfall then feeds into the right elementary, middle, and high school, and ultimately, if all goes as planned, Harvard or Yale. If one can understand the genesis of this gaming attitude, the Varsity Blues scandal starts to, if not make sense, at least seem less outrageously out of context.

The system that produced the Varsity Blues phenomenon was created by helicopter and snowplow parents who have evolved into what I like to call "artisanal parents." They're parents of comfortable means who have spent their lives carefully selecting the perfect Bugaboo stroller and Stokke high chair and toddler music program for their child, and otherwise curating their lives down to the status-signifying Golden Goose sneakers with the perfectly-dyed-to-look-dirty laces they're sent off to third grade in.

"It feels like parents used to think, 'I'm doing my best and hoping for the best,'" said Luisa Donati, the executive director of Cassidy Preschool in Santa Monica, whose tuition starts at $16,000 a year and sends children to private elementary schools like Curtis School, John Thomas Dye, and Brentwood School. "Now I see more, there's a 'right' way to do this parenting thing. 'I just need to be connected to those with answers and then I'll know what the right way is.' And it's missing everything about the truth and reality of parenting, which is that there isn't a 'right' way."

Donati sees this in all kinds of ways—for instance, tutors who charge $350 an hour to help four-year-olds work on their penmanship and fine-motor skills in preparation for a kindergarten assessment at a private elementary school. "Countless systems eat off this anxiety," she said. "So by the time you get to college, the stakes feel so high."

The stakes don't just feel high; they feel almost ridiculously impossible. Most Gen X parents who went to competitive colleges readily admit that the chances that they'd get into those same schools today are minimal. Indeed, several of the parents indicted in the Varsity Blues scandal themselves went to top schools and yet felt their children wouldn't be able to follow that path on their own merits, even with legacy status and connections. Jane Buckingham, the LA entrepreneur and parenting guru who hired Rick Singer to have someone take her son's ACT test for him, is herself a graduate of Duke and has connections at USC. Yet she still agreed to pay Singer $50,000 to ensure that her son received a near-perfect ACT score. Bill McGlashan, the cofounder of a billion-dollar growth fund called the Rise Fund, is a Yale grad and a Stanford business school alum who could have easily used his connections and wealth to get his son into USC. As he bragged to Singer: "Half the board knows me" at USC. Yet he still allegedly relied on Singer to help his son ace the ACT and then package him as a fake football recruit. (McGlashan, who is fighting the charges, claims he pulled out of the scheme before his son actually applied to USC and that he did not know Singer was fixing his son's ACT.) Fashion designer Mossimo Giannulli and his wife, Lori Loughlin, have connections to USC, not to mention are wealthy enough to have made a noteworthy donation to the school. The list goes on. Morrie Tobin, the LA businessman who tipped the Feds off to the scandal, attended Yale and fundraised for the school. But he still tried to get his younger daughter into the school as a fake soccer player. Tobin has not been charged in the Varsity Blues case, but pled guilty and received jail time for his involvement in a securities fraud crime.

Yet one similarity among many parents in the case is that even those who attended Ivy League or other top schools did not come from money, and got into those schools by hard work and sweat. Once their own children, who had grown up with considerable means thanks to their success, were preparing for college, these parents seemed to fear that they wouldn't be able to get in on their own, given how hard it now was to get into top schools. They also seemed to doubt their children's own sense of self-determination. (A common refrain among the children of these parents—the great majority of whom had no idea about their parents' scheming—was "Why didn't you believe in me?") Yet because of how dramatically college had changed their own lives, they desperately wanted the same trajectory for their children. There are also a number of parents, such as Loughlin and Giannulli, who did not attend college, making them all the more passionate about their children going.

Most parents wouldn't go to criminal lengths to get their children into college. But many are frustrated by the fact that getting into college today is nothing like what it was twenty or thirty years ago, and they feel a sense of injustice—justified or not—over that dramatic shift. In my own case, I transferred into Georgetown in the early 1990s, following a public-high-school career that began in earnest sophomore year; freshman year had been a wash. Helping me, I'm sure, was that I had an alumni connection—my mother had graduated from the school (though our family was certainly not on the Big Donor list). But today, there's simply no room for error, let alone an entire year of mediocre performance, even if it's followed by a dramatic turnaround. As Jen Kaifesh, an independent college counselor in LA, reminded me: "There's point one percent chance of you getting into Stanford with B's on your transcript. Because all the other kids don't have those. So why would they take a kid who struggled in something when they can take a kid who never did?"

This reality is evident in college acceptance rates, and it's not just Stanford's that have become chillingly low. Harvard's is 4.9 percent, meaning that of the 40,248 students who applied to be freshmen in the fall of 2020, only 1,980 were given spots. In other words, about nineteen of every twenty applicants were denied. Yale accepts 6 percent of its applicants. Even less competitive schools, like Tulane University in New Orleans, have become a stretch for many. The school accepted just 11 percent of the 44,000 applications it received for the class of 2024, making it more selective than Amherst and the University of California, Berkeley. This has in part been driven by an extremely aggressive—and hip— admissions director, Jeff Schiffman, who posts videos of himself on YouTube: showing up to work in a tank top and black workout tights with white stars on them; high-fiving students on campus before heading to lunch in the French Quarter. Schiffman said he sees himself as a "next-generation admissions director."

"I look at this as a less clandestine experience, for lack of a better word," he said. "My goal is to give students as many resources as possible, rather than have this be a secret process behind a closed curtain." But Tulane has used less transparent tactics as well to goose its numbers, such as sending out "fast applications" or "VIP applications," which are emails sent to preselected high school students based on their test scores and GPAs. The emails enthusiastically encourage students—who are told they are being given "priority consideration"—to apply to the school without having to pay a fee. (In fact, Tulane dropped its application fee for all students in the wake of Hurricane Katrina.) The effect is a marketing ploy to make students feel beloved by a school they might not have even been considering. And to apply is so easy—and free! Some colleges' VIP applications allow students to submit fewer essays and promise a faster verdict. To further drive up application numbers, some years Tulane offers two rounds of early decision.

Schiffman said Tulane has stopped its VIP application program but admitted that it was a "big component" behind why the school's admittance rate has dropped so dramatically. Between 2002 and 2017 Tulane's acceptance rate plummeted 62 percent.

As for why the landscape has become so competitive, experts point to a few factors. First is the growing popularity of the Common Application. Although the form first graced the scene in the 1970s, it wasn't widely accepted until the 2000s. Today nearly nine hundred colleges use it, meaning that applying to multiple schools at once—and not having to laboriously write answers to individualized essay questions—is as simple as clicking a mouse. This has sent the overall application rate to schools skyrocketing, and thus acceptance rates nosediving. Whereas in the early 1990s, students generally applied to three or four schools (one safety, one target, one reach) and those who felt more ambitious might apply to six or seven, today kids often apply to as many as twenty or twenty-five. According to a Pew Research Center study that examined 1,364 four-year colleges, in 2002 there were nearly 4.9 million total applications. By 2017, that number had more than doubled, to almost 10.2 million. As for the most exclusive schools, defined as those that accepted between 10 percent and 20 percent of their 2017 applicants, the application volume rose 110 percent between 2002 and 2017. This tsunami of applicants is being encouraged by colleges, who behind the scenes are direct-mailing prospective students, blasting them with promotional emails, and giving presentations that encourage everyone in the room to apply, regardless of their qualifications.

But even more important to colleges than acceptance rates are their yield figures, i.e., how many in the accepted pool actually show up in the fall to matriculate. This isn't just about prestige and having a high rank on *U.S. News and World Report*'s annual list of the "best" colleges and universities, which remains the preeminent ranking. There is a financial incentive. Colleges are ultimately businesses, and like all businesses, they need to raise money in order to grow. They also need to borrow money. Not every university has a $40 billion endowment like Harvard, and yet even Harvard borrows money by issuing bonds and then repaying them with interest over several years—colleges' principal source of debt funding. But to do this, colleges need a solid bond rating, which is primarily driven by yield.

"Yield dictates your entire admissions model," said Sara Harberson, a former associate dean of admissions at Penn. "So if you have a low yield rate, you know that your acceptance rate needs to be high to be able to bring in your class on target. If the admissions office does not meet their enrollment goals, the whole university model is thrown off, because everything the university does— projects, hiring, housing—is based off of enrollment. The admissions office is the most important office on a college campus."

Indeed, the more impressive enrollment numbers are, the more money colleges are given to build, say, that new athletic facility with its own barbershop and German-engineered lockers (University of Oregon), or a student village featuring a small mall's worth of shops and restaurants (USC), which in turn is used to lure even more prospective students, driving application rates up and selectivity numbers down so that the cycle continues.

The importance of yield explains colleges' push for students to apply early decision, a trend that has been on the rise in recent years. Kids who apply early decision commit to attending the school if accepted, meaning that the yield rate is extremely high. Applying ED has become standard advice from college counselors and anyone telling kids how to play the admissions game. Rick Singer himself wrote in his book, *Getting In: Gaining Admission to Your College of Choice*, "Your chance of acceptance goes up 50% if you apply early, and you can apply to multiple schools with Early Action." One LA mother said that when she went to a private event held by Emory for prospective applicants, the admissions dean straight-out told the gathered parents and students that kids would have a much better chance of being accepted if they applied early. (A development officer was also on hand, in the event anyone wanted to start writing checks to Emory that night.)

The pressure for a high yield explains why Tulane goes to such lengths to attract applicants. For while its tactics are generating a huge number of applicants, driving down its acceptance rate, its actual yield is under 40 percent. Meaning that while the school is drumming up interest, the majority of kids who get in aren't showing up in the fall. Schiffman said Tulane's yield has rebounded mightily since Hurricane Katrina, after which its yield was under 10 percent, and that he is "quite pleased" with its growth.

But perhaps the most anxiety-inducing piece of the process today is what colleges are now looking for in their applicants. Long gone are the days when getting an admissions god to smile down on you meant excelling in a well-rounded portfolio of activities: the star student who's class president, captain of the tennis team, and volunteers at an animal shelter on the side. Today, colleges snooze at such clichéd, dilettantish trappings. What they want is someone who is "pointy," as Mark Sklarow, CEO of the Independent Educational Consultants Association (IECA), puts it.

In other words, someone who takes his or her singular passion and turbocharges it in creative ways.

"It used to be about breadth. Now it's about depth," said counselor Jen Kaifesh. "From the college's point of view, they don't want someone who is on student council, plays an instrument, plays a sport. They want a specialist. So if you're going to do social justice, you need to have worked at the Museum of Tolerance and you need to have marched in everything and organized marches, and you need to be heading things and showing initiative. It's all about going further than any other applicant."

Alexandra Dumas Rhodes, another independent college counselor in LA, echoed this. "I had this wonderful kid who was doing robotics at his high school," she said. "And it turns out that that robotics program was not good enough. So he started his own robotics program. He pulled the best robotics kids from around the city. He did it in his garage. He went on to win the world robotics championship. That kid realized at the world competition that there were no minorities [represented], so he went into the inner city of LA, went to an inner-city high school, and started programs. He trained teachers. That's who's getting into Harvard, Yale, and Princeton."

Ideally, from a college's perspective, this robotics kid entered his freshman college class alongside a world-class cello player, an animal rights activist-turned-entrepreneur, and a kid who patented an app that strives to end homelessness.

"It's a well-rounded class, not a well-rounded student," Dumas Rhodes said.

And yet colleges never say this. Quite the opposite. In the fall of 2019, I attended the admissions presentation that Stanford held at Granada Hills Charter High School, an academically competitive public school located forty minutes north of Los Angeles. A sunny admissions officer talked to the two hundred plus people, many of them minorities, who had gathered in the school's fluorescent-lit auditorium about Stanford's commitment to diversity, "collaborative spirit," and "engaged community members." Guests were also given a glossy brochure packed with impressive statistics, such as how many countries are represented in the class of 2023 (seventy-seven); how much money is being invested in undergraduate research ($5.8 million); and how many MacArthur Fellows are part of the Stanford community (thirty-two). But nowhere, neither in the brochure nor in the talk, was any mention made of that startlingly low acceptance statistic: 4 percent. Instead, the admissions officer stressed Stanford's "holistic" review process. "So we don't have any cutoffs for testing or GPA in our process," she said. "We view every application in whole, regardless of these academic qualifications. We are really looking to know you as a whole person."

On a podcast earlier in the year, Richard Shaw, Stanford's dean of admissions, reiterated these points while adding, "We look at autobiography. We look at their hopes and aspirations."

Stanford is not the only school that waxes on about its holistic approach. The phrase is the current admissions buzzword, trotted out at every turn in a way that makes admissions officers seem like sommeliers taking delicate sips of a vintage pinot noir, trying to determine just how exceptional it is—as opposed to simply looking at the bottle and giving it a grade.

And yet very often that's exactly what they're doing. "Colleges are straight-up lying to prospective students. Every day, in every interaction, they're openly misleading students," said the former Ivy League admissions officer. "The way they're doing that is this narrative of the holistic review."

This person told me about the system he had when he was working in admissions at a top-twenty-ranked private university.

"I had a printout next to my desk that said, 'If a student scores less than twelve hundred on the SAT, stop reading the file.' You're done. Don't pass go. Don't collect two hundred dollars. That's it," he said. "But then when I would go to an information session and speak in front of two hundred fifty families, somebody would always raise their hand and say, 'Hey, do you have any minimum scores?' In my mind I'm thinking, 'Of course we have minimum scores. If you score less than twelve hundred, you're done!' But I couldn't say that."

Colleges' lack of transparency about how they're making decisions coupled with the basic problem of so many applicants for so few spots has parents pulling their hair out, and it's deepening their discouragement. "Colleges have become more and more secretive about who gets in," said Sklarow. It used to be, he continued, that "when you applied, people sort of knew that if you had an A average and a fourteen hundred SAT, you'd go here. If it was a lower GPA and a lower SAT, you went there. That's the way it was. Now suddenly it feels like, well, wait. What's going on? The same school has two kids [with similar profiles]: one gets in, the other doesn't. Wait, their grades are the same. It's raised anxiety through the roof. Nobody can figure out who's getting in."

At Harvard-Westlake, this anxiety was validated during part two of Senior College Night. As Bruni walked off into the wings, the parents were divided into groups and sent to rooms with upper school deans for an information session. Each dean gave a slideshow presentation that broke down colleges into tiers. The top group included Harvard, Yale, Princeton, Stanford, and MIT. The deans then broke students down into two categories: "hooked," industry parlance for kids with special traits that give them a leg up in college applications, such as being a legacy, an athlete, a minority, a development case (i.e., very wealthy), or "first-gen"—

someone who is the first in their family to attend college; and "unhooked." The deans then laid out the different admittance data—GPAs and test scores—for hooked and unhooked kids. The statistics were, of course, much better for the hooked kids.

"It was a big reality check," said one parent. "If you weren't underprivileged or a first-gen student or an athlete," you were basically screwed.

Said another: "What they made clear is that everything has a caveat. You can give a donation, but does Yale really need your money? Sure, you're a legacy, but that may not mean anything. Even the hooks feel tenuous."

The next day parents were sent login information for Naviance, an online tool that provided access to charts and scattergraphs that showed former Harvard-Westlake students' GPAs and test scores and where they had and hadn't gotten into college. (Their names were not included.) This information, too, was broken down between hooked and unhooked categories. So parents could see that, say, a hooked former student who had a 3.9 GPA and got a 1460 on the SAT wasn't accepted by Duke but did get into Vanderbilt.

Immediately, parents began scratching down numbers. "Everyone's doing the calculus," said one parent. "You could plug in your kid's test scores and GPA, what school they're interested in, and you know exactly where your kid is."

Whatever the school's intentions had been to calm fears, seeing the raw data heightened parents' anxiety. "Your kid has a 4.1 and is not even above the cutoff at a non-Ivy," said one. The takeaway for many was that they needed to pull out all the stops, spend as much money as possible, do whatever it took to solve the problem. A private-school education with a bevy of extracurriculars was no longer enough. They had to provide more. Chief among those advantages was hiring an independent college counselor. Someone who, for $20,000 to $30,000—or more—can help a student ace their college application. Part coach, part drill sergeant, part therapist, independent counselors provide feedback on essays, help come up with a list of target schools, and give advice on which courses to take and which extracurriculars to focus on. In an era of intense personalization and outsourcing, they are a complete support system, providing input and guidance, usually in the comfort of a student's home.

As a rule, independent counselors never promise results. "Any good counselor will tell you they cannot guarantee a school," said Dumas Rhodes. "That's on my contract, which only has four little items on it. Number four says, 'Cannot guarantee a particular college.'"

And yet there was one independent counselor, whose name was circulating in LA, who was known as a kind of fixer. He eschewed the language of uncertainty and maybes embraced by everyone else in his business. He spoke in absolutes. "I can get your kid into college X," he would say confidently to parents, whose hearts swelled in relief when they finally heard someone offer them firm ground in an otherwise entirely shaky and unknowable landscape. Indeed, he seemed too good to be true. One Los Angeles mother who was shopping for an independent counselor for her son told me she was "gathering names from all these moms at these competitive schools who [were] using these people," and this man's name kept coming up, again and again. "This guy is a cut above," other parents would tell her. "He's the best. He can get it all done."

His name was Rick Singer.

CHAPTER 2

The Guy

Located on Stone Canyon Road, the Hotel Bel-Air is a pink-stuccoed palace in the exclusive gated neighborhood of the same name. Snugly tucked into a pocket of maniacally manicured greenery, the historic hotel has long been a playground for Hollywood royalty and other members of the one percent, who can pay upwards of $995 a night for a room. There's a suite named for one-time habitué Grace Kelly, and it was here that Marilyn Monroe playfully wrapped herself in diaphanous citrus-colored scarves for a *Vogue* photo shoot just weeks before her death.

But on the evening of September 26, 2017, the famed hotel wasn't host to celebrities of the stage and screen. Several dozen of the wealthiest businessmen and women in Los Angeles were gathered in one of the hotel's ballrooms. They had come to this elegant cream-hued space—with French doors that looked out onto the club's rolling grounds—to hear a man speak. There was something nervous, jumpy, about the man, who was slightly built and had short-cropped salt-and-pepper hair. His piercing brown eyes focused intently on whomever he was addressing and he spoke loudly with a Midwestern twang. As guests flowed into the room, he doled out handshakes and back slaps, but it was clear that he wanted to get down to business. It was time for the show.

Rick Singer was "the CEO and Master Coach of the world's largest private college counseling and life coaching company, the Key Worldwide," according to the flyer announcing the event. The company claimed to have offices in 101 US cities and 5 foreign countries. But what was the most impressive-sounding of all, and the reason people had come tonight, was this titillating statistic: The Key boasted of having gotten 1.5 million students into their first- and second-choice colleges. It was an irresistible data point. Images of acceptance letters from Yale, Harvard, and Princeton flitted through guests' minds as they turned their attention to their host.

Singer may have been a "master coach," but among the people who had gathered there that evening, he was better known as "the guy." As in "he's the guy" you need to hire. Or "Psst, I've got a guy." One parent preferred the term "the kid whisperer." "People were very secretive about him," another parent told me. "The ones who used him would whisper his name and share it only with their friends." The secrecy was born out of strategy: In the ultracompetitive education game in Los Angeles, when someone discovered they had an ace in their hand, they tended to keep it to themselves. This was, after all, the land of "stealth tutors," a term for when a parent hired a tutor to help their child in a subject at school but refrained from sharing the tutor's name with anyone else, lest other kids get a leg up, too. (A practice, by the way, that can begin in first grade.) When it came to independent college counselors, Singer was a similar kind of weapon that people wanted to keep on the DL.

Singer's talk at the Hotel Bel-Air that night was sponsored by the Summa Group, a division of the global investment company Oppenheimer & Co. that oversaw $1.5 billion of its clients' personal wealth. His connection to the company came through Brian Werdesheim, who was the cofounder and CEO of the Summa Group, and who had been recommending Singer to friends and associates for years. Just a few months earlier, Werdesheim had brought Singer onto the board of the Summa Group's children's charity, the Banyan Foundation, which hooked up privileged LA teens with volunteer opportunities of the sort that were socially beneficial but that also added polish to their college applications. Oppenheimer has said it maintained a "very limited" relationship with Singer, under the impression that his business and foundation were legitimate, but the relationship was then severed.

Werdesheim, who is not implicated in the Varsity Blues scandal, had a personal interest in Singer—his daughter was starting high school at the elite Buckley School and would soon be applying to colleges. Werdesheim was on the board at Buckley and had been touting Singer around the school, connecting him to his pal and fellow board member Devin Sloane, the founder of the LA water systems company AquaTecture. Sloane had already hired Singer to help his son Matteo, who was a junior at Buckley, apply to college. But he'd come to the presentation tonight just to hear him speak. He'd been impressed by Singer from their first meeting, liking his no-nonsense approach to tutoring: Singer told Matteo that if he was going to work with him, he would have to adhere to certain rules, like no drinking, no drugs, and getting plenty of sleep (wisdom Singer himself adhered to). Seeing him now in this posh setting, spouting his wisdom to a group of fellow business titans, confirmed in his mind that Singer really was "the guy," according to a source close to Sloane.

Given Singer's mystique, one would have expected him to have a more illustrious presence—or at least someone who showed up at professional events like the one this evening wearing a tie. But part of his allure was that he seemed so ordinary and accessible. A former assistant basketball coach at Sacramento State, Singer, who was then fifty-six, still carried himself like a coach. It was a persona he fully embraced. "He makes everything sound so matter-of-fact," said Dan Larson, who met Singer at a private athletic club in Sacramento in the early 2000s. "It's almost like a coach calling out plays with his team. He's one step away from having a chalkboard and drawing it out." Singer's unvarying uniform completed the image: khakis, a polo shirt, sneakers. Sometimes he dressed the look down further. He sold himself to one Silicon Valley family by showing up to the first meeting wearing an Ironman triathlon T-shirt, which served as a prompt for a litany of athletic boasts. He was relatively small—he measured in at five foot eight—and walked with a slight waddle, owing to his bowed legs. But he had the taut, muscular frame of the exercise junkie that he was. His regular workout regimen included biking, weights, endless laps in outdoor swimming pools, and paddleboarding. Even his diet was defined by discipline. During the day he stuck to water, usually eating a meal only at dinner, which was often takeout. He didn't smoke or drink.

Singer grew up as a scrappy kid in a Chicago suburb. He had nothing in common with the Hermès- and Chanel-drenched milieu he now found himself in. But in the eyes of those who'd gathered to hear him, he was a kind of guru, one who possessed the secret formula of how to land an acceptance letter from a prestigious college—something that was a particularly crowning achievement in certain status-obsessed circles of Los Angeles. Here, where so much was commoditized and labeled, a fancy college name was yet another VIP upgrade, more proof that a student—and, by extension, their parents—was a Somebody. More important, it provided social cred in a culture that revolved around see-and-be-seen fundraisers and galas in LA and winter holidays in Aspen. "Where's your kid going?" was a question tossed out with seeming casualness on the sidelines of a Saturday morning AYSO soccer game, yet it was anything but a throwaway line. In a city that prided itself on, and determined its worth by, flashy exteriors and credits, admittance to USC or Columbia, to say nothing of Harvard or Yale, was currency.

And here was the one person who said he knew how to gain entree to those gilded institutions. Unlike others in his field, Singer spoke in the language of certitude. He was, even in this realm, absolute, in a way that was borderline audacious. As he would tell the crowd tonight: *"Listen to me, and I will get your child into college."*

Singer's talk was grandiosely titled "Demystifying Healthcare & College Admission in Uncertain and Challenging Times: How to Be Proactive in Gaining Access to Game Changing Guidance and Expertise for You and Your Family." It was a confusing (and grammatically challenged) premise, but it boiled down to one thing: how competitive the college admissions landscape was and how Singer could help kids conquer it. He cited abysmal acceptance rate statistics and stressed the importance of a "personal brand" in order to get the attention of college admissions officers, who were inundated with thousands upon thousands of outstanding applicants. In order to stand out, kids needed to build their own narrative, he stressed, and he could help them do that. It was a message he underscored in *Getting In*, the thin guide he self-published in 2014, in which he wrote, "To build your personal brand, you'll need to simplify the story of you. Pick the strongest moments—your shining achievements, your darkest tragedies, the parts of your life that stick in people's minds. Tell that story."

Not all the guests at the Bel-Air Hotel were quite sure what to make of their host. He was mouthy and aggressive, even in the way he paced around the room as he went through his PowerPoint presentation—his style at all the many presentations he was giving around LA at this point. "He was loud. He talked over you," one guest told me. But this person admitted that Singer had a solid grounding in what colleges were looking for, and how to navigate your way through the admissions process. He ticked off insights such as that when a college asks for a list of ten interests or hobbies, to put down only four. Ten would make you look like you were just doing a bunch of clubs, that you weren't devoted to anything in depth. And he had inside knowledge about the colleges themselves: Northwestern was taking fewer students but offering more financial aid. Community members in Durham, North Carolina, where Duke is located, "hated" college kids. The University of Southern California had grown in stature, though it was still at the bottom of what he considered tier-one schools.

But most of all, he made college admissions seem scary. The landscape had changed so much, he said, it was impossible to get in anywhere. You think your kid's brilliant? There are thousands more like him or her. You think a donation to the college will do the trick? Not unless you're talking $50 million or more. As he would tell a client who said he'd given $750,000 to Cornell and thus expected to have some sway there, "Your seven-fifty is diddly dink in the world." Someone else Singer worked with, he said, had given *$50 million* to Cornell.

His message was crystal clear to those in the room: *Use me, and I'll get the job done. Don't use me, and you're screwed.*

❧

By 2017, presentations were just one small prong of Rick Singer's growing empire. The Key had also been running summer workshops on the UCLA campus, where students could "earn college level mastery of their personal career passions" in areas like film, alternative-fuel vehicles, start-ups, and even tech gadgets. One of these workshops, called "The Real Mac Genius," was described as a three-day "total immersion program" that focused "on Apple's four major products." The Key also had contracts with online high schools, supplying them with exclusive college counseling services, providing yet another revenue stream. Singer was also incubating his own tech products, sinking millions into a series of digital start-ups geared around education and college counseling, which he hoped to one day bundle together and sell off, maybe in an IPO. Indeed, he was looking for seemingly any way to translate his crazy drive, discipline, and salesmanship into making a buck.

His charitable arm, the Key Worldwide Foundation (KWF), a nonprofit organization that he set up in 2012 to purportedly help underprivileged kids in California and "needy Cambodians," as stated in its mission statement, had invested in a Welsh soccer team and a Mexican fast-food chain. At one point, he was trying to create his own version of IMG Academy, the elite sports-training prep school in Bradenton, Florida (which is now owned by the Hollywood entertainment conglomerate Endeavor), believing he could create a sports academy that was better. As one former Key employee said of Singer: "He had all kinds of ideas about how to make money."

During this time, Singer was a blur, getting on and off airplanes as he continued to personally tutor kids all over the country while cooking up new business schemes on the side. A new-age Sammy Glick, he seemed to be adhering to his own advice. "Whenever you find yourself waiting in line, or stuck in traffic, or with nothing to do, spend the time working," he wrote in *Getting In*. "Fine-tune your strategies. Carry a notebook to jot down ideas; don't expect to remember them later. Always be doing something."

Although his home base was Newport Beach, California, where he lived in a five-bedroom Mediterranean villa not far from the beach, he was rarely there. To visitors, the place felt like a deserted bachelor pad. "It was pretty sparsely furnished—dark wood, dark floors, dark furniture. The kitchen looked like it was never used," said Bill Templeton, the former president and CEO of the Money Store, who was involved with Singer's digital start-up venture. Another guest remembers opening the refrigerator and seeing nothing but bottled water.

Singer was always in motion, always thrumming. The one thing that focused him was exercise. He got up before dawn to work out and drove around in a white Mercedes Sprinter with his paddleboard secured to the roof. He told associates that the van had a reclining chair inside that he would sleep in, so that when he was in Sacramento, he could drive it to San Francisco and get up early and paddleboard in the bay. When he was home, he paddleboarded in the Newport Beach harbor.

"He was nonstop," Templeton said. "He was always on a plane. To get a ten-minute call with him was a major challenge. 'I'm flying here. I've got this here.' The guy was like a maniac. He never stopped. He was constantly on the go."

Singer was short on specifics, Templeton said, he but would drop the names of whomever he was flying to see. "He mentioned Bill Gates. He said to me at one time that he was tutoring, or was communicating with Michelle Obama about the two girls, which I didn't believe. There were grandiose images of what he was doing with his organization." (There is no evidence that he had any known connection to those individuals.)

But despite his penchant for exaggeration, another practice he preached in *Getting In* ("Branding requires bragging. But don't just brag about everything—brag smart"), he had by now built up an impressive cadre of clients in his main hubs of LA, Orange County, and Silicon Valley. Hollywood actors and studio executives, a famed NFL quarterback, and high-profile VC partners had all hired Singer to help their kids apply to college. As a result, he was now bringing in real money. In 2016, the Key generated $7 million, according to tax documents. But even with a thriving business that he'd almost single-handedly built, he never stopped hustling. One day, he walked up to a well-known billionaire in the men's locker room of the Equinox gym in Palo Alto, according to a source. Knowing the man had high-school-aged kids, he pitched him his services. The man agreed to a meeting.

꿈

As a kid growing up in Lincolnwood, a suburb outside of Chicago, in the late 1960s and '70s, Ricky Singer was technically a "Wooder." That was the term for kids who lived in the affluent Jewish neighborhood, and a marked distinction from the less monied "Grovers" from nearby Morton Grove, which Italian and Polish immigrants had made their home a century before. Wooders tended to have parents who were doctors or dentists or business owners. When they turned sixteen, they drove their own cars. (Grovers rode bikes.) Their parents could afford braces. And many of them lived in Lincolnwood Towers, a stately neighborhood with large Tudor homes and manicured lawns.

"If you think of a John Hughes movie, the kids from Lincolnwood were more privileged," said Arnie Bernstein, a Grover who went to school with Singer. "They had money and really fancy houses. They were the Socs, basically, and they let you know it," he said, referring to the rich kids in S. E. Hinton's coming-of-age novel *The Outsiders*.

But despite Singer's zip code, he was a Wooder in name only. Unlike most of his friends, he lived in a row house in East Lincolnwood, an area decidedly less ritzy than the Towers, with his mother, stepfather, and younger sister. (His parents divorced when he was seven.) Friends say that even though Ricky was a plucky, gregarious kid who had no shortage of confidence, he was self-conscious about the wealth divide he found himself in. He rarely invited friends to play at his house, and took note when other Wooders went off to sleepaway camp over the summer, while he stayed home. Wooders were also known for having extravagant bar mitzvahs at the Hyatt in Lincolnwood, a.k.a. the Purple Hotel, a swank, modern hotel with a lavender brick exterior, where Barry Manilow and Roberta Flack were said to have stayed. Singer never had a bar mitzvah, let alone at a purple hotel, nor did he go to Hebrew school like most of his friends did.

"I don't think religion was a thing in his family," said Mike Wolfe, one of his best pals at the time.

Wolfe met him when Singer moved to Lincolnwood from California in sixth grade. They bonded over sports and played travel baseball together. But even though they were close, Wolfe said he never really knew his friend. Singer never discussed his family or his previous life out west. "He was very hush-hush," Wolfe said. "He didn't talk about where he came from."

Instead he put his verbal energy into spinning stories and telling tall tales geared to impress. "He would try to make up stories just to kind of lift himself up or to make himself look better," Wolfe said. "He did that a lot." But he could also be snide and sarcastic, tossing off put-downs and judgments on people who weren't like him, as a kind of self-protective defense. Namely, his targets were kids who had money or were what he called "NAs"— i.e., nonathletes. To him, the world was broken down between athletes and NAs. Singer proudly considered himself the former, even though, as a chubby short kid, he was hardly a natural.

But his physical shortcomings drove him to play harder than anyone else, to organize more pickup basketball games, and to spend hours practicing free throws with an almost maniacal dedication. "He could shoot," Wolfe said. "He had really good range. I wouldn't say he was quick off the dribble or one of those kind of quick point guards. But he could shoot. I'm telling you. He was probably the best shooter in grade school. He worked on it. He played a lot."

Singer played Little League, but basketball was his passion. He lived it, dreamed it, talked about it incessantly. When he tried out for the team at Lincoln Hall, the middle school he attended in seventh grade, all his friends assumed he was a shoo-in. No one could believe it when he wasn't picked, least of all him. "He was crushed," Wolfe said. "It really hurt him."

Around this time, Singer decided to do something about his weight. As another friend, Cheryl Levin-Folio, recounted in the podcast *Gangster Capitalism: The College Admissions Scandal*, kids teased him about his physique, calling him Fat Man Singer. In a photograph taken when he was in middle school, he has a doughy, cherubic face and thick forearms. He's surrounded by a group of boys who are string beans in comparison.

His transformation began over the summer before high school, when he put himself on a diet of raisins and peanuts, and began jogging every day. He wore thick clothing, to sweat off more pounds. By the end of the summer, he had completely thinned out. "He literally transformed himself," said one peer. "After that, he just took on a new persona. He had that cocky confidence before, but it got more dramatic."

Singer had always been a performer. At one of those fancy bar mitzvahs, after admitting he didn't know how to dance, some boys took him into the bathroom and taught him a few moves. Once he hit the dance floor, he couldn't be stopped. He liked to be the center of attention, and would charm and chat his way into people's good graces. But once he lost the weight, his desire to peacock and show off went into overdrive. "He always embellished," the friend said. "That was a big part of who he became." It was never clear how much he was saying was true, how much he just wanted to impress someone, or how much of it he actually believed himself. As he would write in *Getting In*: "Whenever possible, believe your own story…If you're pretending to be a sanitized version of yourself, think like that person. If you're presenting yourself as a reformed character who can show his or her scars with pride, think like that character. Be a method actor." And now Singer had reformed himself. He was a new person. He'd proven that he could set his mind to something and do it, that he had the ability to change something that had seemed insurmountable. It was as though he possessed a new secret power.

"The only thing that ever bothered Ricky was his weight," the friend went on. "Anything else he could do. He could work his magic or finagle something. But this was something he had to do on his own."

He brought his newfound swagger to Niles West High School, a big public school, where the attitude was, "You gotta succeed, you gotta succeed," said Bernstein. The school consisted of mostly white families from Lincolnwood, Morton Grove, and Skokie, who had been successful enough to move out to the Chicago suburbs. Among the school's alumni are Olympic gymnast Bart Conner, who was two years ahead of Singer; and Merrick Garland, the Supreme Court nominee, who was valedictorian of the class of 1970. A lot of Niles West kids were Jewish, yet there was an underlying anti-Semitism alive and well at the school. Ross Benjoya, one of Singer's classmates, recalled hearing "some nasty things on the wrestling bus. People would say things about Hitler, that he had the right ideas, 'Put your grandmother in an oven.' It was not overt, everyone sat in the student lounge and talked together. But it did exist." Beyond the walls of Niles West, these attitudes were less veiled. In 1977, a year before Singer graduated, a group of neo-Nazis organized a march in Skokie, which at the time had the largest population of Holocaust survivors in the country. Most kids didn't pay much attention to the march, but it created a simmering backdrop of division and hatred.

Among the movers and shakers at Niles West, Singer was mediocre at best. Although he established himself as a sports presence—he played on the football team for four years and the baseball team his freshman year (once again, he didn't make basketball)—he was hardly a star. "I don't remember him being Mr. Athlete," said Benjoya, who played football with him. "The only conversation we had was about curly hair. We both had big heads of dark, curly hair. It was the style back then. But ours was natural, not permed."

Singer's baseball coach Marv Klebba similarly remembers him more for his physical appearance than his athletic prowess: He was the only kid on the team who pinned his baseball cap to his head in order to keep it secure over his big hair. As for his skills, "He could run, but he wasn't very fast," said Klebba. "He could move, he was agile, but he wasn't athletic and smooth by any means."

Off the field, however, he made more of an impression. "He was very boisterous and always talking, to the point that it was annoying to the other team," said Klebba. During one game, against New Trier, the famed North Shore high school whose players had a snooty attitude toward the less sophisticated suburban kids at Niles West, Singer stood on a wooden bench and was particularly noisy, cheering on his teammates and whooping it up. The New Trier players were not amused. "He was always a loudmouth, braggart kind of a guy," Klebba said. "The type of kid that would get you in trouble if you hung around him."

Singer had a decidedly different view of himself. In his senior yearbook in 1978, next to one of the only existing photographs of him wearing a coat and tie, he wrote: "I would most like to be remembered for the outstanding personality I have been given, and being able to get along with others."

Most kids who graduated from Niles West stayed local. So many seniors went on to the University of Illinois that it was known as Niles South. In 1983, when the movie *Risky Business* came out, in which Tom Cruise plays a rich kid from the Chicago suburbs who skids around in his briefs and flubs his chances of getting into Princeton, Niles West kids went crazy when Cruise's character put on a pair of dark sunglasses, flashed a grin, and said: "Looks like University of Illinois!"

"That was a huge laugh line," Bernstein said. "That movie was the perfect embodiment of that area."

But Singer was ready to move on and continue rebranding himself. He also craved a climate that would allow him to exercise outdoors year-round—once he started running for exercise, he never stopped. So he headed south, along with Levin-Folio and Wolfe, and enrolled in the University of Arizona. He has never admitted that he attended U of A, although the university confirmed his attendance. In Singer fashion, it has been almost entirely wiped from the history books—another example of his penchant for inventing his own narrative. Indeed, even when he was sworn under oath while being questioned for a deposition he gave in

2016 (the case was unrelated to Varsity Blues), when asked where he attended college, Singer mentioned only Trinity University in Texas. He did, in fact, attend that school, but not until 1984—about four years after he abruptly left U of A in the middle of his sophomore year. When asked what he did between high school and Trinity, to account for the time lapse, he said he worked for his family's vending-machine business, never mentioning the year and a half he spent in Tucson.

It may be that, not unlike his time at Niles West, his Southwest stint was hardly defining. It was a forgettable blip along the path. At a Division I school like U of A, there was no way he was going to play college sports, so he was relegated to pickup basketball games and his nonstop workout routine. He joined the Jewish fraternity, Alpha Epsilon Pi, but mainly kept to himself.

"You know, it's college. You go out, you go to bars. He would never go out. He said, 'Athletes don't drink,'" said Wolfe, who roomed with Singer in the frat house. "I don't remember him ever taking a sip of liquor. He never went out. He would go to bed early, because he was up really early in the morning running. That's all he did. He was very focused."

His insularity from those around him is on display in the 1979 yearbook photo of AEPi, where he's standing in the front row, wearing white athletic shorts, a UCLA sweatshirt, and sneakers, his hair still a mass of dark curls. The rest of the fraternity is a sea of button-downs and ties, as though the guys were about to head off to a formal event. "That picture says it all," Wolfe said. "He was going to wear what he wore. If we had a fraternity thing or whatever and people were dressed up, it didn't matter. He was wearing shorts, running shoes, T-shirts. That was it.

"He kept apart," Wolfe went on. "I think he wanted it that way. He didn't want to fit in. He had this image of himself that he wasn't like anybody else. He didn't care to fit in. He could care less what anybody thought about him. He had this cocky air about him all the time pretty much."

As his roommate, Wolfe got a firsthand look at Singer's obsessive qualities and quirks. "Every day, all he would do is run. He'd wear these running shoes, running shorts. He only ate raisins, then he switched to peanuts. And he drank Tab. I don't know what was in that Tab, but he just drank Tab." Outside of his dorm, he loaded up on salads at the Wendy's $1.99 all-you-can-eat buffet, not only for the sake of his waistline, but to stick to a budget. "Rick couldn't financially do what everyone else was doing" in college, noted another classmate.

Sharing a room with Singer also meant putting up with unsanitary living conditions, according to his roommate. "He was a slob," Wolfe said. "I'm in this room with him and I'm smelling these socks that he ran in, sweated in. And these clothes, they would just be laying around and they would smell. And then with this Tab—I'm just laying there one day in the room, and he would take these Tab cans and wouldn't throw them out. He made a pyramid with them, the way some kids do with beer cans. He did that with Tab cans. And I remember I'm just laying there, and all of a sudden I'm swatting away bees left and right. I'm going, 'Where are these bees coming from?' And I look, and they're crawling out of these Tab cans. He didn't even wash them out."

He left U of A in December of his sophomore year. Wolfe couldn't recall why, but another friend surmised it was a money issue and that perhaps he could no longer afford out-of-state tuition. Even in Arizona, Singer was the kid who couldn't run with the rest of the crowd, and who made up for his shortcomings with an FU attitude and a loud mouth.

For a few years, he kicked around Chicago. Then he moved

to Dallas, where his father, who'd become sick, was living. (His dad would pass away a few years later.) In Texas, Singer took another shot at college. By now he had a more clear sense of his future, which he'd decided was to become a basketball coach. His idol was Bobby Knight, the hot-blooded, chair-throwing Indiana basketball coach, whom Singer amused people with his uncanny impression of. Trinity University in San Antonio, where Singer transferred after short stints at Brookhaven Community College and Our Lady of the Lake, a small Catholic college, afforded him the perfect environment to do this. The small liberal arts college was in the midst of transitioning from being a Division I school to a Division III school, which meant that he could play on both the varsity basketball team and the baseball team. Trinity also had a robust intramural sports league, and he dove in, playing any sport he could fit into his schedule and even refereeing on the side.

But despite being in his sports element at Trinity, Singer stood out as an arrogant kid from "the wrong side of the tracks," said Paul Hensley, who played on the basketball team with him. Trinity was a rich kids' school—many of the students were from wealthy oil families—where undergrads drove Mercedes, lived in apartments off campus, and had monthly stipends from their parents. Hensley said that Singer was one of the only students without a car; he remembers him having a bike. And while most of the student body wore eighties-style designer shorts and polo shirts, Singer was always either in sweats or workout shorts.

"Rick seemed like he never had any money. Never," Hensley said. "He was barely scraping by." To earn cash, he worked at the front desk of the school's athletic facility, the Sams Center, checking ID cards. It was a convenient gig: When he wasn't behind the desk, he was in the gym playing racquetball, shooting hoops, and lifting weights. He was rarely seen studying, and he failed a course in kinesiology that was required for his phys ed major (he dual majored in English), forcing him to retake it. The professor was known to be tough, but Hensley said that when Singer didn't pass, he took it personally, feeling that the teacher had singled him out and been unfairly tough on him. "He was very upset about that," Hensley said. "It brought him to the point of tears."

At Trinity, Singer didn't bother with fraternities. He scoffed to Hensley and other teammates that he "didn't need them," and once again he threw himself into sports while maintaining an aloof distance from those around him. "He wasn't a shoot-the-shit kind of guy," Hensley said. "You weren't going to have a beer with him. After the games, we'd all hang out, but Rick would go off and do his own thing. He wasn't a team guy.

"He was very abrasive and divisive. Rick was out for Rick."

On the basketball court, he held his own. Although he was by far the shortest player on the team, he'd dedicated himself to the sport for so many years now, and had spent so much time studying technique and strategy, that in some games he was the leading scorer. "He was a grinder," said one classmate. "He wanted to win so badly that he tried harder, worked harder." In an article in the school newspaper, the *Trinitonian*, Singer admitted as much, saying, "I'm definitely not a tremendous player. But when I'm out there I work as hard as I can every single time."

In the same article, he talks about his desire to be a coach, saying, "I'm really interested in youth. I feel that I had a tremendous amount of coaching in my playing days. I've seen the good parts and the bad parts. I think I could do a credible job with kids. I used to definitely want to be a pre-med major, but I'd rather wake up and go to a job that I really enjoy than something I dread.

"Coaching doesn't pay very well, but if you get any amount of real satisfaction, it's a better job. I like teaching and I think I can help kids. I like to communicate with people, and I'm definitely a person who works hard on my own skills. I think that makes it easier for me to teach. I know how hard it is for me sometimes, and I think that helps. If things come really easy for you, then it's sometimes hard for you to teach someone else who isn't as good. A lot of times the guys who have to work really hard make the best teachers."

Singer shared this ambition with his peers, causing them to roll their eyes. "Good luck," they thought. He hardly seemed to have the right temperament to work with kids, and his competitive streak was so extreme it could feel dangerous. "Rick was one of those guys that was just ultra-aggressive," Hensley said. "He would always be trying to slap the ball out of your hands. When you're practicing with your own team, you usually don't want to get somebody hurt. The rest of us would only go seventy percent, because you don't want to kill your own player. But Rick didn't know anything other than turning it all the way up."

Even pickup games at the school gym could turn ugly. One classmate recalled a game when a guy on the opposite team made a breakaway and headed for the basketball hoop. Singer, he said, "came over and cleaned him out. He tackled him rather than let him go do a layup. To me, that's a fight. So I run over, I'm yelling at Rick. He kind of has this look of 'What?' Like he's surprised anyone's pushing back."

"He was a win-at-all-costs guy," this person said. "He could be charming when you were sitting with him in the cafeteria, but when competition was on the line, he turned into this monster."

Losing at Trivial Pursuit was another cause for an explosion. "He'd go absolutely bonkers if you beat him," Hensley said. "It was like, 'Dude, it's Trivial Pursuit.' He'd just go off—he was very temperamental. He'd stomp around and had an acerbic mouth. It was 'Fuck this, fuck that.'"

As for possessing the traits of a coach, Singer clearly believed he had them, but they manifested themselves in strange ways. His style was to shout out critiques to his teammates during practice and games. But to those on the receiving end, it felt more like harassment. "What are you, a wimp?" he'd yell if someone dove for a ball and missed it. One year, when the freshman basketball players showed up for practice, he stood on the sidelines and busted their balls while they ran through drills. "You suck at free throws!" he'd shout. Or, "You can't hit a layup!" In a sign of how obsessive he could be when it came to downloading information, he'd memorized all the freshman players' names, where they'd gone to high school, and what their basketball stats were.

"I think he saw himself as an unofficial coach trying to get the best out of everybody," said Hensley. "But it backfired. Who wants that as a coach? He always saw himself as the player-coach."

Once again, Singer's perception of himself was completely at odds with the way he was seen by others: Around campus, he became known as Rick the Dick.

His down-and-dirty drive found the perfect platform his senior year, when he was a captain of an intramural flag football team. Intramural sports were far more popular and competitive at Trinity than intercollegiate sports, and championship games attracted hundreds of students, who'd come out to cheer the players on. The games and playoffs were dutifully reported in the school paper. "You'd have guys quit the football team" to play flag football "because you couldn't do both," said Grant Scheiner, then a sportswriter for the *Trinitonian*. "Then you'd have basketball and baseball players who played in the league. It was a big deal."

Flag football had long been dominated by fraternity teams, but in Singer's senior year a team of independent misfits came together and created their own team. They called it Etc., a joking reference to its ragtag makeup. Most of the guys were athletes of some kind, but because none of them were part of the Greek system, it made them a kind of David going up against the frat-boy Goliaths. Singer was the team's captain and quarterback, whom the *Trinitonian* dubbed "a strategist." During games, he did his thing, screaming at his teammates ("Why didn't you block that guy?" "You missed coverage!"), calling foul plays, and elbowing everyone in sight. Making the scene even more dramatic was that at the time flag football was a full-contact sport at Trinity. "That meant you could hit people—you could really hit them hard," said Scheiner, who played in the league. "You didn't wear helmets or anything, so it would be full blocking without any helmets or anything."

Ever the renegade, Singer thrived in this free-for-all environment. And when Etc. won the championship game against Omega Phi—marking the first time in nearly a decade that a nonfrat won the event—he became a hero. The yearbook devoted a two-page spread to the game, featuring a photo of him, his legs slightly bowed as he leans into a throw and sends a football blasting across the field. "We took a bunch of independent guys and beat the pants off of the frat brothers," he's quoted as saying.

In a *Trinitonian* article that ran after the game, he was more diplomatic, showing his increasing awareness of the power of the perfect, albeit clichéd, sound bite. "This was a team effort," he said. "There is no 'I' in the word 'team.'"

After graduating in 1986, Singer set his sights on a basketball coaching job, and he landed one, as an assistant coach at Mac-Arthur High School in San Antonio. It didn't last long. His volatile temper led to fights with parents, who felt he was too tough on their kids, according to Hensley. He was canned. It was time, once again, for Singer to rework his brand. So, he headed west.

CHAPTER 3

Breaking Glass

In the fall of 1994, Bill Templeton received a knock at his door. Templeton, who was the CEO of the mortgage lending company the Money Store, had recently relocated from New Jersey to Carmichael, California, an affluent Sacramento suburb that was a fifteen-minute drive from the company's headquarters in a ten-story ziggurat-shaped building overlooking the American River. Templeton lived with his wife and three kids in a gated Victorian home with a rolling lawn in front and a basketball court and guest house out back. When he came to the door, he was met, he said, by "this skinny kid in jeans." The young man (he was actually thirty-four) introduced himself as Rick Singer and said that he understood that Templeton had two daughters in high school. Before Templeton could respond, Singer went on. He explained that he'd recently started a business helping students apply to college. He wondered if Templeton would be interested in having him "coach" his daughters.

Templeton was curious enough about the proposition and curious enough about Singer, whom he found unusually confident and engaging, that he invited him inside. The two men sat down in the living room and talked for half an hour. "What I remember about him back then was he was very caring, supportive, and unique, in a way," Templeton told me. Indeed, Singer was the first so-called independent college counselor Templeton had ever heard of, who worked with students on their college "lists," prepping for standardized tests, and perfecting their résumé, or brand, as Singer called it.

Singer said he'd be willing to work with both of Templeton's daughters—one was a freshman and one was a junior at Rio Americano High School, a well-regarded public school in the area. Templeton suggested starting off with the oldest to see how it went. And so it was that Singer began coming over to Templeton's home a few times a month to sit down with Templeton's oldest daughter to help her map out her college plan. "He'd come and spend maybe two hours with her, going through books, preparing for tests," Templeton said. Afterward, he'd take her down to the basketball court to shoot hoops. "He used that as kind of an example of how you need to be competitive. I liked the way he kind of intertwined sports with the scholastic side of what he was doing."

Singer charged a fee of $1,200 for his services, which extended into senior year. Templeton thought it was a bargain, and soon signed up his second daughter. At the time, Templeton guessed that he was one of Singer's biggest clients and that he was probably tutoring about ten kids tops. "He had to be losing money. It was not a profitable venture," he said. "But he was really spending quality time with my kids. He would never rush. He was more of an inspirational coach kind of a thing."

Templeton was all the more pleased when his daughter got into her school of choice, the University of California at Davis. "He was a pioneer," he said of Singer. "Those things weren't done back in those days. You didn't have coaches working with your kids in high school. He was on the up-and-up."

Singer's business, Future Stars, was a DIY operation that he ran with his wife, Allison, whom he'd married in 1989. Née Allison Karver, Allison, who went by "Allie," had grown up in Sacramento, where she'd attended St. Francis, an all-girls Catholic high school. She went on to San Diego State University before returning home to Sacramento. Like Singer, she was an exercise buff who volunteered at local road races and in 1982 had opened up a fitness club called P.S. Workout with her first husband. (P.S. stood for Park Side, an area in Sacramento.) By the time she met Singer, Allison had segued into real estate, ascending the ranks at Lyon Real Estate, the city's oldest and biggest realty company, to become a training director. "She was very knowledgeable and good with people. She was good at giving classes and helping people start on their real estate careers," said Paula Colombo, a fellow agent at Lyon.

But Allison was also a private person who kept to herself. When Singer started his college counseling business, Allison diverted her management skills into her new husband's business, becoming Singer's number two.

At Future Stars, there was no office, no staff, nor professional trappings of any sort. Group SAT and ACT prep classes were held in churches and rec centers around town. He worked out of his car, which Margie Amott, who was then a volunteer guidance counselor at Rio Americano High School, described as "a junk pile."

"It was some old car, it was not fancy at all," Amott said. "He kept everything in his car. That was his office."

But Singer marketed himself as a one-of-a-kind concierge service. As he told the *Sacramento Bee,* when he worked with students, "I set it all up for them. I call the admissions office and arrange a campus tour. I set up a visit with key professors or department staff. I arrange a stay on campus if possible. For some people, I even set up car rentals, plane reservations, and hotels."

Allison handled the back-end administrative duties, while Singer was the front man and the face of the company. In the early days, the couple worked their respective connections to bring in clients: people Allison knew through her job at Lyon, and Singer's sports contacts. Indeed, much of Singer's early career was spent helping high school athletes land scholarships. He also made inroads with the Jewish community in Sacramento, even though he'd never been religious or associated with any synagogue. Allison was a reserved but steely force, and thus a grounded foil to her loud-mouth husband. She also had a reflective side that he lacked, and she regularly attended services at Unity, a nondenominational church in town. But she shared her husband's ambitions—as well as his love of exercise; they often jogged together—and was eager for their new venture to succeed. One friend said Allison admired Singer's dogged work ethic even when it became obsessive because "he was building a future for them." The couple had recently purchased a modest 1,293-square-foot ranch home for $139,500, in a middle-class neighborhood not far from Sac State, and were talking about adopting a child. As they planned for their future, they lived sensibly, keeping separate bank accounts to maintain independence and putting together a spending and savings plan. But finances were clearly on both their minds. "My husband figured that our vacation this year would cost $1,400, so we both took $700 out of our savings account," Allison told the *Sacramento Bee* in a 1995 article about family budgeting.

"This allows us to take nice vacations, we drive nice cars...and we don't make a lot of money," she went on. "Savings has become a matter of habit for us."

Future Stars was Singer's first attempt at an entrepreneurial venture that he was in control of and that had potential to bring real financial rewards. Although he'd said in college that he was more interested in personal reward than a big paycheck, he was finding that his ambitions superseded what coaching could offer, and so he'd earned a master's degree in school counseling from the University of La Verne. Coaching had also not panned out quite as planned for him when he relocated to Sacramento from San Antonio in the late 1980s. His bombastic behavior on the basketball court led to serial firings—as the head coach at Encina High School, a public school in Sacramento, and as an assistant coach at Sacramento Country Day School, a private K–12 school, where the city's government officials and other local power players sent their children. His explosions were in particularly stark relief at Country Day, where families were more accustomed to country club manners. "Parents complained and said he was abusive to other coaches," said Patricia Fels, who was a guidance counselor at Country Day at the time and attended some of the basketball games that Singer coached. "He wasn't physically abusive, but he did things that were obnoxious. It was considered not to be the proper way to behave, especially at a small independent school."

But if he ruffled the feathers of peers and parents, he connected with kids. His former players at Encina, where he coached for the 1987–88 season—or, almost all of it, as he was fired before the last game—still refer to him fondly as Coach Singer even as they describe grueling workouts, having to show up for practice at six in the morning the day after losing a game (no one hated losing more than Singer), and, of course, his temper. "Coaches are kind of notoriously bad-mouthed, but he cussed plenty, screamed plenty—at us, the refs, the other team, whoever. He was intense," said Saddiq Abdul-Alim, who used to go by Corey Taylor.

Coaches of rival teams were stunned by Singer's behavior and considered him "a first-class asshole," said Pete LeBlanc, a sports-writer for the *Sacramento Bee* at the time. "It was the Bobby Knight style of coaching: very high expectations, a lot of yelling and screaming. Now we're so far away from that, but at that time that was still an accepted practice. As long as you weren't hitting kids, that sort of tough love approach, where the yelling comes with all the other [good] stuff that people don't see," went unchecked. But it did not go unnoticed. LeBlanc said the attitude among coaches was: *What the hell is going on with this guy?*

Encina was located in a middle-class neighborhood that had fallen on hard times. Some of the kids on Singer's team came from broken homes, and it was the kind of school where suspensions were not uncommon due to failing grades and rough behavior. This could affect who showed up for basketball practice and games, putting even more of a burden on a team that was low on power players. But Singer used his fiery antics to motivate his kids, driving them all the harder. "I think he always wanted people to feel that you can do more," said John Meckfessel, another player on the team. "You can do better. Don't settle. He was a guy who approached high school basketball like a college coach."

They believed in themselves even when they had only three guys on the court because players had been fouled or injured. "We all thought we could win, and it was because of him," Meckfessel said.

"He got more out of us than he probably would have got out of us," said Abdul-Alim. "We probably had one notable player on the team, but he got a lot of mileage out of the team he had. We were pretty ragtag."

Singer led by example, showing up early to open the gym and staying later than anyone else to close everything down. "He took a lot of pride in his work," Meckfessel said. "He would do the work. He was the kind of guy who'd be like, 'Hey, let's mop the floor.' He didn't pawn it off on someone else. He was trying to build something."

Beyond teaching basketball skills, he commanded his players to walk onto the court with dignity: to always have their shorts pulled up, not to let them ride low, as was the fashion, and to keep their hair trimmed. This was yet another nugget that would become fodder for *Getting In*, in which he would write: "Never underestimate the importance of a good haircut." Rather than roll their eyes, his team took it in.

"We were kids and we listened to him," Meckfessel went on. "I believed in what he said. He had a big voice. He had a presence. When he started talking, no balls bounced. He commanded respect like the old-school coaches."

Perhaps because he'd always identified himself as an outsider and underdog, Singer seemed to most relate to the kids with less than. He took a special interest in players like Abdul-Alim, who lived with a single mother struggling with drug addiction. "He'd call me to see how I was doing. See how school was going," Abdul-Alim said. "He'd stop by to see me, just to chat, just to see where I was... He was more direct with everyone, but he seemed to have a special connection with us, the poorer minority kids."

Singer gave Abdul-Alim and his friends uniforms for free and offered unsolicited advice about college athletics, a subject he was becoming increasingly expert in, helping one player on the team earn a basketball scholarship to Sacramento State. He once told Abdul-Alim that a degree in sociology was a "suckers' degree." "He said that it was just a degree that they forced the athletes into because it's pretty easy to get. But you can't make money coming out of school with that degree, and that I should go into business or maybe law or something."

In the end, Abdul-Alim, who said he was a terrible student in high school, went on to earn a PhD in genetics. "If you'd known me then, this would have been the most unlikely outcome that you ever imagined—getting a PhD," he said. "I consider Coach instrumental in that."

While coaching at Encina, Singer took on another job as the assistant men's basketball coach at Sierra College. He was also running a lunchtime intramural program at Arden Junior High. He seemed to thrive most when there was too much to do. All of the demands and the relentless schedule kept him singularly focused on performance. Other needs were kept at bay. "At times it gets lonely," Singer told Pete LeBlanc for an article in the *Sacramento Bee*. "I love the kids to death but at times you need a companion. I eat by myself and go to movies by myself. It's tough but I wouldn't trade my life for anything." (In the same article, Singer falsely alleged that he'd attended Texas A&M before transferring to Trinity; graduated magna cum laude from Trinity, where he'd also been the head basketball coach; and that he was friends with Bobby Knight and Magic Johnson and had coached at both of their summer camps.)

John Rankin, the head coach at Sierra, likened Singer to a battery. "He was so energetic," Rankin said. "There was no downtime for him."

Indeed, when he wasn't coaching multiple teams or swimming laps in the pool at Encina at dawn—something he did religiously—he was on the move, always looking for a new venture, trying to hatch a plan of some sort. At Sierra, he reportedly attempted to start a sports vision program that used strobe lights and buzzers to help athletes improve their reaction times. He also had a sideline vending-machine business.

"He bought vending machines and put them in different places," Abdul-Alim said. "I was kind of like, huh, that's not a whole lot of work. People just chuck money into [the machines], you get paid. I mean, obviously there's some work to it. But that kind of stuff meant that he was making money all the time, even when he wasn't with the machine."

"His brain was always active," Abdul-Alim went on. "He just never looked like he relaxed. He's one of those active people. Active brain, active body. They have to be doing something. They have to fix something. Or they have to see angles. They see stuff that other people don't see."

When Abdul-Alim stopped by Singer's place once, he was surprised to see newspapers like the *New York Times* and the *Wall Street Journal* lying around. "It struck me because I was a reader. Bookish. So I remember thinking, huh, *Wall Street Journal*. That he'd delve into those kinds of things. I thought that was interesting. He had the smart newspapers lying around. Not the *Sacramento Bee*. He's very self-educated."

When Singer had first been hired, Encina High School's principal had told him that he'd be "lucky to win one game this year." His team won nine and lost sixteen. They even had a chance of making it to the playoffs, but after Singer was fired at the tail end of the season, the players voted unanimously to forfeit the final game. The last straw had come when he called Abdul-Alim a "son of a bitch" during a game because he was unhappy with Abdul-Alim's performance. When Abdul-Alim then walked, rather than jogged, off the floor, Singer kicked him out of the gym. Singer was let go.

By now his behavior was making headlines. Another *Sacramento Bee* article by LeBlanc began: "Rick Singer. The name alone evokes many images in the minds of local basketball players and fans." The story cast Singer as a colorful rager whose coaching style "crossed the line of discipline and wandered off into the land of lunacy."

Singer told LeBlanc: "I'll tell you what. When you say the name Rick Singer, people start saying, 'Oh my God, Rick Singer.' But after they get to know me, they say, 'That can't be the same guy.' That's after they know me for who I am."

At Sierra, where he continued to coach, Singer toned his temper down. But his shameless self-aggrandizement raged on. When Sierra did well in the junior college state championships in 1988, Jeff Caraska, then a sports editor at the *Auburn Journal*, a local paper in the area, was asked to write a story about Sierra's invigorated coaching staff, which included Singer. Caraska's conversation with him lasted only fifteen minutes, but in that time Singer painted an embellished picture of himself, telling Caraska that he'd been a four-sport athlete at Texas A&M as well as a "successful high school coach" in San Antonio who'd taken the team at MacArthur High to the large-school state playoffs, not once but twice. (Singer was at the school only one year and never took them to the play-offs.) For added measure, he said he'd coached four sports at the school and was the head coach of three—more fallacies.

"I couldn't Google the guy when I was done talking to him," said Caraska, noting the limitations of pre-internet fact-checking. He admits, though, that Singer's claim that he'd been a four-sport athlete in college "should have set off an alarm in my head. Three-and four-sport kids were common in the 1970s, and by the nineties there'd be some two-sport kids, but very rarely three-sport kids.

"But how would a sports editor of a nine-thousand-circulation paper in Auburn fact-check that?" Caraska said. "The paper was designed so you took people at face value. In community journalism, there's a lot of that."

Caraska said his overall impression of Singer was of a guy who was looking down the road. "Rocklin, California, was not where he was going to end his journey," Caraska said.

Singer's opportunity came in 1989, when he got his first shot at coaching Division I at Sacramento State just as that school was transitioning into the big-program category. That job—he was one of two assistant coaches for the men's basketball team—played to his quirks and strengths. Yelling was more accepted at the college level, and much of his role was traveling to high schools and other basketball hubs to recruit kids to Sac State. His fellow assistant coach, Ron McKenna, recalled Singer's ability to travel into tough neighborhoods, walk onto basketball courts, and level with guys who were often twice his size. "He'd go into the playgrounds of East LA and talk to the guys, and he'd play in pickup games. He could do that," McKenna said. "He could talk the talk and walk the walk."

"He was a very good recruiter—that was his full-time job. Coaching and recruiting. He was a straight shooter with the kids. He'd tell them what it was. 'We can do this for you. You can do that for me.' 'Can you do this for me?' 'No, we can't do that.' For kids that live there, if you're straight with them, that's the only way you're gonna get around."

Meanwhile, his penchant for exaggeration continued. When Sac State published a media guide featuring its basketball team and staff, Singer's bio claimed that he'd played varsity basketball, baseball, football, and tennis at Trinity. It also stated that he'd been captain of the basketball team and had won numerous basketball awards and honors—none of which was true.

In 1992, Sac State dissolved its staff, following three dismal seasons during which the school had failed to find its footing in Division I. Singer was once again without a job. But this time he changed course, deciding to take a break from the basketball court, at least for the time being. He also seemed to realize that in order to succeed, he needed to be more in control of his destiny, to be his own boss. And after many years kicking the tires of many different business propositions, he felt he was on to something: a new, untested profession that would combine his ability to connect with kids and his knowledge of how college admissions worked, especially when it came to recruited athletes. He'd been watching the trend of identifying and grooming elite young basketball players and prepping them to attend top college basketball programs, a system that had kicked into gear in the 1980s. Back then, promising basketball players as young as eleven years old were being funneled into elite summer camps and showered with gear by Nike and Adidas, then transferring to high schools that essentially existed solely to be finishing academies for a player's skills before they went on to a powerhouse college team.

Sports aside, he saw a white space. Kids (and their parents) desperately wanted to get into certain schools. And yet, especially at public high schools, there typically weren't enough guidance counselors to help them navigate the college admissions process. Often, just one or two counselors were managing a load of hundreds of students. As for what was offered beyond a high school career center, there were SAT and ACT prep classes, run by companies like the Princeton Review and Kaplan, but these were largely formulaic and impersonal. Nothing was individualized, geared to take into account a kid's particular circumstances, interests, or strengths. But perhaps Singer's most potent insight of all was that parents hated being involved in college applications, and that the ones who could afford to pay someone else to take charge were eager to do so.

"Rick became the intermediary between the parents and the students, which the parents liked because they didn't have to fight with their students to get the material, fill out the applications— do all the kind of work that needs to be done to apply to college," said McKenna, who after coaching at Sac State became a guidance counselor at Kennedy High School in Sacramento and would often meet with his old coaching buddy.

Singer's trajectory as an independent college counselor rose rapidly, thanks to the social fabric of Sacramento. Although the city has its share of Bay Area tech millionaires who have relocated to the quieter and cheaper state capital, Sacramento remains a low-key place. "We're a cow town, an agricultural city," said Kim Perry, a workplace consultant who lives in the area. "So the people who made money here were developers or were in oil or agriculture. But they don't brag about it."

It's also a so-called government town, where people put in their time working for the state at nine-to-five jobs and then retire with generous pensions by the time they're fifty. The city has a laid-back, folksy feel. It's the kind of place that people like to say is easy to live in and a great place to raise kids. There are parks, trees, and ponds. Traffic moves gently along narrow, tree-lined streets. No one seems to be in any hurry. In other words, it was the ideal place for a guy in sneakers and Gap jeans to start peddling his services.

He also benefited from how socially and economically stratified Sacramento is. The city's mostly white upper-class families form a fairly small, tight-knit group, who see one another at the local coffee shops in the morning, at soccer games after school, and at local fundraisers on the weekends. They tend to be liberal and education-minded and deeply focused on where their kids go to school, both at the secondary level and beyond. Many send their children to private schools, including Catholic institutions like St. Francis (the inspiration for the all-girls school in the Oscar-nominated film *Lady Bird*) and Jesuit High School, where most of the kids play sports—providing yet more socializing opportunities.

When a family decides to enroll their child in a new activity—say, synchronized swimming—it suddenly becomes a thing. Similarly, when a family hires a guy to help their child get into college, ears prick up. This was all the more so in the 1990s, when "all the wealthy families in Sacramento knew each other," said Perry. "If one kid did something, everyone knew about it."

This happened at St. Francis, where after one student hired Singer to help them apply to college, dozens followed. "He became very in demand, and all of a sudden word started spreading like wildfire," said Perry. "Not only within the private Catholic school community, but at public schools, where affluent kids were going. All of a sudden, it was like, 'I hired Rick Singer, I got a blah-blah-blah on my SAT, and I improved by doing all these practice tests. So for many people it was a no-brainer to hire him."

He "made common sense for parents who really had nowhere to turn—the school counselors were wonderful but extraordinarily busy," said Margie Amott, who after seeing Singer speak decided to become an independent college counselor herself, figuring she could do better. "So a lot of them started hiring him. A lot of my good friends did."

Perry first met Rick Singer when she ran into a classmate of hers who was sitting with him at Burr's Fountain, a popular ice-cream shop (now closed), going through test-prep materials. Perry walked over to the table, and her friend introduced her to Singer. Soon enough, he was at Perry's house, pitching his company to her parents, who agreed to hire him for $500 to help her prep for the SAT over a period of six months. There was an additional charge to help her with her college applications. Perry couldn't recall what it was but said, "His fee was negligible. It was a hundred times cheaper than getting braces."

Her first impression of Singer was that he was like a track

coach. "Just that kind of guy who looks like he's a marathon runner," she said. "He positioned himself as a mentor. He was very charismatic. Very sharp and shrewd."

Another Future Stars client, Scott Kingston, who attended Country Day and then Rio Americano, where he played golf and basketball, said Singer had "an athletic coach mentality," which he responded to. Singer would sometimes start tutoring sessions with Kingston by shooting hoops with him in front of his house. "It was a different era," Kingston said. "It wasn't safe spaces and everyone gets trophies. It was very much you need to win, and here are the tools to win. I respect that now as an adult looking back on what he was doing then."

Beyond helping Perry prepare for the SAT and come up with her college list, he encouraged her to think about what made her unique, what was her brand. When he learned that Perry had a special-needs sibling whom she'd helped raise, he told her to write about that in her college essay. The advice itself wasn't groundbreaking, but Singer presented it not as a suggestion but as essential marketing. "We as teenagers didn't know what that meant, 'What was our brand?'" she said. "It was really brilliant, because it helped you think about what stood you apart from even your classmates in high school."

Singer also steered Perry away from communications and other majors that he told her were "inundated," to increase her chances of admission. And, proving that he was ultimately not only a coach or tutor but a soup-to-nuts concierge, when she said she was interested in applying to UC Davis, he arranged for her to spend the night at the school with a female former client who was now enrolled there. "He facilitated things," Perry said.

"When he worked with you, he'd do everything," said Amott. "He signed kids up for the SAT or ACT," he figured out their class schedule, when applications were due, organized their college tours. But although he sold himself as the guy who'd get you into the school of your choice, his record wasn't perfect. Perry was disappointed when she didn't get into UCLA (she instead enrolled at UC Davis). But she said, "Never once did it occur to me to blame him."

Other clients took it harder. He encouraged one young woman to apply to the University of North Carolina, apparently unaware of the higher standards for out-of-state applicants. When she was rejected, she was "heartbroken," according to Amott, who knew the family. The sting was made all the worse because Singer had been so confident she'd get in.

These slips made people like Amott begin to question just how much of a miracle worker he actually was. There were times he seemed completely out of touch, such as when he was helping one student with her résumé. The girl had worked as a candy striper at a local hospital, and on the résumé, Singer described the job as "paints stripes on candy."

"We all kind of laughed," said Amott. "'No, Rick. That's not what a candy striper is.'"

She got an even better look at Singer when she hired him to work with her daughter when she was a senior at Rio Americano. After her daughter wrote her college essay and showed it to him, he proclaimed it "Great!" Amott then read the essay herself and had a starkly different opinion. "It was awful," she said. Singer was let go.

As he grew his business and became a known entity around town, these inconsistencies, as well as his overabundance of chutzpah, were becoming impossible to ignore, as was his gnawing persistence, which was invariably centered around one thing: giving him an advantage over everyone else. He would call up high school counselors and pester them about coming to give presentations at their schools, even as he was instructing the families he was working with to not engage with their high school counselors and even ignore what they had to say.

"At that point, I'd never heard of him doing anything unlawful," said Dorothy Missler, who ran the college and career center at Jesuit High School and who was one of the people Singer was always calling up. "But he wasn't following the ethical guidelines of our national organization [the IECA]. He was making promises and having students embellish their résumés. He'd say, 'Oh, well, if you were part of the swim team, say you were captain of the swim team.'"

A former associate of Singer's said that résumé padding was by now routine for him. He'd outright say to a kid he was working with: "You're a little lacking on community service. Let's just throw this item on your résumé."

"It was all very nonchalant," the associate said. "He would ask for permission. 'Do you mind if I do this?' The teenager's sitting there going, 'Yeah, sure.'" This person also heard from families that Singer was writing essays for kids and, in at least one case, had a student list themselves as an underrepresented minority, which they were not. "You don't have to be doing this for very long to realize there are a lot of things you can do to pull levers. There are so many things you can't verify."

It was as though Singer was applying his succeed-at-all-costs sports mentality to college tutoring, invoking the famous line by former Chicago Cubs first baseman Mark Grace: "If you're not cheating, you're not winning." And Singer desperately wanted to win. Not for the glory, and not necessarily for the money (though money was tangible proof of success), but to overcompensate for the flaws and shortcomings of which he was so painfully aware: his lack of wealth growing up; his physical attributes (short and with a tendency to gain weight); his circuitous, stop-and-go career path.

In his mind, a few stretches of the truth here and a few outright lies there were just part of the game, necessary tactics taken by anyone who was truly committed to coming out on top. Not that there was any self-reflection on Singer's part; he operated mostly by knee-jerk hustle. A Darwinian sense of survival. Honesty and hard work alone might get you respect but not much else. And that simply wouldn't do. On the basketball court this justified throwing an elbow or tackling a teammate or being outrageously foulmouthed. But those were ultimately overheated antics that could be shrugged off after a foul was called and everyone dove back into the action. As Singer parlayed this cutting-corners strategy to college counseling, he began getting into much more serious, and dangerous, territory.

❦

Rick Singer was certainly not the first independent college counselor to grace the scene, but he was by all accounts an early pioneer. The profession has been around since the 1970s, when the IECA was founded, but back then independent counselors were primarily hired by families looking to find "the best" private high schools and boarding schools for their children, according to IECA CEO Mark Sklarow. In the 1980s, the shift toward helping families with college admissions began. But the concept of hiring an outside college consultant didn't really take off until the late 1990s and 2000s, driven by the high demand for name-brand colleges and universities, and the increasing difficulty of getting into them. This coincided with colleges' shift from seeking out well-rounded students to those with more narrowly defined interests, leading to more and more bafflement as to why certain kids weren't being admitted to their top choices. Those independent counselors that did exist tended to focus on the basics: standardized test prep, helping kids come up with a list of colleges to apply to and providing information and advice on those schools, and essay help. But Singer amped things up to a new level, stressing not only how a student could stand out and seem appealing to an admissions officer, but how to aggressively sell themselves as though they were a marketable product. As he would write in *Getting In*: "Getting into college is a lot like selling iPads or cans of Coca-Cola. It's all about branding...

"If you don't know what your personal brand is yet, it's time to name it and claim it. Because you need a strong brand."

This was long before branding was a mainstream cultural phenomenon, though the idea, at least, was in the ether—in 1997, Tom Peters published a zeitgeisty essay in *Fast Company* magazine titled "The Brand Called You," in which he argued that everyone from CEOs to receptionists should be in control of their image and careers. Still, these were the days before social media, before digital influencers, before six-year-old YouTube sensations turned their impish charm into a $26 billion toy and media empire (see Ryan's World on YouTube). But Singer presciently plugged into where the culture was headed, just as colleges were focusing more on students who could be defined by a singular catchphrase. He also had a deeply ingrained cynicism about getting into college, believing from the beginning that admissions was an unfair game that could be won with a dash of cunning and, if necessary, rule-breaking.

Today, the demand for independent college counselors has skyrocketed as more and more families perplexed by college admissions have sought guidance. Sklarow estimates that there are now about fifteen thousand independent counselors working in the United States, up from about two thousand in 2005. They are hired almost exclusively by families who can afford to pay thousands of dollars a year for a tutor to help a student navigate every loophole and nuance of the application process, as well as help them plan their high school career: what courses to enroll in, which extracurriculars to pursue. Meetings with families begin as early as when a student is in eighth grade. Following Singer's concierge model, today most college counselors work with students around the clock, available on weekends for texts and Skype or Zoom sessions. Independent counselors don't write a student's college essay, but rounds of edits and proofreading are provided, giving the student a distinct edge over those who are left to their own devices. Indeed, more than anything else, in an era of intense personalization and outsourcing, independent counselors offer a sense of advantage in a landscape where the feeling is that there is little to no chance of winning without one.

For many wealthy parents, the price is negligible, considering the potential returns: admittance to a top-tier school. "As I tell people all the time, if they're going to spend five thousand dollars on a handbag, what is five thousand, ten thousand, to hire a college counselor?" said Bill Rubin, who runs the College Authority, a company in Laguna Beach, California, that provides college tours for high school students. "Everyone wants an edge."

Ten thousand dollars is actually on the low side. In LA, families spend up to $30,000 over the course of four years for a college tutor. In other parts of the country, such as New York and San Francisco, these fees can run into the hundreds of thousands of dollars.

Rubin also works as an independent college counselor, and he jokes about the perception people have of his profession. "The stereotype of the independent counselor is: Jewish middle-aged woman whose husband is loaded and who does this on the side because she enjoys it," he told me. "Because her kids got into really good colleges, she thinks she can do a good job, too.

"I'm now forty-nine, I'm actually Jewish, though I'm not practicing, and my husband is loaded," Rubin added. "So I actually fit the stereotype. But it just cracks me up. There's a lot of that. A lot of parents whose kids have gotten into excellent schools and they all think, 'Oh, I can do this.'"

The industry is, in fact, unregulated, meaning anyone can set up shop—another factor that facilitated Singer, who for all intents and purposes was a basketball coach when he founded Future Stars, despite his degree in counseling. Increasingly, the field has attracted graduates of top-tier schools who have worked in admissions and have relations with admissions officers, but there are no testing or licensing requirements for the job and many who succeed do so simply by being smart, learning the field, and having a knack for interacting with students. Some, like Jill Newman, started up their businesses following careers as high school counselors. Newman began taking on private clients after spending years working at public schools in Sacramento. (She recently returned to high school counseling.) She said her goal was never to mastermind a kid's application, but rather to give a student tools to successfully go through the process themselves. "I'm like a Home Depot. I'm going to teach you how to do it, then you do it," she said. "If you still want me to hold your hand, fine. But I'm really going to encourage you to not have to need me." Newman also did pro bono work on the side, as do many independent counselors, offering her services either for free or for a reduced rate to families who can't afford her rate of $110 an hour. (She generally meets with kids two to three times a year for a few hours at a time over the course of their high school career.)

Her advice to families is similarly reasonable and sound. "When parents and kids come in and say, 'We're going to try for Stanford and our safety is Berkeley,' I say, 'Um...Let me explain to you what I mean by 'range.'

"The job is a lot about calming down the fears, building confidence so that they know they can go through it and it's not going to break them," she went on. "Even if they start at a community college or a local [branch of] California State University or a college that's not a known college in the west, as long as it's the right college for them and they're successful and happy there, then we've succeeded. They've stayed in college, they've completed their degree within four years, and now they're off to whatever their next step is going to be."

Counselors who want more formal legitimacy join organizations such as the Higher Education Consultants Association (HECA) or the IECA. The latter offers membership to independent counselors who have logged a certain number of hours working in the profession, who regularly tour colleges and universities, and who complete an online ethics course. Sklarow said that in the wake of the college admissions scandal, applications to the IECA grew 300 percent. But of the fifteen thousand independent college counselors in the United States today, only twenty-one hundred belong to his group. HECA has a membership of one thousand. (Singer has never been a part of either of these groups.)

But most parents don't care about credentials. They care about referrals and word-of-mouth recommendations and, of course, results. In West LA, one of the most sought-after independent college counselors is Sally Schultz, a woman who has been described to me in almost mythic terms. She lives "up in the hills," where she tutors out of her home, which is "almost like a club—you have to be invited," one parent told me. Schultz even turns clients down, causing people to put in "asks" from friends and do their best to charm her. "People are like, 'Would you mind calling Sally and putting in a word on my behalf?' It's kind of horrifying."

In an interview with the *Harvard-Westlake Chronicle*, Schultz described the methodology of her program. "I teach far beyond the standardized tests," she said. "My sessions include discussing current events, sharing favorite 'good reads,' and encouraging and tracking efforts to volunteer in the community. We are trying to become better citizens while getting a stellar score along the way."

Others are less lofty about what they're selling. Allen Koh, the founder of Cardinal Education in San Francisco, counsels families on the delicate dance with college development offices, telling parents when the best time is to make a donation to a school that their child is applying to. "You don't ever want to insult the development officer by offering money right before they are applying, that would be considered a faux pas," Koh told the *Wall Street Journal*. When I spoke to him, Koh said that he also analyzes a student's "executive function," helping them improve their study habits and school performance. If they're spending too much time on, say, Snapchat, "We have a lot of different apps and things we can do through tech to eliminate the constant parent-child arguments about social media and screen usage in general. We want them to be producers, not consumers." Koh's most popular package is $65,000, but his services go as high as $350,000. In some special cases that Koh described as "complicated situations" involving international students, he charges $1 million.

Independent college counselors tend to keep at a remove from the high school counselors that work with students on their college applications. In fact, most private high schools discourage using them, feeling not only that independent counselors are meddling in a process that the school should oversee but also that their power is ultimately limited. Unlike high school counselors, independent counselors cannot call up admissions officers and discuss applicants, elaborating, say, on why a certain student is a good fit for a school. Some universities, such as Georgetown, are so down on independent counselors that they won't let them take tours of the school and refuse to read any recommendations or other materials that have been prepared by them. But families wind up hiring them anyway, fearful that their child is not getting enough attention from overworked school counselors. This argument is more valid at public schools, where the average caseload for a school counselor is 482 students, according to the American School Counselor Association. In California, the caseload per school counselor is 760. Beyond the pure volume these counselors are grappling with, their jobs also include providing social and emotional support to students, as well as bureaucratic demands such as scheduling.

When Jill Newman was working as a high school counselor at Rio Americano in the early 2000s, she said they had caseloads of 450 students each, and when the economic recession hit in 2008, they got down to thirty counselors in the entire San Juan Unified School District, which serves nine high schools. "It was horrible," she said. "When the economy stabilized and California started putting money back into schools, the district started to hire back a lot of counselors, and we returned to having seventy."

Gwen Meyer is the college and career center coordinator at Alameda High School, a public high school outside of San Francisco. "We have four academic counselors for four hundred thirty kids. For each one of them, they were doing at least a minimum of twenty-five secondary reports. Some did thirtysomething," she told me. "With some kids, there's a letter of recommendation component for the high school counselor, and they have been inundated with so many of these that they have had to create hard deadlines for students, so that they can fill out all of this information and write an individual letter of recommendation. Because each letter of recommendation is crafted individually. They're not recycling them. It's a shit ton of work for a high school counselor."

Meyer says she feels relief when students work with independent counselors. "Because then I can really help serve the kids who don't have anybody," she told me. "They're taking the SAT or the ACT with very little prep—maybe they did some Khan Academy online for free. But it's a different process for them."

At private schools, however, where counselors have a much more manageable load of students, often only about a dozen to thirty per counselor, the feeling toward outside counselors is more antagonistic. "I always tell parents, 'It's up to you whether you want [the high school counselors] to know that I exist,'" said independent counselor Jen Kaifesh. "A lot of it is like, 'I cannot be a ghostwriter, but I'm kind of in the background advising you.' I will tell them, 'Go to the counselor,' because I want them to have a relationship with their school counselor. Because that's who's writing the recommendation. I'm like, 'You can't diss her for me. She is still the primary source. I don't need to exist.'"

"I would use the term 'hated,'" said Andy Lockwood, cofounder of Lockwood College Prep in New York. "A lot of [high school counselors] dislike me or people like me, because their perception is that if they were doing their jobs, parents wouldn't need to go anywhere else. So it's a defensive thing. My position is, 'Listen, the problem is the system, it's not your counselor.'"

Marlborough's head of school, Priscilla Sands, said that she asks parents not to work with independent counselors but that it's impossible to monitor. "We say, 'Don't hire,' but they do." Even when she reminds parents that the school's three in-house counselors [for a class of between eighty and one hundred] have relationships with the students and know them from both an academic and a personal point of view, few listen. The counselors "are intimately working with the girls," Sands said. "They spend a tremendous amount of time with each girl. They know them well. They meet with the families and know all of the teachers who are writing [recommendations] for them. They know them as students."

To her, though, the real tragedy isn't that her counselors aren't being relied on enough; it's that students aren't using an important milestone in life—figuring out a post–high school plan and working to achieve that goal—as an opportunity to develop greater self-reliance and responsibility.

"These girls should be doing it themselves," Sands said. "They're basically hiring sort of a college nanny to do the work."

❧

By the late 1990s, the nonstop hustle required by Rick Singer's job—he'd brought on one partner but was still doing most of the tutoring and test-prep workshops himself—was taking its toll, or at least causing him to once again wonder what other opportunities were out there. At $1,200 a client, he wasn't clearing that much more than a basketball coach. He would later tell the *Sacramento Business Journal* that he was better at coaching than running a business. Furthermore, he and Allison had adopted a son, Bradley, and the family craved more financial return than being a one-man tutor was providing. "Ali wanted him to be successful, and I think at a certain point they didn't think being a teacher was going to make him successful," said one friend of Allison's from that time. Singer was a proud father. He told friends how he would run on a treadmill and work out after putting Bradley in a baby seat on the floor, hoping to motivate his son.

To make ends meet, he was still coaching hoops on the side, working as a PE coach and boys' basketball coach at Marshall High School in downtown Sacramento. But he had grander ambitions. One day, when he showed up at Bill Templeton's house for a session with Templeton's younger daughter, he asked the CEO if he could talk to him for a minute. Templeton led him into the living room. Singer got right to the point.

"Do you think you could get me a job?"

Templeton was surprised by the question, assuming Singer had wanted to talk to him about his daughter. "A job doing what?" he said.

"I'm not sure," Singer replied. "I'd like to get into corporate America. I gotta do something more than I'm currently doing now. Is there something you can do for me?"

Templeton had been consistently impressed by Singer's work ethic and dedication to working with his kids, so he took his request seriously and wound up offering him a job managing call centers for the Money Store. As Templeton explained, "We were a financial services company, but our core competence was marketing. We were spending a hundred twenty million dollars a year in marketing, and a lot of that money was spent on TV ads. We'd always be on TV. 'Call one eight hundred...'"

In the early 1990s, the Money Store brought on Baltimore Orioles pitcher Jim Palmer as a spokesman—and the face of those ads. "We were getting a zillion phone calls," Templeton said. "We had three call centers answering thousands of calls, maybe millions of calls, on a yearly basis. So that was a very, very important aspect of our business."

Singer sold Future Stars and was hired at the Money Store

as a midlevel manager—though he told people he was a senior executive, and even told some he was the company's president. "I brought him into my office and said, 'This is what I want you to do. This is what you have to do. This is the kind of space we have to find. This is the technology,'" Templeton said. "I want you to go out and recruit people and train them how to answer phones. Can you do that?"

Singer responded with enthusiasm. "Yeah, I can do that!"

He got right to work. One of his projects was to open up a call center in New Jersey, where he impressed Templeton by going to schools in the area to try and recruit interns. "That was an unheard-of thing at the time," Templeton said.

Indeed, Singer dove into the work, transferring his signature drive into his new gig. He seemed proud of his job and told one former associate he was netting there what he was grossing in college counseling. His efforts did not go unnoticed. More than one senior Money Store executive walked into Templeton's office and remarked, "Who the hell is this Rick Singer guy?"

"Why?" Templeton would ask.

"He's breaking glass," the person would say. "He's making things happen."

CHAPTER 4

Toddler Admissions Mania

Michele Gathrid, the director of Circle of Children Preschool in Santa Monica, likes to tell this story. One day, a family walked into her office to discuss their child, whom they wanted to send to Circle, as it's generally known. "They were very official. They walked in in lovely clothing—suit and tie for the dad, beautiful dress for the mom," Gathrid said. "They sat down on my bench and they said, 'We are interested in our child going to either Harvard or Yale. And we heard that this is the right school for us to attend for us to get our child there.'"

Gathrid, a soft-spoken former preschool teacher, who has a calm, genteel vibe, was taken aback by the boldness of the statement, but she gently told them, "If that's your goal, I can't help you."

"The reason I said that is not because I don't want the family here," Gathrid told me one winter morning. It was gray and chilly out, and she was wrapped in muted-toned cashmere: a thick scarf wrapped around her neck, and a soft sweater. "Because I don't treat people that way. I said it because nobody can guarantee anything. This is not about what school your child attends or doesn't attend. This is about the morals and values that you instill in your children. That's what matters. That's what gets you from point A to point B."

After Gathrid laid out this argument to the family, she said, "They ended up getting up, and they did not enroll in my school."

Most parents may not be as blunt about their desires as these parents were, but in certain pockets of Los Angeles, it's a given that families select preschools based on what elementary and secondary schools their five-year-old graduates go to and what social and educational milieu they would like to see their children travel through—a path that will culminate in, if all goes as planned, a top-tier college. Circle, which is located on Montana Avenue, a neighborhood awash in designer boutiques and trendy restaurants, where sun-kissed locals decked out in James Perse hoodies and Lululemon yoga pants walk their dogs and enjoy leisurely coffee sessions at the local Peet's, is one such preschool. Families who apply there (past parents include Meryl Streep and Tom Hanks) often do so because they believe it will lead to an acceptance at a prestigious elementary school, such as Carlthorp School or John Thomas Dye, which in turn will lead to an acceptance at Harvard-Westlake or Marlborough and, in turn, a top college. As one LA parent told me, "Circle is totally a feeder to Carlthorp." (Carlthorp, a buttoned-down private school that attracts the children of Hollywood bigwigs, is about a mile from Circle.)

When I ran this comment by Gathrid, she vigorously denied it. "I can by no means get any child into any school," she said. "I am by no means any kind of a feeder school, nor are any of the preschools on the west side of town." (The west side of Los Angeles is a hotbed of wealth and status-minded families of a certain ilk. There is just as much status obsession on the east side, but it comes in the form of Jesse Kamm pants and second homes in Joshua Tree, as opposed to Teslas and memberships at Jonathan Club.)

But whether Gathrid is willing to admit it or not, Circle, along with other "tier-one" preschools in West LA, such as Sunshine, Piper, Cassidy, First Presbyterian, and Little Dolphins by the Sea, is where the education game for the elite begins in Los Angeles. As one preschool mother put it: "It's the light version of what parents will be doing at Brentwood and John Thomas Dye."

Indeed, it is here where families hone the skills that will serve them so well when their toddlers are suddenly high school juniors vying to get into college. For many parents, the environment at these preschools, which cost between $16,000 and $25,000 a year (more, if enrichment programs are added), is an anxiety-ridden buildup to a gilded kindergarten acceptance letter. While children spend their days mastering their fine and gross motor skills, their parents are working with consultants on kindergarten applications, hiring tutors to get their child ready for their kindergarten assessment, and attending lavish parties-slash-fundraisers, where they network and burnish their standing as VIP families, both with directors and other "power families," as one parent put it— i.e., influential families whose connections may be helpful with elementary school admissions.

A few weeks after I met with Gathrid, Circle parents threw a Winter Wonderland party at one of their opulent homes in the Pacific Palisades. Each child was given an exquisite gingerbread house to decorate, invited to interact with a troupe of wandering characters from the movie *Frozen*, and led to a gifting station laden with goody bags. As the children played, their parents enjoyed a catered meal. There was also a glistening walkway of fake snow to heighten the winter illusion in a city where December temperatures hover in the sixties and seventies. The event was a so-called Party Book fundraiser, of which there are many throughout the year (though generally less over-the-top) in order to raise money for school improvements, teacher pension plans, and scholar-ships, Gathrid said. Party Book gatherings—which are even more prevalent at private elementary and high schools—are completely organized by parents and Gathrid said she rarely attends. "It all depends on the people who are choosing to head [Party Book planning] and what their vision is and what they want to raise for the school. As horrible as it may sound, it benefits the school."

For the privileged class, the cultural parallels between preschool and high school when it comes to strategizing a child's next step is lost on no one, least of all those who are in the thick of it. Cassidy Preschool's executive director, Luisa Donati, said that when the Varsity Blues scandal hit in March of 2019, it was on the heels of elementary school application deadlines. She'd spent the previous weeks working around the clock with families on their applica-tions, offering advice and guidance to a very stressed-out group of parents. "I remember thinking, 'Every day I am seeing the baby version, the embryo of what just happened,'" she said. "Not neces-sarily the wrongdoing part, or that there is any wrongdoing at this level. But what I'm saying is that the seed of anxiety that blossoms into the insanity of what happened with Varsity Blues is present already in the preschool and elementary application process."

❧

It's easy to completely miss Circle while strolling down Montana Avenue in Santa Monica. Despite its location in one of LA's toniest neighborhoods, the school—which is sandwiched between an up-scale dry cleaner and a beauty and wellness store called the Detox Market—has an unassuming exterior, devoid of any signage or advertising. The only clue as to its identity is a solid orange circle affixed to the side of its gray concrete exterior. Upon entering, visitors walk past a small sand area and into a warren-like group of rooms, where young teachers wearing Ugg boots are corralling children from activity to activity.

In other words, Circle is not the kind of space that, at first glance, one would ooh and aah over. And yet that is exactly what enamored parents do. "It's like Neverland!" one mother who applied there gushed to me. "There's a tortoise that walks around!" This mother called Michele Gathrid a "genius," saying how when the mother visited the school with her daughter, Gathrid gamely jumped into the sandbox with the girl and showed her the most effective way to shovel.

She also appreciated Gathrid's folksy vibe with prospective parents. "She said, 'Come visit! Bring your kid!' Other directors say, 'Make an appointment,'" and are much more formal. This mother was well aware of Gathrid's reputation as a respected elder in the preschool circuit. A longtime director—she's had her job for almost twenty years—Gathrid possesses that rare combination of a deep grounding in early child development and education, and the sophistication and temperament to deal with parents who often require as much handholding as their children. Perhaps most importantly, she's a trusted voice among elementary school admissions officers.

For many parents, Gathrid is Circle's main draw, and they are willing to do anything to get their child into the school—which itself is no simple act. In order to enroll in Circle's toddler program, which ensures admittance to the preschool itself, parents have to take a tour of the school when their child is one (the toddler program is for two-year-olds, with the youngest children starting at twenty-one months), fill out an application, and then call Gathrid once every four to six weeks to show their interest. They can call and chat or call after hours and simply leave a message.

The point is to prove their interest and dedication to the school, i.e., that they want it that badly.

One parent called the requirements "absurd," but to Gathrid it is simply a means of separating out people who are applying just to apply from those who will be more invested in the school should their children be admitted. Who wouldn't want an incoming class of parents who are eager to participate and who are, on a very basic level, just happy to be there? "In all honesty, I can flip through my application book and know who wants to be a part of my school and who doesn't," Gathrid said. "And that's who gets in. There's no picking, no first come, first served."

The only caveat is reserved for siblings and legacies. "I don't care if you're on your third marriage with your third set of kids," Gathrid said. "You're still a part of my community."

But parents who do apply rarely leave their chances to a few phone calls, seeing preschool admissions as a game that requires working every connection and advantage. To increase their odds, they solicit recommendations from current or former Circle families as well as, in some cases, endorsements from influencers in the West LA baby and toddler scene. These include women like Donna Holloran, who runs a highly selective baby group for mothers and their infants, and consultants like Betsy Brown Braun and Michelle Nitka, who help parents come up with a list of preschools to apply to and walk them through the application process. (Brown Braun is also a child development consultant who advises parents on things like sleep training and behavior issues.) A call from Betsy—everyone in this ecosystem is on a first-name-only basis—to a preschool is the equivalent of a tag implying that the child's application deserves serious consideration.

"I don't think that just a random person who lives on the west side, who doesn't know anyone, can just apply and get in [to a competitive preschool]," said Christina Simon, the coauthor of *Beyond the Brochure: An Insider's Guide to Private Elementary Schools in Los Angeles*. "That would be very surprising. You have to be connected."

"Oh, no," laughed a mother whose child attended Sunshine Preschool in Brentwood, when I asked her about an unconnected family getting into the school. "It's all who you know." (Sunshine is considered one of the most selective schools in the area and attracts an inordinate number of übermonied families.)

Stories about getting into elite preschools in LA range from humorous to frightening to eyebrow-raising. At the Center for Early Education, whose preschool feeds into its famed elementary school (Beyoncé performed at a school gala, and former head of school Reveta Bowers was on the Disney board), one mother who was applying for the school's preschool program said she was asked whether she had delivered her child via C-section or vaginal birth. The mother considered the question not only strange and invasive, but inappropriate and ended up not applying.

According to Mark Brooks, the Center's head of school, the question is more of a conversation starter with couples, no different from asking parents what the first six months was like with their child. "It's more like, how can we engage with you in a conversation about your child? It's a way to try to make people feel like they can share with us. 'How was that? What's going on with you?'

"It's just a way to get people to share with us."

Preschool directors like to say that they look for families who are a "good fit." But at some schools this means *parents* who are a good fit, much more than children. "Directors want to engineer a certain class," said one former Sunshine mother, who said that factors like wealth and ability to donate, as well as social cachet and connections, all play a part. At one west side preschool, the school's admissions director was known to take notes on what kind of handbag mothers toted on a tour, and to look up the value of a family's home on Zillow.

At Piper, another elite preschool in Santa Monica, which has an outdoor creek and which pipes in tunes by GNR and the Dave Matthews Band during school hours (Reese Witherspoon and Jessica Alba sent their kids here), parents who hope to enroll their children are subject to a cheeky personality test, meant to filter out the uncool. Application questions include: "Rate your crazy," and "You got front row sold-out tickets for Bon Jovi...new sitter...your child begins a quick dramatic spiral. You are more likely to..." Among the possible answers given for the Bon Jovi question: "Kiss your finger, touch their forehead, and dash. 'Livin' on a Prayer' is only great live" and "Explain that we really need this night together because Jon's smile gives Mommy chills. Tuck them in, then leave."

At Sunshine, in Brentwood, which boasts on its website that its "graduates attend the most prominent West Los Angeles private and public schools," some parents feel the attitude toward prospective families is "You're lucky to be in our midst," according to one mother. "I felt like I was applying to Stanford," she said. She was nonetheless caught up in the mystique of the school, which looks like a mini version of Tara nestled alongside Sunset Boulevard, firmly believing that "in order to go to Stanford or Harvard or other Ivy League schools, [her child] had to go to Sunshine." And so she gave the admissions interview her all, ticking off her and her husband's own Ivy League credentials and their impressive résumés, which were laden with the names of Fortune 500 companies. "I name-dropped everything and everyone I'd ever met in my entire life," she said.

It worked, and her child was admitted to the preschool's toddler program, a "Parent and Me" group that met two days a week for one hour and forty-five minutes each day. The cost of the program was over $4,000 for a year. "It was literally doing little sponge paintings, singing a couple of songs, and sitting around chatting with other stay-at-home moms, sharing and lamenting our rough lives," this mother joked.

Unlike at Circle, however, admittance did not ensure that the child would move on to the actual preschool program, making the toddler program feel less about child development and more an opportunity to schmooze and grease the wheels for admission. "The toddler group was the way to get invited to the fundraisers, the Party Books, the galas," the mother said. "There was this veiled sort of understanding that you had to make donations in order to get in full-time."

Rita Cornyn, Sunshine's longtime owner and former director, denied this and said, "I'm sorry that's the way it came off. It shouldn't be that way. It is hard to get in, though. Usually siblings get in first and I only have so many places. There are too many applicants. But it should never be a matter of money to get in."

This mother felt otherwise, particularly when she, along with other toddler program parents, were invited to Sunshine's annual fundraiser, which that year was held at the Riviera Country Club—the golf mecca in the Pacific Palisades where Mark Wahlberg, Adam Sandler, and Larry David all tee off—and asked to solicit donations for the auction. "It can be anything from a meet and greet with Oprah to a gift certificate to your favorite nail spa," read an email that was sent to the toddler group members. "And if this isn't up your alley, angel donations are greatly appreciated as well."

A form spelled out what "angel donations" entailed: "gifts"

ranging from $1,500 (bronze member) to $10,000 (platinum member). Those who went all out and attained platinum-member status were given two tickets to the party, a full-page ad in the gala program, a website banner ad, special acknowledgment at the event, and acknowledgment on the school website. This mother was so stressed by the request that she reached out to her preschool consultant, who told her that she should not feel she had to make a donation, seeing as her child wasn't enrolled in the preschool.

Yet the mother did attend the gala, where "people raise a paddle and pay fifty thousand dollars for the front parking spot [at the school]," said another former Sunshine parent. "It's a drop in the bucket for these people. It's twenty thousand this, twenty thousand that."

The toddler program mother also attended a number of Party Book events, racking up more payments to the school, mainly to get face time with the preschool's higher-ups. "It's all about access," she said. "Guess who's at the parties? The admissions director is there. The head of the school is there. We were definitely trying to get our child in."

Perhaps the most important goal for parents at top preschools is to hit it off with the school's director, who is viewed as the ultimate gatekeeper to a child's future, the understanding being that, come time for elementary school applications, the director will advocate—or not—for a student. Parents, after all, are well aware that directors have deep relationships with elementary school admissions officers, with whom they communicate when families are applying to their schools. Some have even deeper ties. When Piper's cofounder Crystal Free was running Cassidy, which she also cofounded, it was lost on no one that she had connections to Brentwood School, where she previously worked as a school psychologist. This led one parent to tell *Los Angeles* magazine, "Crystal equals Brentwood."

Michele Gathrid is viewed as a similar kind of arbiter. "It's all about winning favor with Michele," said one Circle parent. "She has power and relationships. She can either help you or hurt you." Parents are even willing to pay for that favor. One Party Book event at Circle—"Tacos and Tequila with Michele"—cost hundreds of dollars to attend.

"A preschool director has a tremendous amount of power in the recommendations they make to the elementary school regarding a particular child," said Anne Simon, who cowrote *Beyond the Brochure* and is a former dean at Crossroads and the former head of Wildwood Elementary School. She went on to say that if a preschool has "five kids applying to Curtis, and the preschool director says, 'Lola, Isabel, and Hank are well equipped for Curtis,' and says, 'Lila and John will be fine,' Lila and John are probably not going to get in."

"Directors are the rulers of their fiefdoms," said *Beyond the Brochure* coauthor Christina Simon. "If you have a bad preschool experience and you're on their bad side for whatever reason, you can just forget about them helping you get into school. You have to understand that you're going to need their help."

Consultant Betsy Brown Braun, a former preschool director herself, said that the fixation on directors and the sense that they are almighty gods determining a child's future has not come from directors. "Directors, in my mind, have the well-being of children and their parents in mind," she said. "They are trying to be reassuring and calming and not fueling this fury. This idea that has evolved—'Don't do anything that might get you on the bad side of a director, because she won't get you into elementary school'— that has come from parents."

Said Gathrid: "My job is to guide and help parents through this process. To maybe even manage some expectations and maybe set them on a track or a path that is going to provide them with all the information that they need to apply to these schools. There's no secret. There's no right word to say. There's no essay to write. Everybody is different.

"My parents would like the process to begin the minute they walk through the door of preschool," she went on. "I really slow them down a little bit, and what I do is ask them to not do anything until the year before their child is applying to school."

As for her connections to admissions directors, she said, "Because I've been in the field for so long, I have relationships with these elementary schools, these heads of admissions and their headmasters... It's a relationship, just like I have relationships with preschool directors. But I wouldn't say that my relationship with anybody gives me any priority at all."

When I asked her if parents *think* it does, she didn't hesitate. "Of course they do," she said.

When Luisa Donati, a youthful and bubbly mother of two who favors jeans and hoodies, took over Cassidy in 2015, it was coming off of a legal battle between the school's former co-owners. A much-buzzed-about story by Claire Martin in *Los Angeles* magazine about the conflict revealed the cozy relations between parents at the preschool and the couple who ran the school at the time—Crystal Free and Jesse Bilitz, who were also co-owners—but the juicy details were unrelated to the lawsuit. There were tales by parents of Jacuzzi parties, private jet rides, and vacations together. The school, which has a Serena & Lily vibe (paper lanterns, perfectly framed artwork, an edible garden where the children grow lemon lettuce), was considered one of the worst offenders when it came to allowing parents to hold sway with the director via their wealth and resources. Donati has been working hard to rid the school of this VIP veneer and to democratize its roster. Now, about 35 percent of Cassidy families—as opposed to 5 percent before she started—send their kids to public school, and the school offers a toddler class on weekends so that working parents can attend. Being admitted to the toddler program does not ensure a slot at the preschool, another means of attracting a broader range of families. "We strive to be reflective of the world around us," Donati said. "Not everyone can do a toddler program, for whatever reason. I wasn't able to do that as a working mother, but my kids still deserved a great preschool."

Nonetheless, her job still is about helping parents navigate elementary school admissions, which bears an uncanny parallel to the kind of strategizing that goes on at the high school level among the privileged class. She said she spends a good five hours a week between September and March (the month when acceptance notices go out) consulting with parents and coming up with a list of elementary schools to apply to. "It's a little bit therapy. It's a little bit guiding them down the path. And then it turns into, 'Oh my gosh, this school or that school—what's the right fit?' Or the dad really wants this one, the mom wants that one," Donati said. "So there's a lot of counseling. Like, literally, counseling, and grounding them in the reality that they and their children will be okay regardless of what the result is."

She also helps parents figure out what connections a family has at a school: Do they know a board member? An influential family with pull that goes there? "There are people who collapse before the process even starts because of how competitive they perceive it to be," she said. "They'll say, 'We don't have any connections,' or 'We don't know a board member, but we know this person.' This creates so much stress for parents every year. I'm not going to be naive and say that connections are never a factor, but I have seen plenty of 'nonconnected' families get into multiple schools, including their 'first choice.'" Donati also shares more basic tips like sending a handwritten thank-you note to an elementary school following a tour.

"I used to detest this aspect of my work," Donati said. "The expectations and the pressure of it felt crushing. As if what we were doing with the kids all day, with so much thoughtfulness and inspiration, didn't ultimately matter as much as what private schools they got into." She said she knew had to find a way to reframe it for herself and her school, or else she would have had to find a new job.

Instead, she started enrolling families who were less singularly focused on elementary school admissions and who "held similar core values about children and education." As a result, she said, "I can feel good about being able to bring some element of sanity and perspective to it."

Most parents, however, struggle to find such peace. One mother said that when she applied to John Thomas Dye—whose campus looks like a sprawling Cape Cod estate—she made the mistake of not sending in letters of recommendation, as is advised on the school's website. Some of her friends, meanwhile, had up to six different families vouch for them. Their children were admitted; this mother's child was not. "I was so naive," she said. "I thought, 'My daughter is so bright and curious. That'll be enough.'"

But even preschool directors balk at some of the turns that elementary school admissions have taken in recent years as the landscape has become so competitive, in part because of the decline in the quality of public-school education in LA, particularly at the middle and high school levels. As more and more families opt for private education, there simply aren't enough slots to accommodate them all. Schools typically first fill a kindergarten class with siblings and legacies and, in some cases, the children of faculty. By the time that happens, half the class may be filled. "There's more anxiety because there's less space," said Gathrid. "Because there are so many applicants. These families are walking into open houses with twenty of their best friends. So that in itself creates anxiety."

∝

Perhaps nothing breeds as much fear and paranoia as the kindergarten assessment, when children are invited to spend time at an elementary school during the admissions process in order to be observed. Depending on the school and how academically rigorous it is, children might be asked to demonstrate their reading and writing abilities. They'll also play and interact with other children, in order to get a sense of their temperament and social skills.

Parents, who are not with their child during the assessment, describe the painful hours of the ordeal in horrific terms. There are fears "that if your child cries during the assessment, they're not getting in," one mother told me. There are the rumors of art assignments where if the child fails to draw a person with a neck, they're out. Ditto for a stick figure that is "floating in the air and not standing on the ground."

These fears may be overblown, but parents' anxiety about the assessment isn't totally unfounded. Elementary schools continue to raise the bar when it comes to what they expect from preschoolers, in part because they simply need to winnow down the huge number of applicants. One director said that the notes she would get back from schools would say things like, "I saw that when he was writing his name, he looked to the teacher for confirmation that he was doing it right. Does he have low confidence?"

The director was dumbfounded. "It's because it's the third week of September and he's four. What are we talking about? This is insane."

To help their kid ace the assessment, many parents turn to consultants. Indeed, there is a budding industry of kindergarten-prep tutors and companies—the toddler version of independent college counselors—marketing themselves to freaked-out parents. One of the most popular is Kinder Ready, which offers one-on-one tutoring, for $350 an hour, to help children master the skills they will need for kindergarten. Many parents, however, employ the service solely to help their kid prepare for the assessment. The company also holds summer camps with "customizable curriculums" for ages three through twelve, which includes coding, Mandarin, and manners. The company's marketing materials include enthusiastic quotes from Adam Sandler and Tom Arnold.

Elizabeth Fraley, Kinder Ready's founder and CEO, insists her services are not geared toward the kindergarten assessment test but offer a broader, academic grounding in things like handwriting and "communication skills" that will prepare children for the demands of elementary school. A former kindergarten teacher, Fraley said she saw the need for a "transitional program for preschoolers going into kindergarten, so they may have the skills, confidence, and skill sets to thrive and build a strong foundation early on." She said each child's curriculum is different depending on their needs—whether they are, say, visual or auditory learners—and what type of preschool program they're enrolled in, either academic or more play-based.

Most parents enlist tutors because other parents are doing it, but keep it on the DL at preschool. "[Parents] choose not to share that information with me, because I make it very clear that it's unnecessary," said Michele Gathrid. "The reason I find it unnecessary is because if we're tutoring our child to get in [to kindergarten], that means that a child is not ready for an environment like that. So that requires you to continue to tutor your child for the rest of their elementary career."

Luisa Donati is more blunt with her families, telling them, "Look, there are a bunch of people out there that are looking to make money off your anxiety. I know you think they're providing a needed service, but no self-respecting educator will tell you it's a good idea to introduce academic concepts to kids when they're not ready for it. And also, who wants to tutor a child to a test when they're four?"

Most parents listen and even agree with her—but they don't fire the tutor.

By the time applications are finally due, families are frazzled. Some aren't speaking to one another. "There's so much animosity in relationships," said one mother. "I had a friend try to steer me away from a school she was applying to." To soothe nerves and prepare everyone for the verdict they've been so desperately awaiting, Donati emails a letter to her families a week before elementary school acceptance letters are sent out. In the spring of 2020, her letter began: "Dear Parents, We know that this week is an exhausting culmination of months of school visits, filling out applications, trying desperately to keep your child healthy and rested for his/her assessment days, sending thank you notes and making calls, and generally jumping through more hoops than you probably ever thought you would be part of applying for school for a 5-year-old."

The letter offered dos and don'ts for how to handle being accepted, rejected, or wait-listed, and urged parents to act promptly and graciously whatever their news. "It is a good idea to write a note thanking each school you applied to for considering your child. Admissions directors take a lot of time to consider and get to know each family, and so it is a kind gesture to acknowledge and thank them."

She also quoted admissions consultant Rob Stone: "One thing families can do during that terrible limbo of waiting for the decision is to embrace the premise that everything is going to be okay. The biggest trap is thinking that a child's whole future hinges on getting into a certain school. The second-biggest trap is allowing the stakes of the admissions decisions to create so much pressure in the home that it begins to trickle down to the children."

And then it's decision day, the Friday afternoon in late March when admissions notices go out. Donati sits down in what her husband jokingly calls the War Room at home, her phone on a table in front of her. Just after five o'clock, when the emails go out, the phone starts ringing. There are the calls from the jubilant parents who can't thank her enough, never could have done it without her, are literally crying in ecstasy, and the calls from devastated parents who are beside themselves with grief and, at times, angry at her and the preschool, wondering why she couldn't have done more. Then there are the families whose children are waitlisted, caught in a state of uncertainty and desperate for advice. This requires back-and-forth communication with the elementary schools to find out whether the wait-list status is simply a courtesy or whether the family actually has a shot at getting in. The phone calls go well into the weekend.

Parents find D-day equally unpleasant. "You find out at five p.m. on a Friday," said one mother. "You're with your kids. It's dinnertime. You have to log in to their site. For the last six months, everything in your life has been about working towards this." And now it all comes down to checking a website right before the weekend (it's also usually the eve of spring break). "The whole process is horrible," she added.

Rejections don't affect just families; they can affect a preschool's reputation, too. One top-tier preschool that started to have less success placing children at elite elementary schools caused concern among parents. "Over the last three years, families were not getting into kindergarten," said one mother. "There was one woman who dumped so much money into the school—she worked on every party, she did the auction, she did everything. And she was rejected from five schools. It became the talk of Brentwood."

❧

Betsy Brown Braun chalks up the frenzy over getting kids into the right schools, whether it's preschool or college, to "competitive parenting."

"What's happened is, parents started waiting longer to get married, because they were working very hard to have a career and they were doing whatever it took to claw their ways to the top in that career mode. They kind of attacked their lives much like they attacked their careers," she says. "You know, you've got your watch, you've got your car, you've got your apartment— now I've got to get my wife or my husband, and I've got to get my kids...

"They have this plan for themselves in a way that people didn't used to. I admire a planner, but we're talking about people, and you don't get to plan—you have to parent that child. You can't create the child and then parent it in your image, in your idea, or to meet your need."

It's a rainy Saturday morning in November, and Brown Braun is sitting across from me at a diner in Santa Monica. It's a place she goes with her husband and grandkids all the time, and the waiters all know her and her order: oatmeal with raisins, milk and brown sugar on the side. Brown Braun looks chic and youthful in a navy-and-white-striped T-shirt and fitted jean jacket. Like Michele Gathrid, Brown Braun has her share of parents who sit on her couch and ask which preschools will get their children into Harvard-Westlake and then Penn. Brown Braun shudders when she hears this and proceeds to lecture the parents ("It's usually the fathers, by the way," she says), not just debunking the idea of a feeder preschool, but asking them how they can possibly know that their kid could even handle the intensity of these schools. "I say, 'How do you know your kid is not going to be diagnosed with a learning difference? How do you know he's not going to get messed up in drugs or alcohol or whatever?'" she tells me.

"I have a client who is currently in high school and has been on track his whole life," she goes on, "who has gone to whatever it means to say 'the best.' He went to an 'it' nursery school and an 'it' elementary school and he is now at an 'it' high school. And he's just come back from, let's just call it a home. A facility for kids who have so much anxiety and stress and are literally depressed. They may be trying to kill themselves. Right now, his parents are glad he's alive. He might or might not go to the best college, but that has nothing to do with anything right now. But that could have been a parent who [years ago] said, 'Just tell me [how to get into the right nursery school].'"

In the world of LA toddlerdom, Brown Braun is an institution. A former kindergarten teacher and preschool director, she currently runs eighteen parenting groups for families with kids between the ages of two and sixteen, in addition to being a private parenting consultant, for which she charges $300 an hour. She also offers a "preschool blitz" seminar, where she lectures parents for two and a half hours on the dos and don'ts of applying to preschool.

Through her parenting empire, Parenting Pathways, Inc., which she created in 2011, she is a nonstop purveyor of advice and how-to-isms, which her followers can access via podcast, blog, video seminar, public and private talks, books, and a column in the *Palisadian-Post*. Among a certain set of parents, Brown Braun is a must-have accessory. Jane Buckingham, one of the parents indicted in Varsity Blues, referred to her as her "parenting guru." These parents crave Brown Braun's advice as well as the validation that comes from working with someone who's considered an icon in the field.

But let it be known that there is nothing superficial or trendy about what Brown Braun has to say. Her bottom line is tough, sensible love. The mother of triplets, who raised them herself back in the pre-nanny 1970s, she firmly believes in empowering children to be independent self-starters, no matter how many tears or tantrums that might induce. She likes to say, "You already have a child. You're raising an adult."

A kid doesn't want to eat their dinner? Brown Braun's advice: Let them starve. They want to go to school in their pajamas? Take them and drop them off in their jammies. Siblings are fighting? Don't get involved unless there's blood.

Dare to tell her you're still cosleeping with your five-year-old? Most won't. Or even ask her just a basic question, like what she thinks of the elementary school you're sending your kids to, and brace yourself for the answer.

I put this to Brown Braun at breakfast, tossing out the name of my kids' school, which is considered a top public school in the area.

"It's good *enough*," she says plainly, taking a bite of oatmeal. "Is it the best? No."

I change the subject before she has a chance to explain why.

Clients describe Brown Braun as a Jewish grandmother who's nurturing but direct, the advisor who says what you don't necessarily want to hear but, down deep, you know speaks the truth. Particularly with celebrities and the ultrawealthy, who tend to be surrounded by fawning sycophants and yea-sayers, Brown Braun is often the only person in the room who dares to stand up to them or offer a contrarian opinion. Ultimately, she is the voice of old-fashioned hard-line parenting in a culture that veers heavily toward overaccommodation.

"She's blunt. Not everybody loves that," said Meredith Alexander, a mother who's in a mommy group led by Brown Braun. "There is a small community of moms who find her polarizing. But she comes at it with love. She feels like a family member. She really has that nurturing-mom piece that makes you feel like everything is going to be okay."

Some LA moms, however, avoid her, precisely because of her truth-serum approach. "I'm not going to Betsy because I don't want to hear what I *should* do. I want to hear what I want to do," one mother who had used Brown Braun in the past said to me. Another mother called her "too aggressive."

When I run this by Brown Braun, she doesn't flinch. "I know what people say about me," she says.

"I kind of cut to the chase," she adds. "I tell it like it is. I don't want to waste your time. I don't care if I hurt your feelings. We should all be productive, and if you don't like it and go to someone else, that's okay. Once that baby has been born, the train has left the station."

She says she first started noticing signs of competitive parenting in the early 2000s. "I used the word 'affluenza' before it was a word. I have a seminar called "Affluenza: The Perils of Privilege" that I created eighteen years ago. I was responding to the overprivilege that I was seeing. I think [Varsity Blues] is just an outgrowth of that."

To Brown Braun, the term means "an addiction to wealth" and the relentless pursuit of bigger and better things (cars, houses, vacations). She told the *Malibu Times* back in 2007 that it "comes from a society that promotes consumerism and materialism. The message our children hear is 'Gimme, gimme, gimme.' And parents become incapable of distinguishing 'I want' from 'I need.'" Affluenza affects children who are raised by parents with these values, she explained, and it is made worse by the outsourcing of care that often takes place in these households.

"Wealthy parents feel they should pay for 'experts' to train their kids, so they abdicate their own authority," Brown Braun told the *Times*. "Then you have nannies and tennis coaches and all sorts of other care-givers, and you end up with kids lacking identity."

On the other end of the spectrum are parents who are aggressively hands-on with their kids to the point that there's a blurring of lines when it comes to the child's and the parents' identities. These parents can fall into the trap of pushing kids for more accolades (that in turn reflect on them), a pursuit that is now rewarded on a minute-by-minute basis thanks to Facebook and Instagram. (*Look, Lola won her first tennis match! #WimbledonHereWeCome.* Or: *Here's a photo of Benji with his acceptance letter from Dartmouth.*)

Overparenting can run so amok that parents completely take over their child's lives, leaving kids feeling helpless and in some cases incapable of completing basic tasks, like homework or showing up on time for an outside job. Julie Lythcott-Haims saw this firsthand when she was a dean of freshmen and undergraduate advising at Stanford, which propelled her to write *How to Raise an Adult*. In it, she advises parents to give their children more independence—let them walk to school once they're school-age, for instance—as a means of fostering more self-reliance. But she admits it's an uphill battle in our culture. "We treat our kids like rare and precious botanical specimens and provide a deliberate, measured amount of care and feeding while running interference on all that might toughen and weather them...," she says in the book. "Without experiencing the rougher spots of life, our kids become exquisite, like orchids, yet are incapable, sometimes terribly incapable, of thriving in the real world on their own. Why did parenting change from preparing our kids *for* life to protecting them *from* life, which means they're not prepared to live life on their own?"

In a recent interview, Lythcott-Haims told me: "It's like 'I can buy you that toy that no one else can get their hands on. I can give you a birthday party that includes a helicopter trip to wherever. And I can buy you this college experience.' But if parents are doing that, it's an insecurity. It's 'My child only loves me if I'm buying them the right experiences.' It's 'My peers will think less of me if I don't make these things happen for my kid.' So ultimately, it's an unwellness in the parents. And, on top of that, what parents have lost sight of is that they're undermining their kids' mental health, too."

Even the best-intentioned parents, who don't give a damn about Instagram, can fall into this well of insecurity, leaving them to seek outside expertise on just about everything. As Sophie Robertson, the former director of Westwood Presbyterian Church Preschool, a play-based nursery school in West LA that accepts families off a wait list (many mothers call to procure a spot from the hospital, after delivering their child), told me, "There's increasing insecurity in parents' own ability to parent. There's a lot of 'Am I doing this right?' I think that comes from a culture of don't trust your instincts. You need to go out and attend this group, and read this blog, and read this article and this book, in order to be a good parent.

"Whereas parenting used to be like, 'Hey, you're the parent. You parent the way you think you should be parenting,'" Robertson added. "It wasn't always right. I'm not saying it was better. But I think that's something that I see a lot more of, parents coming in to see me and saying, 'Look, this is what's going on, and I just don't know whether I'm doing the right thing about it.'" (Disclaimer: My two children attended WPCP.)

The anxiety follows parents from preschool all the way to college. In Betsy Brown Braun's groups whose parents have high-school-aged kids, the discussion inevitably turns toward college admissions. "I had a mom in one group," she tells me, "and we go around and talk about what's going on. I said, 'You've been so quiet. What's going on?' She has twins. They're seniors. She burst into tears. 'I have no help. How am I going to get my kids in [to college]? I'm so worried, I can't do this.'

"I said, 'Why is this on you?' She says, 'I can't help it, I feel like it's on me. I have to help them.'

"They both go to private schools where there are counselors," Brown Braun adds, "but she felt so responsible for doing anything she could to help them complete the college application. It's competitive parenting of a sort. It's making sure your kid has every advantage that every other kid has to the extent of your ability."

CHAPTER 5

Welcome to the Gold Coast

Rick Singer's dream of becoming a corporate executive was brief and never quite fulfilled. His gig setting up call centers at the Money Store came to an end after the company was sold in 1998 to First Union, and so he packed up shop and got another call center job working for West Corporation in Omaha, Nebraska. (On the side, he coached a middle-school-aged basketball team at the local JCC, running grueling four-hour practices and referring to certain kids on the team as "meat-packers.") Looking to gain more professional cred, he enrolled in an online PhD program in organization and management at Capella University, though he never finished his degree. Instead, he was on to the next thing: more call center work, this time in India, where US companies were outsourcing their call centers in droves, drawn by cheap labor and operating expenses. Singer got a job as CEO at a company called FirstRing, which, like many other local call center businesses, was eager to hire native English speakers to train its staff. He brought his hard-driving ways to the company, telling his existing employees that they needed to work harder in order to be as productive and competent as the "A team" of hires that he'd brought on. "He made us feel like we were not up to potential," said Prab Singh, then a senior vice president at the company. Singh said that Singer's own work ethic was dizzying and that he stopped moving only to take brief naps while in a car or an airplane. "It would be for maximum fifteen minutes and then he would be awake, plugging back into some work."

Singh respected Singer, who he said seemed to know the business inside and out, but resented some of his tactics. For instance, Singer insisted that Singh spend an hour a day on the phone with callers—a grueling and thankless job—in order to better understand how the company worked and to build team morale. "I was heading up all operations, so I thought it was demeaning," Singh said. "It did not seem like the best use of my time." It was demands like this that ultimately led Singh to quit. But Singer stayed on until FirstRing was sold to an Indian bank, ICICI OneSource, in 2003. As CEO with preferred shares in FirstRing, Singer did well in the exit—something he would crow about for years.

Armed with more cash and even more confidence, Singer returned to Sacramento to begin his next chapter: another stab at college counseling. He was well aware of the valuable network he'd left behind, as well as a career that was becoming potentially more lucrative as the desire for A-list colleges and universities went into overdrive. The noncompete that he'd signed when he sold Future Stars had also expired, meaning he was free to get back in the game. He and Allison bought an attractive but modest four-bedroom ranch home for $579,000. The house was on a quiet, tree-lined street, around the corner from a large park, where Allison often went walking.

Singer returned to California with outsized ambitions. He called up one former associate and remarked that he was amazed that a college consultant in Manhattan was charging $30,000 a client. Sacramento was a far cry from New York, and there was no way he could charge that kind of money in the easygoing government town, but he thought he could move in that direction. The CollegeSource, his new company, charged some families as much as $10,000, according to the former associate. When Singer met anyone whom he even remotely sensed was well-off, he pounced. Once, on an airplane, he found himself sitting next to the CEO of a Sacramento bank. Noticing that she was working on a Hebrew-language crossword puzzle, he struck up a conversation with her about it. Two hours after they landed, he emailed her to continue the conversation. Soon, he was coaching her three kids.

Word quickly got out that Singer was back in action, causing high school guidance counselors to moan. "We didn't know the second [company] existed until we started seeing him come around again," said Jill Newman, who was still working as a high school counselor at Rio Americano. "There was a time where it was like, 'Cool, no Rick!' Then he comes back."

In no time, he was once again a ubiquitous figure around town. He would show up at Sacramento Country Day and sit down with students he was working with on a bench in the campus quad or in the library after school. At Granite Bay High School, which is located in a rolling Sacramento suburb of McMansions and gated communities, he "was a pretty regular presence, coming through the counseling area, coming through the administration area," according to Karl Grubaugh, who began teaching government, economics, and journalism at the school in 1998. Although by now, there were other independent counselors in town, a counselor constantly showing up on campus "was to some degree a little unusual," Grubaugh said. "It wasn't 'Call the cops, nine-one-one, there's a weird guy.' But it was not the norm."

If Singer had been an aggressive operator who was starting to dabble in dishonesty when he ran Future Stars, his slide into unethical territory at the CollegeSource became far more brazen. Now he made no bones about telling students to exaggerate or lie on their applications, and when the process went digital, he would ask for their passwords and log on to fill out student information himself (unlike with paper applications, no signature was required on online paperwork at the time). This would become standard protocol for Singer going forward. There were still clients who swore he did nothing but motivate them to work harder and be more strategic about applying to college, but the tales of his shady behavior were piling up.

Newman experienced this when she was counseling a senior athlete at Rio Americano who'd struggled in math. The boy hadn't passed Algebra 1, and therefore hadn't been able to progress to Geometry or Algebra 2, which was required by the well-known Division I school the student had his heart set on attending. (Newman did not want to reveal the university or the sport in order to protect the student's identity.) The student had also received a poor grade in another class his junior year. The plan that Newman and the boy and his family had come up with was for him to attend a local community college and then transfer to the university.

"And then they hired Rick," Newman said.

Soon afterward, the student and his parents came to school to meet with Newman, with Singer in tow. Newman sensed a new vibe in the room. "They deferred everything over to Rick and said, 'You didn't do your job. You should have put our son into Algebra 2,'" Newman told me. "I explained that I couldn't do that for the reason that he didn't pass Algebra 1."

Singer then interrupted her, saying, "No problem. I'm going to put him into all three math classes online, and he's going to redo that junior class online, too."

Newman was shocked. "I said, 'Hold on. He has a full day with us, taking senior classes. And now you're going to give him three on-line math classes in the course of senior year? That's impossible.'"

"That's not impossible," Singer shot back. "We're going to make it happen. He's going to pass, and then he'll be eligible to play at the university."

"I was in disbelief," Newman said. "Complete disbelief."

During the meeting, the student had remained completely silent. But a few days later, he stopped by Newman's office. "I really want to apologize," he told her. "I know we've always had a good working relationship with you. Rick coached my parents to behave that way."

When Newman asked the boy what he thought of the situation, he said, "I don't know. My parents hired him and told me I had to do whatever he told me to do."

Newman then asked him how he thought he was going to do in college, seeing as he wasn't going to be fully prepared for a college-level class like Precalculus. "Well," the student replied, "Rick's going to get me tutors in college."

In the end, the student attended his university of choice after getting credits for the online classes that Singer enrolled him in. Whether he actually took the classes, though, remains unknown. (Singer would go on to have his employees take online classes for students, as would be revealed in the Varsity Blues scandal.) "I think the classes were taken," Newman said. "I don't know who took them."

This wasn't Newman's only run-in with Singer. "I'd have a family I'd be working with as a Rio counselor, and we'd have a plan. 'You're going to apply to these six colleges. Two of them are reaches, two are targets, two are safeties.' And it was a good variety. And then they'd come back in and Rick would be with them, and their tone would change. They'd be almost like 'You sold us down the wrong road. You're not doing for us what Rick is doing for us.'"

Singer's pull with families came down to one simple thing. He promised that he could get their child into a specific school. This promise made him a kind of Svengali, whom even the most reasonable and educated people found themselves swayed by. Whatever about him seemed off or too good to be true was shrouded by his certainty about something that parents felt so anxious, insecure, and perplexed by: how their child was going to get into college. As long as he repeated his promise, they were sold. "That was his big line," said Margie Amott, who by then had become an independent counselor and was Singer's main competition. "'I can get you into a specific school.' And people chose to believe it."

Amott admits that she may have been seen as a "jealous competitor," given that for families deciding on a college counselor in Sacramento in the early 2000s, the choice was simple: him or her. But the reality is that she sensed long before anyone else that something wasn't just fishy about Singer; it was deeply wrong. Driven by this hunch, she began taking notes on interactions with him that both she and others had, and started keeping hard copies of his promotional materials and mentions in the media. All these years later, she still has them, and when I met with her one morning at a Temple Coffee shop in Sacramento, she laid the printouts neatly on the table, like a scholar displaying years' worth of meticulous research. "People turned a blind eye. They didn't want to hear that he was a fraud," said Amott, a former CPA who speaks in calm, deliberate tones. "I've been screaming about Rick for years and years and years."

One of his methods was to try to ingratiate himself in communities by warming up to school principals and administrators. In at least one case, he made headway. "Our administration loved him, because he was helping kids get into competitive schools," said Karl Grubaugh. Beyond his tutoring work, Rick Singer lobbied for curriculum changes at high schools in order to make the schools more competitive—and, by extension, the students he was coaching. He wanted Granite Bay to have an International Baccalaureate program (it has since adopted one), and Rio Americano to offer more AP and honors classes, telling administrators that if they didn't have certain advanced classes at the school, they should at least offer them online.

But his tactics ultimately came down to what would most benefit him, and if he wasn't able to get what he wanted through ethical channels, he forged another route. At Granite Bay, he became unhappy with a math teacher at the school, presumably because the kids Singer was coaching weren't doing well in the class. "He didn't like the teacher," Grubaugh said. "Rick decided that he was not a math teacher that his kids were going to have, so he told parents of his clients, 'You have to go in and demand that your child be changed to another class.'"

Things got so tense that a meeting was called with the teacher, another member of the math department, a school counselor, and a student and his family. Singer was also in attendance, as was the student's uncle. During the meeting, Singer and the student's family "pushed, pushed, pushed," said Grubaugh. "They said how terrible this class was, how bad this teacher was. The meeting was awful."

Afterward, it was revealed that the man who'd been introduced as the student's uncle was not, in fact, a relative. He was someone who worked for Singer. A letter was then sent out to all of the faculty at Granite Bay, declaring Singer persona non grata.

"That was classic Rick Singer back in the day," said Grubaugh. "He would push and do what he could to grease the system."

Another Granite Bay student who worked with Singer bragged

about the fact that he'd checked the Hispanic box on his application to UCLA. "This kid was as Anglo as you could be," Grubaugh said. "Who knows how else he was cooking the books?"

As it turns out, very creatively. According to Amott, Singer filled out the college application for the son of a friend of hers who'd hired him, spinning all kinds of stories. "He said the kid organized a fantasy football club. That he raised money to build playground equipment in Helen Keller Park. There's no such thing as Helen Keller Park in Sacramento," Amott said. "That he was ranked top fifty in junior tennis. The kid probably was on the tennis team. That he wrote all these scripts that were on TV. Well, he did write scripts—that was his hobby—but they were not on TV. They were huge lies. The application also said that he spoke Spanish in the home. Well, he did not."

The application also stated that the boy had been the "regional social media director/blogger for the Aspen Ideas Festival." When the student and his mother saw the application, they were horrified. The mother paid Singer for his services but then changed the password on her son's online account to lock Singer out, and the student filled out the application truthfully.

Almost anyone working in college counseling in Sacramento around this time has a Singer story. Patricia Fels, who was then a counselor at Sacramento Country Day, had a student being coached by him who told her that Singer had advised him to say that he'd founded a youth group at his synagogue. "It was untrue," Fels said. "The kid was in it, he participated, but that was it. But the pitch from Rick was that just to be a member of a group is not impressive. You have to say you founded it. Well, yeah, except that it's a lie."

He told another student at Country Day to "put down that he had a patent for something," Fels said.

Meanwhile, Singer kept blowing his own horn, churning out marketing materials and statistics intended to embellish the size and scope of his operation, which he was trying desperately to grow and diversify. He would hold speaker events, inviting local attorneys and other business leaders to address his students. Then he'd instruct the kids who'd sat in the session that they should say they were in an entrepreneurial club on their college application— the proof being the one presentation they'd listened to. He talked about approaching companies like Intel to offer his college counseling services as an opt-in perk to their employees. (It never went anywhere.) And he spoke with Luis Robles, an education specialist and engineer, about tutoring his students in math and science, with Singer skimming five dollars off of every hour that Robles charged for. "But when he realized it wasn't going to make him any money," Robles told me, "the idea went away."

Robles's impression of him was that he was all show. "He was never about education," he said. "It was all sales. He was always trying to make a buck."

Singer even called up Prab Singh, his old pal from his Indian call center days, and asked him to start up an Indian arm of the College Source. Singh signed on and began working with local families who were looking to help their kids get into American colleges. Singer charged $2,500 for two years of counseling, which was considered high in India, and he wound up having to give some of the families discounts. The business ultimately failed to take off. Over the course of a year, Singh worked with only eight families, seeing as "there were just not that many families looking at the U.S. for undergraduate education," he said. The slow growth frustrated Singer, who told Singh that he couldn't understand why Singh couldn't get as many clients as he could in the United States, where he bragged he was signing up "thirty students overnight."

"He did not understand why it was taking so long in India to build the client base," Singh said, who added that Allison was frustrated by having to deal with differences between Indian and American accounting practices.

Outwardly, Singer told acquaintances in Sacramento that he was building a booming business in India, something that seemed credible given how often he was getting on a plane. "He was traveling to India all the time," said one. "He was never home."

But in 2005, Singer conceded defeat and handed the Indian piece of the business to Singh.

Singer was spinning his wheels, trying to think up ways to become something much bigger than just a college tutoring company. But if he was hitting walls, he wasn't letting it show. He took out a full-page ad in *Sacramento Magazine*, showing himself standing next to high school seniors he'd helped get into college, who are beaming in their USC and University of Arizona sweatshirts. "Getting into college isn't an art," the ad declared. "It's a science." According to his website at the time, he'd coached over twenty-five thousand college applicants. And in a glowing profile that ran in the *Sacramento Business Journal* in February 2005, he said that the CollegeSource had generated more than $1 million in 2004 and was expected to double that the following year. The story also featured a quote from Ted Mitchell, then the president of Occidental College, saying: "Rick has an encyclopedic knowledge of colleges and universities. Far more important, Rick is really great at getting at the heart of what kids and families want—and finding the right match."

Mitchell was one of a handful of higher-education dignitaries that Singer said he'd assembled on his advisory board, which he touted on his website. Others were Bill Bowen, the former president of Princeton; Donald Kennedy, the former president of Stanford;

Charles Young, the former UCLA chancellor; and Fred Hargadon, the former dean of admissions at Stanford and Princeton.

When Margie Amott saw this, she was horrified and called up Jon Reider, a former admissions officer at Stanford, who was similarly unnerved, having heard tales of Rick Singer over the years. "He was name-dropping Stanford," Reider said. "And I happened to know people on the list." Reider then emailed those people— Kennedy, Mitchell, and Hargadon—writing, "Do you want to be associated with this guy? He is the epitome of sleaze in the private counseling business.

"How did he get your names onto his website? There are some decent independent counselors, but he isn't one of them...We can't stop this guy, but we can slow him down a bit."

Mitchell owned up to his association with him, emailing back that Singer was "a decent guy," whom he'd gotten involved with when Singer was working with poor kids, trying to get them access to college. Kennedy wrote in an email: "Several years ago I agreed to be on an advisory board for his venture, which looked promising. Unfortunately since that time I have had no contact with him whatever, so I cannot vouch for what he is doing with respect to providing counseling services."

Reider couldn't recall what the exact response was from Hargadon, who has since passed away. "I believe he said he had no connection with Singer and had not authorized the use of his name," Reider said. "That would not have been his style, anyway. He never endorsed anything and never put his name on anything.

"Fred was a legendary guy, and it certainly looked good to have his name on the roster with the others."

Steve Repsher, then the head of school at Country Day, who'd also been irritated when he saw the advisory board list, reached out to Kennedy, too. He said that Kennedy told him that he had met Singer only once, at a cocktail party in the Bay Area, which is presumably when Singer asked him to be on his board.

Even if Kennedy had agreed to allow Singer to use his name, Repsher was dismayed. "He was blatantly using well-known people's names indiscriminately," he told me.

Singer had already gotten under the head of school's skin when he'd heard that the college counselor had been bad-mouthing Country Day's math department around town. "In some sense, the math department had been weak back in the late nineties and early aughts," Repsher said. "But by the time I was hearing this, the program was much, much better. We had a great staff."

Eager to set the record straight and challenge Singer about his board claims, Repsher called him and set up a meeting. But Singer never showed. "And then I set up another time and he no-showed again," Repsher said.

Repsher then spread the word to his staff: Singer was not permitted on the Country Day campus. Rio Americano had stopped allowing him to speak at the school, and the math department at Granite Bay was still peeved, meaning that three of his main hubs in Sacramento were now enemy zones.

He also had a falling-out with Billy Downing, whom he'd hired as his COO. Downing had been tutored by Singer when he was a student at Jesuit High School. He then worked for Singer after he graduated from Berkeley, eventually becoming his second-in-command. There's no indication that Downing engaged in Singer's unethical tactics. But according to a source, when Downing wanted to break away and start his own company, Singer turned ugly, withholding his pay. Downing threatened to sue and eventually did start his own company, but Singer's closest business relationship was now severed. (Downing, who has not been implicated in the Varsity Blues scandal, did not respond to multiple requests for comment for this book.) In the close-knit community of Sacramento, where everyone knew everyone and gossip spread like wildfire, Singer's reputation was beginning to catch up to him.

But he was needing Sacramento less and less. One attempt to grow his company that had panned out was a deal with the Sagemont School, a private school in Weston, Florida, that was getting a college counseling program up and running. Brent Goldman, who cofounded the school, told me he hired Singer because "he knew what he was talking about. He seemed to have a lot of contacts. He'd say, 'I know the athletic director here.' 'I know the president here.'"

Singer did a little bit of counseling for Sagemont, according to Goldman, but he mostly helped the school set up its program. "The guy was either working, working out, or sleeping very little," Goldman said. "He was a different bird."

When Sagemont started a virtual school, where students could take classes online, Singer got involved with that, too, hiring tutors to provide college counseling to Sagemont's online students through the CollegeSource. When Sagemont Virtual merged with a division of the University of Miami to become the University of Miami Online High School, he remained the school's college counseling vendor until the school was sold to Kaplan. (He would later tell clients that an ownership stake in the online school had netted him $100 million.) But having found a new revenue source that required little of his time—his tutors handled the students—he sought contracts with other online schools, and he landed his next one with Laurel Springs School, based in West Chester, Pennsylvania.

He also began offering his services at IMG Academy, the elite sports-training center in Bradenton, Florida, which doubles as a boarding school for young athletes looking to nab a sports scholarship to college or who simply have enough money to attend the school.

But even as the company expanded into a bigger business proposition, the CollegeSource remained an odd, dysfunctional company. There was little transparency or communication among its few employees, including half a dozen coaches, bookkeeper Steven Masera, accountant Mikaela Sanford, and an assistant. (Masera and Sanford have pled guilty to charges in the Varsity Blues scandal.) This was not a company of town halls or annual performance reviews. As for Singer, he was mostly on a plane or in another state or country, advising families or drumming up business. One employee who worked for the company as a coach at the time said Singer never offered any benefits or insurance, and that dealings with him were minimal and often incoherent. "It was all one or two sentences," the former employee said. "None of his stuff ever really made sense. You would ask him a question, but he never had a straight answer." A former assistant of Singer's told *The Price of Admission* author Daniel Golden that he would text employees at all hours of the day and night, in what they called "Rick code"—i.e., confusing orders that they would have to discern, such as "Call Miami," which could either mean the University of Miami in Florida, or Miami University in Ohio. As for why insurance was not offered to all employees, the former employee said, "Rick didn't see any value in [what we did]. We were just the worker bees. We weren't big players."

Singer generally split fees with his online coaches 50-50. But when the former employee asked for a greater portion, seeing as Singer had no involvement with their clients, he grew hostile. "There was no discussion. He was basically like, 'If you don't like it, you can leave.' He played hardball."

In 2010, a New York–based independent college counselor, Andy Lockwood, arranged a meeting with Rick Singer. Lockwood, a chatty New Yorker with an easygoing vibe, was friends with Brent Goldman of the Sagemont School, who'd praised Singer as someone who knew a lot about the education field and was doing interesting things. Goldman thought Lockwood, who was working with affluent families in a Long Island suburb, and Singer might be able to collaborate in some way; at the very least, he thought Singer was someone that Lockwood should know, though after saying how great Singer was, he'd added: "I only believe eighty percent of what comes out of his mouth."

Singer blasted into the meeting, dropping names and talking up his business—how it took him all over the place, how rich his clients were. "It was a torrent of nonstop words," said Lockwood, who described Singer as "this little, wiry guy with a backpack. He looked, basically, like a college student with salt-and-pepper hair."

Singer presented himself as someone who provided college counseling for the wealthiest of the wealthy, mentioning names like Steve Jobs to get his point across. "As I understood it, he was still in Sacramento," Lockwood told me, "but he flew all over the place and was brokering donations to college [for his clients]."

The meeting itself is barely a footnote in Singer's story—no business or collaboration ended up coming of it. But it shows how Singer had started to dramatically pivot his business, positioning himself as a college coach not just to affluent families in Sacramento, but to CEOs and other business leaders in the Bay Area, Southern California, New York, and other exceedingly wealthy areas of the world. These weren't parents who were CEOs of a local bank; they were CEOs and COOs of global corporations. They were hedge fund managers and VC founders and other business titans, whose names were recognizable to readers of the *Wall Street Journal* and the *Financial Times*. They were families who had not one nanny, but several, and who were zipping around on private jets—often using them to fly Singer out to one of their many homes for tutoring sessions.

To reflect this shift, and perhaps to appeal more directly to a more powerful and results-oriented clientele, he had recently changed the name of his company to the Edge College & Career Network, though he called it simply "the Key." Lockwood said Singer bragged that he'd had a trademark infringement dispute with motivational guru Tony Robbins over the company's name (Robbins has a series of books and videos called *The Edge*), but that he'd won. "He was like, 'Yeah, he sued me because' we had the same name, and he had to buy the name from me,'" Lockwood said. "Which didn't make sense, because Rick was still using it...He made it like he'd gotten some big victory, like he'd put one over on Tony Robbins."

If anything, Singer saw himself as a Robbins-like figure: a larger-than-life, inspirational coach-slash-mentor who had the answers to life's messy problems and could break them down in a series of simple steps; someone people looked to for advice and help, and who had tremendous influence over their followers, regardless of how powerful those followers were in their own right.

He was obsessed with motivational gurus, and in the late aughts he had sent a group of his employees to Seattle to see Lou Tice give a presentation. Tice had founded the Pacific Institute, which specializes "in creating high performance mindsets for individuals, teams and organizations," and Singer hoped some of his practices would rub off on members of the Key.

Inspired by these public pontificators, he now referred to himself as a "master coach" and a "life coach" in his marketing materials. In a deposition unrelated to Varsity Blues, when he was asked to define the term *master coach*, he said, "Somebody that works with the overall person, both professionally and personally." There is no evidence that Singer ever provided such services to anyone, and when he was asked in the deposition if he had any background in psychology or any other mental health profession, he replied, "No, sir."

Singer's interest in big ideas and how to enact them was not entirely disingenuous. On some level, he did seem to have a passion for education and ways to innovate around it. He engaged in lively discussions about online education and the digital future of learning. He talked about how to provide college-prep help to kids who couldn't afford it and how he'd started a basketball program for disadvantaged kids in Oakland, California. In an ideal world, he would combine these altruistic notions with big moneymaking opportunities—if only he could figure out how.

In the meantime, he would pursue a more lucrative route that had nothing to do with helping kids and everything to do with his own financial aggrandizement. In the meeting with Andy Lockwood, Singer talked a lot about the so-called development angle to college admissions—i.e., making donations to a college in advance of, or while, a student is applying for admission to that school—in order to help get them admitted. He called that approach "the back door" and cast aspersions on it, saying that these days it didn't work, that the checks that would have to be written were simply too much. As proof, he mentioned a foreign family who had called him up, upset that their child was wait-listed at a top university. They wanted to write a $6 million check to the school, which they did, but the kid wasn't moved off the wait list.

According to Singer, to get in the back door at elite schools would cost nine times as much. "Harvard's asking for forty-five million," he would tell one client. "Stanford's asking for fifty million. And they're getting it," he went on. "That's the crazy thing. They're getting it from the Bay Area and New York. Crazy."

He told Lockwood he had a more surefire, and far less costly, approach, which he called "the side door." He didn't spell out exactly what that meant, but he said, "Instead of [a family] donating a couple million, I can get them in for two hundred fifty thousand."

Unbeknownst to Lockwood, Singer was already putting his side-door strategy to work in one of his new business hot spots: Orange County in Southern California, where he had tapped into a community of affluent families in coastal hubs like Newport Beach and Laguna Beach. It would be a crucial foothold. Here, money was proudly flaunted in the form of Maseratis, Teslas, multiple vacation homes, and enrollment in private high schools like Sage Hill School, a $42,000-a-year prep school, where a family might kick in $1 million to upgrade the school's playing turf and running track, and where fundraisers are held at the Balboa Bay Resort, a members-only club and golf course overlooking the Pacific Ocean. As he had at high schools in Sacramento, Singer began ingratiating himself at Sage Hill, and through word-of-mouth referrals got in with members of the school's board of trustees, who wielded considerable influence.

Orange County provided another, even more crucial, gateway for him. Through his growing connections he had started giving college admissions presentations at investment firms in the area for the companies' wealthiest clients. In 2008, he'd given one such talk at Newport Beach–based Pacific Investment Management Company (PIMCO), one of the world's largest bond companies.

According to the *Wall Street Journal*, Singer had gained entree to the company through William Powers, then the company's cohead of mortgages, who'd hired him to work with his daughters on their college applications. Powers had called him "a fabulous resource," according to the *Journal*, and recommended him to PIMCO's head of human resources, which led to Singer speaking at the company in June.

Investment firms like PIMCO served as an ultraefficient and a streamlined business conduit for Singer, cutting out all the hustle and legwork he was accustomed to doing in order to land new clients. Better yet, these clients were one-percenters. By giving a talk or even simply breezing through the office and schmoozing with wealth management advisors, he suddenly had access to clients who relied on the company to invest and manage their sizable income and assets. Those advisors, meanwhile, were eager to lavish their high-paying clients with perks and amenities—such as a college counselor skilled at getting kids into top schools.

Given this dynamic, it's understandable why he attempted to forge a professional relationship with PIMCO in order to keep steadily presenting at the company. But he was reportedly too aggressive in his pitch; PIMCO declined. At that point, it didn't matter. He had already made what would be one of the most significant, lucrative—and illicit—connections of his career so far.

One day, William Powers brought up Rick Singer to his longtime friend Douglas Hodge, who would go on to become PIMCO's COO and then CEO. Their friendship dated back to 1978, when Powers had encouraged Hodge to apply to PIMCO. Hodge, a Harvard MBA, then had five children. His oldest daughter was attending the Cate School, a boarding school in Carpinteria, California, and was getting ready to apply to college. Powers touted Singer as "the best possible mentor and guide," according to court documents, and soon he was working with Hodge's daughter, sitting down for weekly tutoring sessions, planning college trips, editing her essays, and advising her on what classes to take at school.

Hodge was a business titan who'd cleanly and steadily risen through the ranks, first as a bond trader at Salomon Brothers, then at PIMCO, where he spent most of his career. For several years, he was based in Tokyo, where he grew the company's Asia business, and then in 2009, he was appointed COO and returned to Southern California, settling into a $12.2 million home in the gated community of Emerald Bay in Laguna Beach. His philanthropy credentials were as impressive as his résumé. He and his wife, Kylie, founded an international nonprofit that provides mentoring and healthcare education to girls and young women in impoverished countries around the world. He'd even built schools and an orphanage in Cambodia, where his kids would volunteer over the summer. So moved were he and his wife by the hardships he saw children endure in poor countries that he and Kylie adopted their youngest two daughters from a Moroccan orphanage.

Hodge's philanthropic work gave Singer another entree with him, one that he would seize on. Indeed, when Singer would go on to found his own purported charity, he would claim that it was in support of "needy Cambodians"—an inspiration that presumably came from talking to Hodge, who donated large sums of money every year to schools and universities and other programs to assist disadvantaged youth. Between 2007 and 2018, Hodge gave over $30 million to one hundred different organizations, according to legal documents. Singer often used philanthropy as a way to bond with clients, as well as to suss out their financial bandwidth and present himself as a do-gooder. He would tout his own work that he claimed he was doing with needy kids—that basketball program in Oakland, or sports camps he ran for kids who couldn't afford to pay—and effectively create a halo that masked his other activities, which were becoming increasingly sinister.

Hodge would later write that when he first met Singer, the college coach "struck [him] as capable, confident and knowledgeable about the admissions process."

"With thousands of students vying for a limited number of places at every top college," Hodge wrote, "having someone like him on my side seemed smart. His sales pitch had two elements. First, he would create a 'brand' for my child to help separate the application from the legions of others. Second, he touted his many 'connections' at top colleges."

Singer was "good at getting inside these guys' heads," said one source. "He'd talk about famous, wealthy kids who went to certain universities and say, 'You think they got in on their smarts?' He made it sound like everyone got into college through connections and giving money, building libraries. And he seemed to really believe it. I don't think he ever, ever thought he was doing anything out of the norm. That was his psychology."

Another trick Singer employed was to cast severe doubt on a child's ability to get into their college of choice on their own. In this way he preyed on one of parents' biggest fears: having to watch their child's heart break. Who wants to watch their kid go through the demeaning process of receiving emoji-laden text messages from their friends who are celebrating their good news about Stanford and Penn, while they stand by with a wait-list letter? And who wants to accept the fact that after so much has gone into paving the way for the "right" college for their child—not to mention the "right" extracurricular activities and summer internships—it might not, actually, have been worth it? The answer, Singer knew, is no one.

And so he dealt his blow bluntly, making it clear that without his help, his clients' children were, in short, screwed. Although Hodge's oldest daughter was an AP Scholar with Honor, meaning she'd scored at least 3 out of 5 on four or more Advance Placement tests, when she identified Georgetown as her top college choice, Singer informed Hodge that she had "only a 50% chance at best" of getting in.

But there was an alternative, he said, and it was one that sounded so innocuous, so gentle, as though he were simply offering his hand to help a parent cross the road. "I spoke to my connection at Georgetown and he will work with us," Singer wrote Hodge in an email in February of 2008. "He helped me get two girls in last week."

CHAPTER 6

The Sports Connection

Ryan Downes is a six foot three quarterback who weighs 195 pounds. He has a boyish face and short-clipped brown hair, and wears a cross around his neck. In 2019, he was ranked seventh in the country in youth football, earning him two Division I offers to play football in college. He was thirteen years old.

Downes is a member of the 2024 class at IMG Academy, the ultraelite boarding school for young athletes that's located on an immaculate six-hundred-acre campus in Bradenton, Florida. IMG Academy morphed out of famed coach Nick Bollettieri's tennis academy, which groomed icons like Andre Agassi and Monica Seles back in the 1980s. But today, the school is nothing like Bollettieri's homespun, if grueling, tennis boot camp, where Bollettieri would yell and berate his young protégés into Wimbledon champions. "It used to be Nick and company teaching and having kids down there," said a player who attended Bollettieri's camp in the late 1980s. "Now it's more of a factory."

A very posh factory, that is. The tennis academy was bought in 1987 by the powerhouse sports and marketing agency IMG, which was in turn gobbled up by the Hollywood talent agency and media company Endeavor in 2013. These days, IMG Academy is as much a five-star luxury resort for aspiring recruits as it is a cutting-edge training facility. The school trains athletes in nine sports, including football, basketball, lacrosse, and golf, and kids dedicate nearly five hours a day to their respective sport. The school's twelve hundred students live in gleaming "villas," surrounded by an Olympic-sized pool, sand volleyball courts, basketball courts, and an enormous flat-screen TV to watch games on. There's also a giant fire pit for late-night socializing. The gym—the size of five Equinoxes—includes weight machines that are equipped with camera systems to monitor bench-press technique and a "hydration center," where students can stock up on sports drinks, bars, and chews—supplied by Gatorade, which, along with Under Armour, is a corporate sponsor of the school. (No other athletic logos are permitted to be worn on campus other than Under Armour.) There's also a "mind gym," where kids perfect their mental agility and fortitude by playing matching games with cards and reacting to a DynaBoard— a large square with dozens of tiny lights that flash on and off. The idea is to quickly hit each light as it blinks on in order to improve reaction time. The board also strengthens an athlete's eye-hand coordination and peripheral vision. The football locker room, lit by neon-blue strobe lights, looks like a futuristic nightclub. And, perhaps inevitably, there is a wellness spa on campus.

The price of attending this sports Shangri-La is $79,900 and up for just one year, meaning that the school attracts an inordinate number of very wealthy families, many of whom come from abroad. Parking lots at the school are dotted with luxury cars; one tutor recalls a student saying, "I need to get an A in this course, because if I do my dad said he'd buy me a [vintage] Mustang Cobra." A promotional video on YouTube shows a white SUV stretch limo pulling up to take IMG seniors to their prom at the Ritz-Carlton Beach Club in Sarasota.

IMG Academy is one of the most hyperbolic and distilled examples of the emphasis our culture places on youth specialization, the idea that to succeed in life, young people need to be trophy-winning prodigies with one specific area of expertise. It is the next logical step for the child whose parents made her give up soccer at age three because she couldn't skillfully dribble the ball, instead investing in swimming, which led to school teams, club teams, private lessons, personal nutritionists, and expensive summer training camps. The process is not only demanding for kids and parents (who are schlepping their youngsters around to practice day and night), but costly. One New York–based father who sent his son to summer baseball camp for "8- to 10-year-old prospects" at USC in 2019 spent $500 on the camp, $800 on a hotel room, and $1,200 on airfare for him and his son. The camp was for three days.

But for the upper-middle-class and wealthy families who can afford this kind of grooming, it's become the de rigueur route for anyone dreaming of a college scholarship, or simply an easier entree to a top university. According to figures that were released in a lawsuit against Harvard in 2018, over a period of six years, recruited athletes had an 86 percent acceptance rate. This data, which has invigorated parents who spot even a glimmer of advanced eye-hand coordination in their progeny, has led to a gradual, yet very extreme shift in the culture. The days of kids dabbling in multiple sports and not getting very serious about any of them until they're at least ten are long over. Today in sports, the goal is to excel at one at an early age, with parents eagerly strategizing about how all those junior championship titles will translate to a full ride to Stanford. "Parents are thinking about [sports specialization] as early as when their child is six, as a way to look better in the college admissions process," said Travis Dorsch, associate professor of human development and family studies at Utah State University, where he conducts research on sports and youth. "They're rating that as highly as other goals, like having fun and learning new skills and making friends. For parents, this is definitely at the forefront of their thoughts: How do I get my kid into college?"

And for parents who can afford it, IMG Academy is a tantalizing and expedient facilitator. Because of the caliber of athletes that the school attracts and its rigorous focus on making them better to the point of attempting to engineer a flawless athlete, the school is swarming with college recruiters. And, as Ryan Downes is proof, these conversations start very, very early. In 2019, of the 260 students in IMG Academy's graduating class, 165 were accepted by Division I schools. The school proudly touts this statistic, as it does the fact that IMG Academy grads "have attended 90 of the *U.S. News & World Report* Top 100 universities since 2012," as it states on its website.

This combination of aggressive results-oriented parents, extreme wealth, and athletics made IMG Academy an irresistible place for Rick Singer to ingratiate himself, which is what he did in 2003, when he started offering college counseling services through the CollegeSource to academy students. IMG also provided him the opportunity to get even closer to the college recruitment business and to forge relationships with key people within that business. Through contacts at IMG, he would identify and get close with college coaches who would become crucial points of entry for him and his clients at some of the country's top universities, paving the way for his side-door scheme. He would also better understand the weaknesses in the college recruitment process and where the holes were in the admissions system, as well as coaches' simultaneous power and vulnerabilities. He would learn how they often felt underappreciated and undervalued, and in many cases were low-paid, and how they were put-upon and pulled in so many directions already, from development offices and wealthy alumni, making them disillusioned about their jobs that at the same time afforded them tremendous levels of influence. If Singer had begun to glean all of this at Sacramento State, at IMG things become all the more crystallized. The school was his gateway to the major leagues.

When he started at IMG, he was only a contractor, but he quickly became a presence at the school, which at the time was just starting to expand its education offerings. Historically, IMG Academy students attended classes at nearby schools Saint Stephen's Episcopal School and Bradenton Preparatory Academy. But in 2000, the Pendleton School opened on the IMG Academy campus. It wasn't owned by IMG, but it was specifically geared to serve academy students, by allowing them to take classes either in the morning or afternoon, leaving the rest of their schedule open for sports training. As a result, enrollment quickly grew.

The challenge from the onset was to change the perception that a school focused on athletes wasn't serious. "People would say, 'It's just a jock-o-rama school,'" said Richard Odell, the school's headmaster and cofounder, who went on to become IMG Academy's vice president of student affairs. "So we had to work every day to improve the quality of the academics."

This did, in fact, require work. According to a former teacher at the school, many students were there solely to play their sport. They went to class because they had to but put little effort into it. The wealth factor meant that many kids weren't worried about their future. "They thought they were going to make it big in sports," the teacher said, and if not, then their parents' money and connections would provide them with a secure future.

Besides, if they received low grades, parents would often show up and demand they be changed. "They would fly down and tell the teachers what they were going to do," this teacher said. "They'd say, 'I'm spending a hundred thousand dollars here, and my daughter is not going to get a B." And if it came down to it, the teacher said, administrators would cede to the parents.

In one class, a student who would go on to be a professional golfer took part in a science project that required students to sit outside and draw or photograph what they observed, the idea being that scientists must learn to be sensitive to their surroundings. "Each page had a sun with a smiley face, and then it had little V-shaped birds—like in kindergarten," said the former teacher about the assignment the student turned in. She was given an F. Her parents then flew down and complained, and the teacher was asked by an administrator to "give her credit anyway, because at least she did the assignment."

Another student who would go on to be a professional tennis player was once asked to build a three-dimensional project. Her mother showed up and told the teacher to give her daughter worksheets, that the girl was not going to do any other kind of assignment. When the teacher refused, the girl was switched into another class.

Pushy, demanding parents were ideal clients for Singer, who found the perfect hole to fill at IMG Academy. Although Pendleton had its own college counseling staff, the department was still young, and so IMG brought him on as an additional perk for families who were interested in paying for his counseling. Singer sold himself with his usual self-promotional schtick.

"He said he had relationships everywhere," said Greg Breunich, Pendleton cofounder and former IMG senior executive, who said that Singer charged families about $3,500 for his services. Richard

Odell recalls the pitch being even more finely tuned. "I've got great relationships with college coaches," Singer would say.

To help him with his new clients, Singer brought on two IMG insiders, Mark Riddell and Scott Treibly. Riddell was an impeccably groomed local from a prominent family in town. His father, Jefferson, was a real estate attorney, and his mother, Julie, managed Riddell Title & Escrow and graced the pages of the local society magazines, which featured her in spreads about charity luncheons and Junior League events. In 2006, *Sarasota* magazine reported that she had attended Pique-nique sur la Baie, a spring luncheon to raise money for a local library that required attendees to wear fashionable headgear. "Julie Riddell has 10 or 12 hats," the story read. "Her hat of the day came from Neiman's."

Mark Riddell—who would become one of Singer's most instrumental cohorts in the Varsity Blues scandal—grew up playing tennis at the Field Club, a country club near his home. As a kid, he'd ride his bike over to the club to hit balls and talk older kids into playing a game. He then started training more seriously at IMG, where his dad would drop him off every morning at seven and where he caught the attention of Nick Bollettieri. He attended Sarasota High School, where he was known as an affable, somewhat goofy guy. For one school talent show, Riddell got onstage in a full tuxedo and kicked balls around the stage while jamming out to AC/DC's "Big Balls," according to a classmate. He was a straight-A student who took part in the school's magnet STEM program and was a member of the National Honor Society. But where he really stood out was on the tennis court. "He had a pretty amazing slice serve that seemed to defy physics," said one former teammate, who credited Riddell, who was the school's number one singles and doubles player, with helping the team win the state championship in 1999.

After graduating from high school, Riddell spent the summer playing tournaments in Europe and the Caribbean, and then headed off to Harvard, where he enrolled in premed courses. Matt Butler, founder and CEO of the college counseling company the Butler Method International, recalls meeting Riddell on the first day of college, when he walked into Eliot House, where he and Riddell lived. "He was this nice, very suave tennis player from Florida," Butler told me. "He had a bright-white smile, and was always in a good mood. Always friendly. He kind of kept with the cool crowd."

Despite his blue blood, Riddell didn't coast at Harvard, where by his senior year he was the number three singles player and number two doubles player. While back home for a match against IMG (his parents hosted the Crimson team for a barbecue), he told the *Sarasota Herald-Tribune*, "For me, this year has been the most difficult. I honestly skip practice frequently so I can study. Except for tennis, that is about all I do.

"There's a lot of students who are studying 24-7," he went on. "Tennis takes us on the road quite a bit, and that is a little bit difficult. That's why it's not unusual to see a van full of players heading back to campus after a match with books open and flashlights beaming."

Riddell told the paper that he'd decided not to be a doctor—he'd switched over to a biology major—and that he wanted to give professional tennis a try. "I am looking forward to getting out there and playing," Riddell told a reporter. But his dream was short-lived. He didn't win any of the ten pro matches he played, earning him just $892, according to ATP records. And so he returned to Florida.

When Singer met him, Riddell was in the midst of this identity crisis. Tennis as a career was off the table. He still played around country clubs in Sarasota, where there is a thriving community of serious tennis players, many of them former college athletes, who play in local tournaments and coach on the side. But it was clear that he was not on the Andy Roddick track (someone Riddell had beaten as a junior player). According to Richard Odell, Singer used his charm on Mark Riddell, playing the flattery game hard and making it clear how impressed he was by Riddell's credentials. "I think the connection Rick made with him was he was a Harvard grad," Odell said. "He touted that. 'We have a Harvard grad on our staff.' I think that's part of what got Mark sucked into this."

But Riddell had something even more critical to Singer: He was a standardized-test whiz kid. He knew the SAT and ACT "up one side and down the other," according to Odell. "He just had that kind of mind." When he worked as a test-prep tutor for Singer, he would patiently go through test questions with kids, at times even making questions up himself.

It was during this time that Mark Riddell met Scott Treibly, another tutor, who would also become an important partner in crime for Singer. A blond, boyish former assistant college tennis coach at Texas A&M, Treibly was working as a coach at IMG when he was first recruited by Singer. Whereas Riddell was more of a sunny people pleaser, Treibly was a straight shooter, who was skilled at delivering hard truths to parents who were neither accustomed to, nor interested in, hearing them. Said one IMG executive: "Sometimes with our families, you have to be really careful. They're really successful, and you have to be more delicate. You have to be a little political. You have to choose your words carefully. Scott could just tell it the way it is—that was his skill."

According to the *Wall Street Journal*, Singer split his fees with his tutors, writing in one email to Treibly: "250 an hour for my time, 200 for yours."

That fee wasn't solely for test prep. Riddell, and especially Treibly, had relationships with college coaches, which made them even more of an asset to Singer. "Scott helped with placing tennis players [at colleges and universities] because he had such incredible connections in collegiate tennis," the IMG executive said. "He'd been a player and coach at the academy, and he would broadcast the SEC tournament, because he was just incredibly knowledgeable about the world of tennis."

❧

A key introduction that Scott Treibly would make for Rick Singer was with Gordon Ernst, whom Treibly knew from tennis circles and whom he interviewed for the December 2007 issue of *Tennis Life* magazine. A graduate of Brown, where he'd played varsity tennis and hockey, Ernst had become Georgetown's head men's and women's tennis coach in 2006. Named after hockey Hall of Famer Gordie Howe, Ernst came from a family of tennis and hockey players. His father, Dick, was a legendary high school and college coach around the family's hometown of Cranston, Rhode Island. And as a sporty kid growing up in the early 1980s, Gordie, as he was known, was a local phenomenon. He racked up tennis state championship titles, was a hockey All-Stater, and was named an Honor Roll Boy by the *Providence Journal-Bulletin*. Out of high school, he was drafted to play pro hockey for the Minnesota North Stars but opted for an Ivy League education instead. But sports, not school, was more Ernst's thing. He would later joke to his tennis players that while at Brown he'd been in a class where everyone was copying off everyone else's answers on a test. Ernst was apparently the only one who got caught, but he laughed the story off, reveling in the anecdote's power to entertain—which, to him, was of utmost value—rather than its ethical implications. After graduating, he embarked on a brief Wall Street career, working in municipal bonds at Lehman Brothers. Unhappy in a desk job, he'd returned to sports, settling into a tennis coaching career, first at Northwestern, where he was an assistant, and then at Penn, where he was the head tennis coach between 1998 and 2000. Before arriving at Georgetown, he'd been the executive director of the Vineyard Youth Tennis program on Martha's Vineyard.

Chatty and personable, Ernst was a well-liked, even beloved, coach at Georgetown. He was always cracking jokes in meetings, always had a gap-toothed smile on his face. His players were so devoted to him, and vice versa, that they all invited him to their weddings. One young couple even asked him to officiate their marriage. He dressed up for Halloween—one year he wore an orange prison jumpsuit—and invited his teams over to his home to watch the Super Bowl with his wife and two young daughters. He played baseline tennis games with his players, giving them twenty bucks if they beat him. At recruiting events, when coaches descend on a high school gymnasium and prospective players sit down and chat, eager to tick off their impressive stats and wow the coaches, Ernst stood out from other coaches by asking questions like "What's your favorite movie?" He wanted to know kids as kids, not just how well they played tennis.

"I considered Gordie in between a second father and a goofy uncle," said Casey Marx, who played tennis at Georgetown and graduated in 2018. "The whole team had an absolute family vibe."

Marx described Ernst as someone who loved to entertain and make everyone feel comfortable. He also had an irrepressible silly streak. At one dinner that a player's parents hosted at a fancy restaurant, the host asked everyone to go around the table and share their favorite poem. When it was Ernst's turn, he said with a straight face, "Yellow Stream by I. P. Daily," sending his team into giggles.

But this cheery exterior belied a less glossy reality for Ernst. Although Georgetown was a Division I school with a world-famous basketball team, smaller sports received far less fanfare and resources. This situation is typical at universities, where football and basketball are the real money geysers, bringing in funds through ticket sales, media rights, and sponsorship deals, and underwriting all the other athletic programs. But the squeeze on smaller sports, particularly nonmarquee sports like tennis, was even more intense at Georgetown, seeing as the university lacked a high-profile football team. Georgetown's approach to athletics was also much more broad-based than many of its Big East competitors. As a Jesuit university, the school believes in offering as many athletic opportunities as it can to its students—10 percent of whom play on varsity teams—as opposed to investing heavily in a smaller number of sports with an eye toward across-the-board national championship wins.

The school offers close to 130 athletic scholarships each year, but they are more generously allocated to teams that compete nationally, such as basketball, soccer, lacrosse, and track and field. Smaller so-called Olympic sports, like tennis and golf, are not funded at the same level and receive far fewer resources and scholarships. Over the years, there have been complaints from Georgetown coaches who have argued that the school should cut back on the number of sports it carries—twenty-nine—in order to invest more in each of its teams. In 2013, Georgetown's field hockey team, which had just two scholarships to offer prospective athletes—compared to the eight to twelve that its competitors had—started a petition to have the university take the program more seriously. At the time, they were practicing at American University and competing at the University of Maryland, because Georgetown didn't have a field with appropriate turf for the sport. The team also demanded a sit-down with Georgetown president John J. DeGioia and raised $45,000 in donations from parents. As a result of their campaign, the next year the team returned to practicing and competing on campus on a field that had been upgraded.

Georgetown's response, based on conversations with people familiar with the school's philosophy, is that it's not trying to compete with sports-focused schools in the Big East. Rather, it sees itself as a peer of schools in the Ivy League and of other top-tier academic universities like Northwestern and Boston College. Those schools similarly take a broader approach and carry large rosters of varsity teams in order to offer a wider variety of sports, including squash and sailing. Yale, for instance, has thirty-five varsity teams; Cornell has thirty-seven. In contrast, Villanova and Notre Dame have twenty-one and thirteen, respectively. George-town's view of athletics as deeply entwined in a greater mission at the school is clear in a video the university created called *Ethos of Georgetown Athletics*. In the video DeGioia somberly says: "We are animated by the Jesuit idea of *cura personalis*—care for the whole person, heart, body, and mind."

Whatever the bigger picture was, Ernst was nonetheless frustrated by the constraints on his budget. According to one source, he had no travel budget, thus preventing him from traveling around the country to scout for new players; and limited resources for equipment. "Gordie was struggling just to buy cans of balls," said this source. "Most programs, they get all the equipment for their players, all the gear [such as tennis rackets, balls, uniforms, and sneakers], but Georgetown was really minimal on that. The budget was just way too low." Assistant coaches came and went, year to year, due to a lack of resources.

Ernst's low rung on the ladder was underscored by his salary of less than $65,000 annually, according to court documents. Although he supplemented it by running lucrative tennis camps over the summer, it was a far cry from the almost $2 million base salary that Georgetown's men's basketball coach at the time, John Thompson III, was reportedly making.

Ernst felt the most hamstrung in his ability, or lack thereof, to recruit players to his teams. Unlike most of Georgetown's Big East competitors, which had fully funded tennis teams, meaning they had eight full scholarships available for the women's team and 4.5 scholarships for the men's team, he had one-half of a women's scholarship and no men's scholarships, according to two sources. As a result, when he was trying to recruit players, he would often lose out to other schools.

When Ernst started coaching at Georgetown, there were eight outdoor tennis courts on campus. But when it rained or snowed, the team would have to play on the four indoor courts at Yates Field House, the facility where Georgetown students and members of the community worked out. One Big East coach whose team played against Georgetown was dumbfounded when the match was held at Yates. The tennis courts, which doubled as basketball courts, were in the center of the gym with a running track around them, and Ernst had to transform the area, pulling thick curtains around the courts to block off the track, where kids would still be running laps. "It was that rubberized indoor surface that had basketball lines on it," said the coach. "It was kind of crazy to have a collegiate match played on that."

Georgetown's athletic facilities on campus have always been

compromised due to the school's physically constrained location. The campus, which also houses the university's medical school and hospital, is sandwiched into a one-hundred-acre plot of land, which is surrounded by upscale residences, meaning that more than half of the school's teams practice and play off campus. In 2014, when Georgetown broke ground on its new athletic facility to replace Yates, the John R. Thompson Jr. Intercollegiate Athletic Center, Ernst would lose his courts completely. The new building was being constructed where the outdoor tennis courts had been, and there were no plans to build new courts on campus. Instead, the school rented courts at Georgetown Visitation, an all-girls prep school nearby.

Ernst was aware of these realities when he arrived at Georgetown, but the source close to him said he believed he could improve the situation. There was also hope that because he had a connection with the head of the athletic department at the time—Bernard Muir, who had played basketball at Brown while Ernst was there—his program might get a little more love than it had in the past. He was wrong.

Early in his tenure, Ernst scoured up enough donations from alumni and team parents to fund a four-year men's tennis scholarship worth $100,000. But when he brought it to the attention of Muir, he was told that the money had to be donated to Georgetown's overall athletic fund, and that it could not be used solely for tennis. University athletic departments often adhere to a centralized fundraising model, whereby donations are put toward a general fund and then dispersed among teams. This is done in part to try to generate bigger donations from alumni and parents—to get, say, a donor to give $50,000 toward the school's overall athletics as opposed to $10,000 for baseball—as well as to keep coaches from "nickel and diming alumni," said one former senior associate athletic director at a Division I university. But Ernst found the system discouraging. In an email, Muir said he could not recall the incident.

"I think Gordie may have gotten really frustrated by that experience," the source said. "He felt like, 'I raise money, they take it, and I can't even use it.' Maybe at some point, I don't know when, I don't know the details, but we all know it's a really slippery slope…"

The slipping seems to have started quite early. By the time Singer met Ernst, he may have already been taking liberties with his job and admitting kids into Georgetown as tennis recruits as a favor to friends, according to the latest edition of journalist Daniel Golden's book *The Price of Admission*. There's no evidence that money was involved. Ernst would allegedly simply present the students as having Division I tennis chops when they actually didn't. But Singer offered Ernst a new opportunity. He was willing to pay for the coach's dishonesty.

Douglas Hodge, Singer's client who was the COO at PIMCO as well as a philanthropy bigwig who'd built an orphanage in Cambodia, became the first test case. Hodge's oldest daughter had her heart set on Georgetown. But Singer said that the school was too much of a reach. In February of 2008, after he told Hodge that his daughter had a 50 percent chance at best of getting into Georgetown, he added: "There may be an Olympic Sports angle we can use."

The "angle" was to sell her as a tennis recruit. According to Hodge's sentencing memo, Singer didn't quite spell it out this way at first: He told Hodge that by making a targeted donation to a specific program at a university, his daughter's admission chances would be increased. He made it all sound perfunctory, even dull— as though it were yet another loophole that he understood better than most in the tangled web of college admissions, thanks to his years of experience as a college counselor. As he would tell another parent in an email, "Side door is not improper nor is back door both are how all schools fund their special programs or needs." He then told Hodge that he had a connection at Georgetown—Gordon Ernst—and that if Hodge donated money to the "perennially underfunded" women's tennis program, Ernst would promote Hodge's daughter's application. Singer then created a false tennis profile for Hodge's daughter that stated that she had enjoyed victories in multiple United States Tennis Association tournaments. In fact, she had never played one. Singer took things even further in his depiction of a young tennis prodigy: The application that was submitted to Georgetown on November 4, 2008, mentioned a tennis court in the Cambodian jungle that Hodge's daughter had purportedly helped build.

The next month, Georgetown sent out a "likely letter" to Hodge's daughter, which is a letter sent to recruited athletes and others who have been conditionally accepted to a school. The letters go out much earlier than they do to regular applicants—the latter don't hear until March of their senior year in high school—and are considered as close as one can get to a flat-out admission. According to an affidavit filed in the Varsity Blues case, Georgetown candidates who receive a likely letter have more than a 95 percent chance of admission; a student would usually have to do something drastic, such as suddenly fail out of school or commit a felony, in order to have his or her likely status overturned. Occasionally, coaches underestimate how many students will accept their offers and have to rescind "likely" status, but in general, they are considered a dependable promise.

If Hodge had no idea that Singer was involving him in anything unethical when he first discussed making a "targeted" donation, by this time, he was clued in to the scheme and fully understood what Singer had meant when he said he needed to "brand" his daughter. As the date for his daughter's interview with Georgetown approached, Hodge confided to Singer about the meeting: "It would NOT be good at all if tennis in Cambodia came up." Singer had other concerns about the interview. He told Hodge's daughter to "stay under the radar" about her provisional acceptance and to not "say anything" about it during the interview.

In the end, both men's concerns were moot. Hodge's daughter was officially accepted, and she enrolled in Georgetown in the fall of 2009. Satisfied by the turn of events, Hodge wrote out two checks for $75,000 each and mailed them to Ernst at his home address.

Singer had found a new business model: the side door. And he had found his first coach to ensnare in it, capitalizing on Ernst's frustration with his job, his seeming willingness to defy protocol and ethics, and his desire for a lifestyle more high-flying than the one he was enjoying as a modestly paid coach. There was the trip to New York City to compete against St. Johns when Ernst booked rooms at the Gansevoort Hotel, a boutique hotel in the Meatpacking District, where rooms start at several hundred dollars a night. Ernst told his players that he wanted them to experience nice things, and took them out to a fancy dinner. But after one night the team relocated to less posh digs: someone's house.

"He would say, 'We only have so many funds. If we want to go to nice places, we have to do this"—meaning crash at a team member's family's pad. "There was definitely a mentality of, if we could get away without paying for something, we would. It'd be like, 'Oh, I have this connection, we can stay in their basement.' And then later, we'd stay at a resort."

When this player mentioned the tennis team's travel itinerary to a friend on the soccer team, the friend's eyebrows shot up. The soccer team's "mentality was very much like, you take the team bus wherever you go, you eat at the chain restaurant and stay at the Holiday Inn. It was very standard." And according to the *Wall Street Journal*, Ernst once said to a father who asked him where his $400,000 donation to Georgetown's tennis program would be going, "Well, a coach has to eat."

"He was really concerned about making money," said a coach who knows Ernst. This person added that Ernst was "a little bit sloppy" in the way he managed things. In other words, he was perfect prey for Singer.

In many ways, Ernst—who has pled not guilty in the Varsity Blues case—epitomized the wearied, put-upon college coach that is largely hidden from the public eye. To most observers, and in the cultural imagination, coaches are those inspirational mantra-spewing figures who inculcate the values of hard work and blood-sweat-and-tears grit in their devoted players. They are the tough-as-steel figures who whip their minions into shape and guide them to nail-biting victories, after which they're hoisted onto shoulders and carried through an adoring crowd, sometimes winding up on the receiving end of an upturned bucket of Gatorade. Some, like Georgetown's own former basketball coach John Thompson, have achieved larger-than-life mythical status, and are celebrities in their own right.

But the underbelly of coaching, particularly for coaches of smaller, off-the-radar sports, isn't nearly so glamourous. Nor, for many coaches, is the job primarily about recruiting players and training them. Coaches can feel intense pressure to fundraise in order to increase their team's resources and even pay for equipment. Pressure also comes from the development office, which is constantly reminding coaches which donors' children are about to apply, suggesting coaches take them for tours and sit down and meet with them. "There's a lot of, 'Hey, so-and-so's coming on campus with their parents, or with an uncle or a friend of the family. Can you meet with them briefly, either in your office, or can you give them a quick tour of the school?'" said one former Division I college coach. "So suddenly you're doing a campus tour with the kid, and it's not really someone you want. It can feel like a bit of a waste of time if you're competitive."

Then there are parents of players, calling up about their prospective student or their kid who's already on the team but isn't seeing enough playing time. "Parents are very involved," this coach said. "You hear from them when there's a change in the lineup." Parents all but assault coaches during games or at scouting events, in the name of getting on their radar. One former Ivy League coach said she stopped wearing a T-shirt with the school's logo to scouting events because parents would corner her into thirty-minute conversations while she was trying to observe students play. "It was so distracting," she said. "I couldn't even watch."

At academically rigorous colleges, coaches also have to deal with declining rosters as students ditch the team once they're enrolled at the school, finding it difficult to balance schoolwork and their sport. This leaves coaches feeling they have to proceed with delicacy and not push their players too hard, for fear of losing them. Said one disillusioned coach: "The job is just figuring out how to keep everyone happy."

❧

It's not clear what pushed Rick Singer to cross the line into territory that was flat-out illegal, how he went from padding a student's résumé to offering bribes to coaches so that they could usher a kid into a college under false pretenses. What is clear is that when he reached this juncture he was in a world of rarefied wealth, surrounded by a new breed of parent who expected results in a way that his Sacramento clients presumably didn't. "They want this thing done," he would explain to one of his new prospective clients. "They don't want to be messing around with this thing. And so they want in at certain schools...My families want a guarantee." Through coaches like Gordon Ernst, Singer had figured out how to secure that guarantee. And as an always-hustling con man, he understood the value of that guarantee to these families, who were just as desperate about college admissions as families without their wealth and connections.

If anything, they were more desperate. Because of their high-profile names and the company they kept—the jobs they held, the philanthropy circles they ran in, the country clubs they were members of—having their child anointed by a top-tier school wasn't a preferable option; it was considered essential in order to keep the family name intact, and the aura of success and perfection. It was status maintenance of the highest order. In many cases, parents simply felt it was their right, something they were entitled to, regardless of what means were required to reach the end. They were used to sitting on board seats at private high schools, where their influence was all but absolute, where no one questioned their actions or motives. As one Varsity Blues–indicted mother, Michelle Janavs—who served on the board at Sage Hill School—would audaciously say to Singer about the prospect of the school asking questions about a side-door scheme she was pursuing with him: "They're not stupid...But whatever, I don't care. They can't say anything to me."

But what Singer most capitalized on, and where the real brilliance of what would become a $25 million master scheme lay, was that he was an expert at the ins and outs—the ten-thousand-foot view as well as the most granular of details—surrounding college athletics. He understood how athletic departments worked and how they interacted with admissions offices. He knew the pressures that coaches were under and the unglamorous reality of their jobs—including that their salaries were "slightly better than the priesthood," as one source joked. In short, he knew where the weaknesses in the system were. And using his charm, approachability, and almost psychotic doggedness, he was going to exploit the hell out of them.

The most basic fact that he knew as well as anyone was how much easier it was for an athlete to get into school than a nonathlete. Even among other VIP or tagged applicants—legacies, children of wealthy parents, first-generation students—athletes hold the most sway. As he would tell one client over the phone: "You know, the easiest way [to be admitted] is being a student athlete, because you can...overlap and overplay...the legacy."

"The athlete," Singer said, "gets first priority."

According to a former admissions officer at an Ivy League school: "The single biggest influencer in college admissions is athletics. If you get the support of the coach and you make it through the many—you have to jump through many, many hoops to get there. But if you do jump through all those hoops and the coach is still supporting you, you're almost at a one hundred percent acceptance rate in the admissions process."

Athletic recruits still have to meet certain minimums in terms of standardized test scores and transcripts, but those test scores can be two hundred—or more—points lower than nonathletes, and there is a lot of "wiggle room," the admissions officer said. For one thing, recruits often start communicating with coaches in tenth grade, in some cases even earlier, and are given feedback as to how to improve their application. They might be told they need to retake the ACT or the SAT, or that they need to take a more advanced science class. These students then have time to burnish their credentials and ultimately get an okay from the admissions department.

At most Division I schools, a coach will bring his or her list of recruits to the admissions coordinator for athletics, to vet them and make sure they are academically qualified. A prioritized list is then submitted to the admissions committee, which has the final say. The Ivy League adheres to a measure called the Academic Index, which determines an academic average that a specific team has to maintain. In other words, kids can have varying levels of academic transcripts, but together they must average a certain standardized test score and GPA. Thus an academically high-achieving kid can help balance out the roster and make room for a kid with low scores.

But there is still a lot of smoke and mirrors at work. One coach said that when they worked at a school in the top ten in *U.S. News and World Report*'s ranking of the best colleges, coaches were asked to rank their recruits academically with a number from one through five—one being the best students, five being the worst. "You could have as many number ones as you wanted, but you only got one number five." The idea was to drive up the level of academics among student athletes. But extra points were given to students who were underrepresented minorities, meaning those kids could rise to the top of the list even with lower academic qualifications. "Then you'd move up the scale," the coach said. "Because [the college] wanted to diversify."

The sheets of paper were then taken away by the admissions committee, and coaches were told they couldn't photocopy or take pictures of them, for fear they'd be leaked to the public.

This coach said that the public would be shocked by the

disparity in academics between athletes and nonathletes, particularly at more athletically competitive schools, where this coach also worked. "There's no way these recruits would have gotten in on their own—there's just no way," the coach said. "But if you didn't [allow for lower academics], you really couldn't compete. There really are no athletes that have those kind of scores. I don't want to say none, but it's just such a small number, when you think about the kind of scores you need to get into these schools. You have to be perfect on the SAT...So they have to lower the standards. If they didn't, I actually don't know how you could field a team."

Whatever vetting of student athletes is being done—or not—by admissions committees, when it comes to an applicant's athletic abilities, trust is put entirely in the coach. Both the admissions office and the athletic department take a coach's word on a student's athletic credentials. If there is any concern or scrutiny, it tends to be about whether a student meets academic requirements. "If a coach wants John Smith and he's a soccer player, I totally trust my coach," said one former associate director of athletics at a top-ranked school. This makes the system almost ridiculously easy to exploit. For instance, at Georgetown, Gordon Ernst would allegedly give admissions and athletics two different profiles of his recruits. He'd hand admissions his profiles of Rick Singer kids but share his actual recruits only with athletics, filling up the slots he was planning to use for Singer's clients with other nonrecruits who were still decent players. "He deceived everybody," one source told Daniel Golden, as reported in *The Price of Admission*. "It's not that hard to do. There's no coordination between athletics and admissions. These are minor sports, low on visibility, beneath the radar."

Since the Varsity Blues scandal hit, many schools—including

Georgetown, USC, UCLA, and Stanford—have put new systems in place that reinforce the communication between athletics and admissions, as well as the fact-checking that goes on with applicants' athletic credentials. But the former associate athletic director said that not even that is enough. "A lot of schools are saying the administration has to vet the recruit," he explained. "That's fine and good. But even assuming they're straight and ethical and don't cheat, the system is still not foolproof." For instance, a coach could put a good but not necessarily great athlete—considered a "walk-on"—on their roster not for a bribe, but with the understanding that the parent was going to donate to the program.

"Coaches play walk-ons for fundraising and their own purposes," said one former Division I men's basketball coach. "You won't take a fake athlete. But you'll take a subpar athlete, thinking, 'The family will donate to the program.' That happens all the time."

Indeed, few, if any, coaches would ever give one of their scholarship slots to a student who wasn't going to be a strength to the team. That would be throwing money away as well as hurting the team (and the coach's reputation). But in addition to offering scholarships, coaches are able to recruit walk-on athletes to fill out their rosters, giving them additional slots. Historically, the term *walk-on* meant exactly what it sounds like. "If you were at a university, the coach in a sport would put up a notice. 'People who want to try out for three spots on the football team, come out on Wednesday at three o'clock,'" said Fred Stroock, who served as associate athletic director for academic and student services at both USC and UCLA. "So if you were already a student, you would literally walk onto the team."

This still remains true in some college sports, mainly in sports like rowing, which rely on kids who have never rowed in high school to fill out their large rosters. But Stroock said that as tuition, particularly at private colleges and universities, has skyrocketed (USC costs $77,459 a year if you factor in housing, books, and meals), coaches are unable to get as many strong walk-on athletes. "It's so expensive to go there, you don't get the same wide profile of student," he said. Thus walk-ons are actively recruited out of high school.

Walk-ons are not strong enough in their sport to merit a scholarship and may not be starters on a team, but they are good enough to round out the program. Many sports, such as water polo and track and field, need far more athletes to practice and compete than coaches are able to recruit, making walk-ons essential. At USC, for example, the women's cross-country team has two scholarships (which are technically allotted to track and field), meaning that the rest of the dozen or so members of the team are walk-ons. "We relied heavily on getting quality walk-ons, because that was ninety percent of our team, and we had to go up against the Pac-12, which was loaded with scholarship athletes," said former USC coach Tom Walsh. "You have to recruit them, but also say, 'You've got to pay the high tuition, pay your own way.'"

Playing walk-ons for fundraising purposes came to light in a UCLA-issued investigative report detailing how the university recruited a walk-on athlete to its track-and-field program in 2013 despite the fact that the girl's race times didn't qualify her for a spot on the team. Her entree to the school was secured by her parents' pledge to donate $100,000 to the track-and-field program. The case underscores how unregulated recruiting and development processes have been at colleges, and how easily—indeed, breezily—they often interacted. Michael Maynard, UCLA's track-and-field coach at the time, later wrote in a letter that he had approved the decision to recruit the student based on a request from Josh Rebholz, a member of UCLA's athletics fundraising staff, who is now the school's senior associate athletic director.

"Josh asked me if I had any room on my team for a female athlete, and if so would I assist with her admission," Maynard wrote. "Josh indicated that he wasn't sure what events she did in track, but that she was the daughter of major donors...Josh indicated to me once again that her parents were major donors to UCLA, and it was very important to development.

"In my opinion, [the student] was not athletically up to the performance level to participate in indoor or outdoor T&F. At this time I felt that I had been manipulated into coding her under false pretenses."

UCLA opened an investigation into this and another recruiting inconsistency—involving Rick Singer—in 2014, and determined that the timing of the pledge "together with the revelation that [the student] was intended to be only a manager...removes any reasonable doubt that the contribution from the parents was obtained quid pro quo for the daughter's admission." Yet the school did not accuse either the student or her parents of any wrongdoing, and the student graduated in 2017. According to a statement from UCLA, unnamed coaches at the school were "determined to be directly responsible for policy violations" and subjected to unspecified discipline as a result of the investigation. The statement also said that UCLA retained the $100,000 donation.

❧

In 2009, when IMG underwent a management shift, it ended all of its vendor contracts, including its deal with Rick Singer. The company brought all of its outside services in-house, absorbing the Pendleton School. As part of this consolidation, the company built up its own college preparatory department, hiring Mark Riddell to oversee test prep and Scott Treibly to focus on college placement along with one other tutor. The shift coincided with a growing frustration with Singer at IMG. Pendleton's headmaster, Richard Odell, had never cared much for him and his pushy, name-dropping ways, and felt that having him on campus undermined the college-prep services that Pendleton offered. "I said, 'There's no need for this. This is a very mixed message to parents, because the fact that you would have him on campus implies that what parents are paying for through tuition to Pendleton and IMG is not enough to get them [in] someplace.'"

But exile from IMG was no matter for Singer, who was moving on to his biggest rebranding yet. Unbeknownst to IMG, Riddell would continue working for him, only in a new, unorthodox capacity. Treibly would also remain a close colleague, who would continue to help him expand his network of college coaches.

Meanwhile, Singer was rapidly expanding and upgrading his business. Although he continued to deliver sermons on college counseling anywhere he could drum up business—in 2012, he gave a speech at the I Hotel on the campus of the University of Illinois at Urbana-Champaign for members of the global leadership group YPO—he had his eyes on a much bigger prize. His foray into Southern California was leading to more überwealthy clients and toeholds at more desirable schools, including UCLA and USC. Starry-eyed by Hollywood, he had even auditioned for a reality TV show about the pressures of getting into college. In the audition reel, Singer is tanned and revved up, dressed in a baby-blue V-neck sweater over a white Polo T-shirt. "This is a game," he jabbers into the camera. "You have to realize, this is a game.

"This process brings out all the good, and a lot of the bad that goes on in people's homes," he goes on. "Saturday night, it's an amazing night. Why? Because Mom and Dad go to a dinner party. They hear about every kid who's getting into this school, getting into this summer program. Doing this, doing that. Sunday morning, my phone rings off the hook. Why? 'How come we're not doing this? I heard this kid has a three-point-four [GPA] and they're gonna get into Harvard. How come we're not doing this and that?'

"They're out of control. They wake up their kid at seven a.m. on a Sunday morning, saying, 'C'mon, we gotta go, we gotta go! We gotta do stuff!'"

His new business in Orange County and LA was rife with so much potential—and so much more money—that Singer himself relocated to Newport Beach in 2012, buying a five-bedroom Mediterranean villa near the ocean for $1.5 million. He moved into his palatial new home alone. His twenty-two-year marriage with Allison had recently ended in divorce, and their son, Bradley, had left to study at DePaul University, cutting off Singer's primary roots in Sacramento. A source told me that after Allison stopped working for the CollegeSource in the early aughts, she and her husband had been "just coexisting."

But just existing wasn't Singer's style. He registered his company the Edge as a for-profit counseling business in California, and then created the Key Worldwide Foundation, his tax-exempt nonprofit organization that claimed to help "needy Cambodians" and to help underserved youth get into college. As its mission statement read, "Our contributions to major athletic university programs may help to provide placement to students that may not have access under normal channels." Setting up a philanthropic arm would give Singer more of an in with his new caliber of clients, most of whom, like Hodge, were major charity donors. But it would also serve his own purposes, which, at this point, were in no way at all normal.

CHAPTER 7

The Fall of Troy

On February 13, 2013, Ali Khosroshahin, the head women's
soccer coach at USC, emailed Donna Heinel, a senior associate athletic director at the school, about a young soccer player
he was looking to recruit. "TOP DRAWER ESTIMATED #3
RECRUITING CLASS IN NATION," he wrote. He noted that she
was an "All Ex Patriot Japan National Select Team Player," as well
as a member of the "All National Championship Tournament
Team." This student, Khosroshahin went on to say, "is comfortable on the ball with both feet and plays center midfield. Her
knowledge of the game, awareness and vision of the field will set
her apart from most at the college level. These qualities are what
will make her a[n] asset to our team."

The student in question was one of Douglas Hodge's younger
daughters. She was not a high school soccer player, let alone
a nationally ranked one. Nonetheless, the very next day, Heinel
presented her to the subcommittee for athletic admissions, which
vets recruiting candidates, giving them either a green light to the
school or denying them admission as a soccer recruit. In March,
Hodge's daughter was accepted.

Five years after Hodge first started working with Rick Singer—

and the same year that his eldest daughter received her diploma from Georgetown, having never attended tennis practice—he was back for what he would call "the Rick magic." Singer's side-door scheme had worked so flawlessly, and Hodge was so pleased by the results, that he was ponying up his next child. (She would not be the last.) It wasn't quite a rinse-and-repeat cycle. Singer had finessed his operation significantly. This time, he wouldn't ask Hodge to mail a check to a coach directly, as he had with Gordon Ernst. The tennis coach had just gotten another Singer client, the daughter of TV executive Elisabeth Kimmel, into Georgetown through the side door and was now on Singer's payroll, receiving monthly installments of between $11,000 and $24,000. Singer now covered his tracks more adroitly, funneling checks to universities and coaches through his new empire.

On April 5, he instructed Hodge to send a payment of $150,000 to his for-profit, along with a $50,000 payment to the Key Worldwide Foundation, his nonprofit organization. The next day, Singer's bookkeeper, Steven Masera, sent Hodge a letter stating that "no goods or services were exchanged" for his payment to the nonprofit, clearing the path for Hodge to write off the payment as tax-deductible. Singer, in turn, sent two checks of $50,000 each to a soccer club that Khosroshahin ran with his assistant soccer coach, Laura Janke. Sporty and ponytailed, with freckles sprinkled across her face, Janke had played soccer for Khosroshahin when he was a coach at Cal State Fullerton before becoming his assistant there. When he was hired by USC in 2007, he brought her with him, and once described her as "the glue that keeps this program running."

A Persian American with deep-set Clooney-esque eyes and a thick mane of black hair that was starting to gray at the temples, Khosroshahin—like Ernst—coached a low-profile college sport. But unlike Ernst, he was at a school where sports are king. Primarily, this means football, which is less a game than an institution at USC. The morning after a Trojan loss, the voicemail of USC's president is full of rants from fans, alumni, and casual observers. Some even dial in from the Los Angeles Memorial Coliseum, the historic stadium where USC plays, to vent during the game. "I'll tell you, Mr. President. You gotta get rid of your coach. The quarterback's an idiot—he can't even run a play. Did you guys even practice?" But at USC, which is Division I and part of the Pac-12, even non-revenue-generating sports are a source of pride. Inside Heritage Hall, USC's main athletic building, the lobby's Hall of Champions has a museum's worth of trophies, plaques, and gilded cups proudly arranged around a bronze statue of a kneeling Trojan warrior with his arms forming a U-shaped victory sign. Half a dozen Heisman Trophies are propped up on pedestals, and the walls of the circular space are lined with gold medals, representing wins by USC athletes for every Olympic Games dating back a whole century. A special nod is given to women's sports, and in one case is the women's Capital One Cup, which USC won in 2016 after eight of its women's teams finished in the top ten in NCAA championship play. Outside the building, crimson-and-gold banners blare statistics to remind passersby of how central sports is to the Trojan identity: 451 Olympians, 19 Hall of Famers, 507 conference champions.

When Khosroshahin arrived at USC in 2007, he contributed to this tradition, leading the women's soccer team to its first-ever NCAA championship win. The team had come off a lackluster period; it had never made it past the second round of the NCAA tournament for eight straight years. The unexpected turnaround by a newbie coach from Cal State Fullerton was nothing short of historic. Khosroshahin was named NSCAA National Coach of the

Year and was described in the *Orange County Register* as "one of women's soccer's hottest coaches."

"He looked like the most amazing coach of all time," said one acquaintance.

The only trouble was, USC's winning moment never turned into a streak. In 2009, the team didn't make it beyond the first round of the NCAA tournament. In 2011, after his team had suffered eight straight losses of a total of thirteen, marking the first losing season in the program's history, Khosroshahin was openly distressed. "This has been the most difficult season of my coaching career," he told the *Daily Trojan*. "It's been challenging. Most of all, it's been hard to see the kids suffer. It's made me feel absolutely helpless at times.

"This type of season is something this school hasn't seen before," he went on. "And I haven't either. It's out of character for both of us." Soccer was the thing that had saved Khosroshahin when he was growing up in Utah, where his family immigrated from Iran when he was six. As a Persian kid in one of the most Anglo parts of the country, he was an outsider. Indeed, he could barely string together sentences in English: the only words he knew were *hello* and *shut up*. Being able to kick a ball around with other kids, and then eventually compete on the field with them, allowed him to blend in and not appear so out of place. He had a new, shared language, one that didn't require speaking but hustling, jostling, winning, and losing. Khosroshahin got very good at that language. He went on to play soccer in college—first Cal State Fullerton and then Cal State LA, where he played for the man who would become his mentor, Leo Cuéllar, an icon in Mexico and the former coach of Mexico's national women's team. Khosroshahin has said that Cuéllar "taught me everything about soccer.

"Leo has a spirit of the game in him. In this country we know all the tactical stuff, all the drills," Khosroshahin went on. "But we don't have the spirit of the game that they have in other countries. Leo has that spirit, a passion."

Khosroshahin imbibed that passion and brought it to his own coaching style. "Ali talked about soccer like it was a religion. He'd say things like, 'You need to do what the game asks of you,'" said a former USC soccer player. Before some practices, he'd light an incense stick and walk around the field saying "prayers for success," the player said.

But several of Khosroshahin's former players at USC say that his zeal bled into something more extreme. In many ways, as a coach, Khosroshahin was a lot like Rick Singer. Impassioned and charismatic on the best of days, on the worst—of which there were more and more as the team's record worsened—Khosroshahin could be explosive. He was known for throwing chairs on the sidelines at games and breaking clipboards in half when he was angry about the way a game was going. He yelled at his players— once calling them "cream puffs," much to the shock of the team dietician who was in earshot of the remark. At times he became so overcome by anger or frustration that he'd openly weep.

Also like Singer, he believed in grueling training sessions that seemed extreme even for Division I athletes who were accustomed to pushing themselves beyond their limits. Practices were held at 5:30 a.m., and Khosroshahin once brought in a team of ex-Marines to lead his team in a series of torturous exercises, such as treading water for twelve minutes in a swimming pool while wearing sweat-pants and sweatshirts. At one point the players had to take off their sweatshirts (they had bathing suits on underneath) and trade them with another player's while still treading water to keep afloat. "It was so hard," recalled another former player. "I'm a good swim-mer and I can remember swallowing water and being like, 'This is insane.' " Another drill called for players to physically lift a teammate into a fireman's carry and run with them across the soccer field.

Khosroshahin's most infamous practice ritual, according to several players, was a game he called "WWE." A strong believer in building mental and emotional grit, he organized the exercise after the team had lost or when they were gearing up for a big game and he wanted to toughen the team up. He'd have the women stand around the center circle of the soccer field and select two players at a time to oppose each other. Khosroshahin would often pick two women who he knew were bickering or at odds as a way to up the drama. He'd then throw the ball into the middle of the circle and the players would run at it. The idea was to see who could steal away the ball and get it back to him first. As to how that was achieved, there were essentially no rules. Players could body-slam, hit—whatever it took. They were highly motivated do just that, seeing as whoever lost the game would have to run a "Cooper"—that is, a Cooper Test, a much-loathed drill that involves running two miles in under twelve minutes. In other words, running like hell.

Samantha Johnson, who played on a soccer scholarship at USC between 2009 and 2013, recalled the most brutal WWE game of all. It was her senior year and she'd become burned out on soccer and burned out on Khosroshahin, whom she privately referred to as "Satan."

"It was a week before we were going to play UCLA in the Coliseum and he's like, 'We're playing WWE,'" Johnson said. "We're like, 'Ugh, God. No one wants to run a Cooper. We're going to kill one another to not be the loser.'

"He throws the ball in and in my logical brain I'm thinking, 'Why go after the ball? If [the other player] can't get it, then I win,'" Johnson went on. "I was like, 'That's my strategy—to just beat the girl up so she can't get the ball.' You're in the environ-ment of survival, that's where my mind was. So he throws the ball out and I ran straight to her and body-slammed her. I'm doing all these crazy things, bouncing her head on the ground, whooping her ass, thinking, 'This is just part of the game.'"

Another player who witnessed the scene recalled that the other player "had the ball and Sam tackled her to the ground and she refused to let it go. Sam then grabbed her hair and smashed her head into the ground like four times. She was dazed and couldn't hold the ball anymore."

As the girl lay on the ground, Khosroshahin didn't seem at all fazed, according to multiple players. He calmly called the trainer over to help. Taking their cue from their coach, the rest of the team just stood there, unsure of what to do. Eventually the young woman was taken off the field and was told she'd suffered a concussion, according to multiple sources. She'd had concussions before, it was a condition, but this one appeared to be the limit—doctors recommended she never play collegiate soccer again.

"Honestly, at the time I didn't care," Johnson said of the incident. "I was in survival mode. I was like, I'm not running a fucking Cooper."

Several players echoed Johnson's sentiments, saying that play-ing for Khosroshahin was akin to being in a war zone and that even years later they felt PTSD-like effects. It wasn't just that he worked them so hard. He was moody, irritable, and, according to Johnson, "mentally abusive." He'd give the team the silent treatment if he was unhappy with their performance. He once called a player into his office and told her to tell her roommate, who was dealing with family issues, to "snap out of it" and get her head back in the game. He gave the team written quizzes to take on the soccer terminology that he used—some words were in Farsi—that they had to complete on top of their academic load. Indifferent to boundaries, he'd call players on their phones on weekends and during the off-season to talk about a game or an aspect of training.

"I'd see his number on my phone and freak out, but be like, 'I have to answer this.' He'd just want to talk about something that happened at practice. During my senior year, I was with my mom when he called and she was like, 'Don't answer it.'"

Berating and driving players in an extreme way wasn't unheard of at USC. The men's and women's water polo coach, Jovan Vavic, was an infamous screamer of profanities during practice and games. But unlike Khosroshahin, "Jovan was winning," said Johnson. Furthermore, "the water polo environment is very intense, their sport is really nasty—what goes on under the water is crazy. So in a way that behavior is part of the sport. But in soccer," a more gentlemanly sport, she said, a raging coach is "foreign as hell."

Khosroshahin's behavior seemed to be quietly endorsed by Laura Janke, his assistant and the team's goalie coach. The two had been professionally intertwined since their time at UC Fullerton—the bond intensified when they won the 2007 national championship together at USC—and together they created a kind of yin-and-yang dynamic that was overlaid with deep, mutual trust and loyalty. One former player said their connection was so strong that Janke seemed to have "a blind allegiance" to her boss, despite the stark differences in their personalities. Janke was sweet-natured and reserved, though hardly a pushover. She had the tough inner spirit of a trained athlete (she'd been a star goalie at UC Fullerton) and didn't take anyone's bullshit.

As the primary maternal figure on the coaching staff, Janke was able to connect with the players emotionally, and they often confided in her, talking to her about issues they were dealing with. But her loyalty was ultimately with Khosroshahin. "She would always have his back," said Johnson.

Janke never objected to Khosroshahin's crazy workout ideas. If anything, she served as a kind of enabler for his unprofessionalism. "If he cussed us out and then left the room, Laura would talk to us and try to pick up the pieces," said Johnson. "She'd try to explain his behavior. But sometimes, she'd walk out of the room with him."

As the Trojans continued to lose, chatter within USC Athletics was that Khosroshahin had won the national championship with soccer players he'd inherited from USC's previous women's soccer coach, and that he was having trouble recruiting his own batch of superstars. "There was a feeling that Ali was a good coach but not a good recruiter," said one source.

Khosroshahin was vocal about the institutional pressure he felt to win at USC, where, he told the *Daily Trojan* in another interview, "the goal is to win a national championship." He said that USC's athletic director Pat Haden (whose son Khosroshahin had coached as a kid, once benching him for forgetting his cleats) constantly asked him: "What are you doing today to help us win the national championship?"

Tom Walsh, who was USC's women's cross-country head coach and assistant track coach at the time, said that even for minor sports at USC, "the pressure to win is real.

"It comes from the AD, it comes from alums—depending on the sport, certain alums are more cutthroat than others. USC has always had a storied track-and-field team, so there was definitely a pressure for us to be successful and to live up to previous championships."

This focus on winning, made worse by Khosroshahin's dismal

streak, made him feel jaded about his job, according to a source close to him. It was a dramatic comedown from the elation he'd felt upon his arrival at USC. He'd shown up as a glorified coach at low-profile school—having turned the flailing women's program at Cal State Fullerton around, leading it to multiple trips to the NCAA tournament. But Fullerton was Fullerton. Khosroshahin had dreamed of the bigger leagues, and after seeing a job posting for a women's soccer coach on USC's website, he'd sent in an application. He told his players that during his interview with Steve Lopes, who was then associate athletic director, he'd put his elbows on Lopes's desk, leaned over and looked Lopes in the eye, and said, "I'm the guy."

"He was always telling us to be confident, no matter what, even if you're not," said Johnson, who nonetheless thought the story exemplified Khosroshahin's arrogance.

But in a sign that Khosroshahin wasn't just cocky but deeply grateful for his new job, when Lopes called him to offer him the job, he fell to his knees.

USC "changed him," the source close to Khosroshahin told me. "The worst thing in the world that happened to him is going there and, in his first season, winning the national championship." From then on, he was always expected to succeed. "Anywhere else, he would have been seen as the next coming. And there it was, 'What are you going to do next?' There was a climate there that made him feel underappreciated."

Unlike Gordon Ernst at Georgetown, Ali Khosroshahin made good money at USC. According to legal documents, his salary in 2012 was about $200,000. (Assistant coach Laura Janke's was $59,000.) But as pressure mounted for him to turn around his team, he began worrying that his job was at stake. As a result, his antics grew worse, according to players. There was more yelling and, at times, tears. "He was pretty vocal about the fact that he might lose his job. He'd say things like, 'You guys are messing with my livelihood. This is how I pay my bills and provide for my family.' Like it was our fault that he might get fired. He would outright say that," said a former player. He'd also talk about his father, an immigrant from Iran who'd built a successful life for his family in the United States and introduced Khosroshahin to soccer. "He'd say his dad was getting old. 'I just want him to be happy, so we need to win.' He was always guilting us."

By the spring of 2012, Khosroshahin was so concerned about his job that he asked players on the team to talk to Lopes and plead his case. "Our record was so bad, he wanted us to talk to one of the ADs and say, 'We really like Ali, please keep him around. Give him another chance,'" said one of the players. She admitted that she had mixed feelings about the request, given how she felt about Khosroshahin. But, she said, "I was under his spell. A lot of us felt that way."

The plea worked, at least for a time. But Khosroshahin was too familiar with USC's sports culture—"excellence or nothing," as one former soccer player put it—to know that his stint was almost over. Not that he was going to roll over and quit; that wasn't his style. But his anger, coupled with a sense of indomitability that Johnson thinks he imbibed at USC, put him in a new head space.

"You can get away with a lot of shit at USC because at SC, the Trojans always have your back, no matter what," said Johnson. "That's what they teach us. You're part of the Trojan family. You meet someone and they're a Trojan, they have your back. That's the narrative. Ali probably felt like he was invincible." Thus when Rick Singer approached him in the fall of 2012 and floated the idea of ushering in a fake recruit in exchange for money, his timing was impeccable.

After Douglas Hodge's daughter was ushered through the gates, Singer pressed on with another client, the daughter of Toby MacFarlane, a senior executive at a title insurance company who lived in a ritzy area of Del Mar, California. MacFarlane, himself a USC alum who felt anxiety over the college admissions process, had started working with him in 2012 in order to have his daughter's college applications be a "problem solved," according to MacFarlane's sentencing memo. MacFarlane was also at the "nadir" of his life, his attorney said at MacFarlane's sentencing hearing, and in the midst of a "crushing divorce." Singer "offered him an easy way out of one of his stresses."

Originally, Singer provided only basic tutoring and test prep for MacFarlane's daughter, who attended La Jolla Country Day School in San Diego. But he eventually floated the side-door option, saying that if MacFarlane donated $200,000 to his non-profit, he'd use his connections at USC to get his daughter in as a soccer recruit. It didn't matter that she didn't play on her high school team (although she played club soccer) and was not talented enough to play for a highly competitive college team. Singer reassured MacFarlane that his charity was legitimate and supported athletics at various universities and, more specifically, disadvantaged student athletes.

On November 4, 2013, MacFarlane's daughter was presented to the USC athletic admissions subcommittee as a "US Club Soccer All American" in tenth, eleventh, and twelfth grades. Her profile also included a photograph of her playing soccer, which MacFarlane's wife had provided, along with a draft of an essay—written by Singer in his flat, clichéd prose—that read: "On the soccer or lacrosse field I am the one who looks like a boy amongst girls with my hair tied up, arms sleeveless, and blood and bruises from head to toe. My parents have a hard time attending my soccer matches because our opponent's parents are always making rude remarks about that number 8 player who plays without a care for her body or anyone else's on the field. It is true that I can be a bit intense out there on the field."

Khosroshahin and Janke embellished further, writing that they believed MacFarlane's daughter was "a diamond in the rough and as she develops we think that she will be able to help our team at USC." They added that she "would come into our program and will compete for a role as an outside midfielder."

Less than a week later, Khosroshahin was fired—not for taking bribes, but for losing. "Based on the past few years, we felt it was time to go in a new direction," Pat Haden said in a press release. "We need to invigorate our program and get back to contending for NCAA and conference championships."

In the release, Khosroshahin thanked Haden and USC for the opportunity to coach and said, "It was tremendous to be part of the Trojan Family." (Janke was terminated soon afterward.) But inwardly he was crushed. According to the book *Unacceptable* by Melissa Korn and Jennifer Levitz, Khosroshahin was so devastated that he filled up trash bags with all of his USC-logo gear and got rid of them.

Four months later, in March 2014, MacFarlane's daughter was accepted for admission at USC for the following spring. Khosroshahin and Janke received a total payment of $100,000 from Singer through their soccer club. MacFarlane, in turn, wrote a $200,000 check to the Key Worldwide Foundation. The subject memo on the check read "Real Estate Consulting Analysis." Both Khosroshahin and Janke have pled guilty in the Varsity Blues case.

More so than any other school where Rick Singer made inroads, USC would become his hub, the institution that he had more snugly and lucratively in his pocket than any other. Georgetown's tennis program was the minor leagues in comparison, seeing as he had just one point of entry at that school, Gordon Ernst's tennis program. At USC, Singer would not only tap into a network of coaches who were allegedly willing to accept bribes, but prosecutors claim he would forge a partnership with the key liaison between USC's athletic and admissions departments.

Making the situation all the more perfect was that among the übermonied Californians who were becoming Singer's most valuable clients, USC held a special allure. Long gone were the days when the school was referred to, unjokingly, as the University of Spoiled Children and thought of as a finishing school for the Orange County elite—or, as one former USC staffer put it, a school for "the almost-wases of Mission Viejo." Under the leadership of university president Steve Sample and then, especially, Max Nikias, who took the reins at USC in 2010, the school had gone through a meteoric transformation, replacing its reputation for "affluent mediocrity," as a *Los Angeles* magazine cover story put it, into a top-ranked university overflowing with resources. USC's sports program had always been legendary—Trojan football games, with the pomp and noise of the brass band and the high-kicking Song Girls, were an institution. But for once, its SAT scores were higher than its less glamorous crosstown rival, UCLA, giving USC's cultish alums a new set of bragging rights. For the class entering in the fall of 2020, USC accepted just 16 percent of nearly 60,000 applicants. In 1987, it accepted 75 percent.

No one mistook USC for Harvard. But it had become a sought-after prize for wealthy West Coasters, in part because it so seamlessly extended the country club experience of their lives.

Located incongruously in a run-down neighborhood near down-town Los Angeles, the USC campus is an academic utopia of expansive green fields and redbrick Gothic buildings mimicking Ivy League campuses back east. Under Nikias's tenure, USC erected, in addition to a state-of-the-art biomechanics lab and nearly a dozen other new research centers, a fifteen-acre student village, replete with a Trader Joe's, an Abercrombie & Fitch, a Starbucks, and other cafés and restaurants, all meticulously designed to movie-set perfection. Nikias, a Greek-born engineer with lavish tastes and a love of the classics, decided that gracing the center of the space would be a twenty-foot-tall statue of Hecuba, the legendary queen of ancient Troy.

"USC Village is designed for eighteen-year-olds to say to their parents, 'I want to go here! And live in a dorm on top of a Trader Joe's!'" one USC senior faculty member told me, who also said that Nikias "lived in superlatives." "USC wasn't just going to be an important new school," the faculty member went on. "We were going to be the Oxford of the twenty-first century."

The locals, in particular, lapped it up. So many students from the Buckley School in LA go on to USC that Buckley kids refer to their school as a "feeder" to the university. Harvard-Westlake School, meanwhile, has sent eighty-three graduates to USC between 2014 and 2019, compared to the fifty-one who enrolled at Harvard. In LA, the pull is tied to USC's deep roots in the entertainment industry. George Lucas, Robert Zemeckis, and Judd Apatow all graduated from its famed film school, as have a good percentage of Hollywood screenwriters, producers, and executives. But USC's sway extends up the coast beyond Southern California movie buffs, to Bay Area nouveaux riches digerati and venture capitalists. Over the last three years, Menlo School, which has connections to two indicted parents, and which is located in Atherton (the most expensive zip code in the United States in 2019), sent twenty-four kids to USC—the same number it sent to Stanford.

USC's skyrocketing growth was fueled by money, and more and more demands for it. Max Nikias's visions for fundraising and donations were as outsized as his dreams of rebuilding ancient Greece or Oxford in downtown LA. Under his tenure, USC's fundraising staff doubled, and in the first six and a half years of Nikias's position at the helm, the university raised more than it had in the previous six and a half decades. One oft-told story was how, soon after Nikias became president, he had a conference with a group of fundraising consultants he'd hired to help him plan for USC's future. The consultants recommended that USC set a goal of raising $3 billion. "All right then," Nikias said, pounding his fist on the table. "Six billion it is!"

It was the largest fundraising goal ever announced in higher education, and Nikias would fulfill it eighteen months ahead of schedule.

The culture was one of enrichment at all costs, and multiple scandals would come to light down the road as a result. In the meantime, every department across the university felt intense pressure to fundraise, and the athletic department was no exception. In a 2011 interview, athletic director Pat Haden described the need to "feed the beast" and how the athletic department was working with USC's central development office to up its donor game. "The hundred-thousand-dollar asks are one thing," Haden said, "but how are you going to get that pyramid to work to be able to raise six billion dollars, in our case, or whatever our assigned number is?"

Gentlemanly and charismatic, with the easy affability of the aging athlete that he was, Haden was a USC family treasure, who'd led the Trojan football team to double national championship wins in the 1970s before playing for the Los Angeles Rams and then embarking on a successful career as an attorney and a venture capitalist. Adding to his Renaissance man credentials, he'd also been a Rhodes Scholar. The one thing he lacked was experience running an athletic department. Haden returned to USC as a kind of knight in shining armor to help redeem USC athletics, which had been dealt a major black eye with the Reggie Bush scandal—the USC running back was found to have accepted over $100,000 in gifts from agents, causing the NCAA to bar USC from bowl games in 2010 and 2011 and to dock the school thirty scholarships. (Bush denied any wrongdoing.) Haden's mission to redeem Trojan athletics was nothing short of "Herculean," USC said in a press release at the time, and he immediately embarked on ambitious projects to burnish USC's standing with the NCAA, including creating a large NCAA compliance program.

Haden brought a new grace and stateliness to the athletic department and immediately began transferring that into fundraising—the primary job of an AD. As William Tierney, a USC professor of higher education, put it: "The reason Pat Haden was the golden boy was that he was phenomenal at bringing in money." He had his work cut out for him. In 2012 Haden announced a $300 million fundraising drive for athletic scholarships and other amenities (including a beach volleyball facility with palm trees and sand imported from the U.S. Olympic Training Center). He would hit the goal in just three years and keep on going, ultimately raising nearly $750 million. But the actual nuts-and-bolts operation of the athletic department was less polished. According to one person who worked there for several years, USC's fast rise meant that while its brand had become akin to Google, in terms of prestige, the athletic department "was being run like Providence College." In other words, it was being run more like a mom-and-pop shop than an entity generating over $120 million in revenue annually, thanks to football. (As all athletic departments do, USC strives to operate at break-even, investing as much money back into the program as it makes.) Leadership was in the hands of very few, and most were USC lifers, who had grown up within the clubby insider culture of the school but had minimal executive experience elsewhere. Steve Lopes, who was Haden's number two and ran the day-to-day operations, had worked his way up the ranks, starting as an assistant strength coach in the early 1980s. Ron Orr, a former All-American swimmer at USC, had been with the department for three decades when he was hired to oversee the Trojan Athletic Fund in 2010. Major revenue sources like ticketing were being run "out of a couple of cubicles," said the source. And USC was one of the last schools to outsource sponsorships, so at the time, multi-million-dollar deals with companies like Nike were being handled by a single individual who was still using Excel spreadsheets. "It was a lot of people who didn't know any better. They'd never worked anywhere else," the former employee told me. "They weren't corrupt, but the SC culture was all they knew. The inmates were running the asylum."

Individuals close to USC disagree with this characterization, saying that Haden in fact brought in outsiders with experience and substance, including John McKay Jr., a trial attorney who then worked as general manager of the Los Angeles Xtreme, an XFL team. (Though he, too, had Trojan blood. His father was legendary USC football coach John McKay, and McKay Jr. was a former USC and NFL football player himself.) These people point out that Haden had been in private equity and was a skilled businessman whose style was to delegate responsibility to those he trusted. Because Haden was so busy between meetings and outreach and attending USC sporting events—he tried to go to as many as he could—he relied heavily on those below him, including Lopes, Orr, and Donna Heinel.

Overlaying the athletic department was the drumbeat to raise more funds. Pat Haden had access to plenty of wealthy alums and members of the LA business community, and he'd hired five new staffers to have more "bodies on the street" and do outreach to younger USC fans and families, he said in the 2011 interview. As at most schools, the development game at USC was played with aggressive shamelessness. Just how shameless—and how crass—came to light through documents that were revealed as part of the discovery process in one Varsity Blues case. The dozens of emails and spreadsheets that were released laid out a complex color-coded system whereby USC tracked its VIP or flagged candidates across the university. Many of the applicants were prospective student athletes, and emails between members of the athletics, admissions, and development offices flew back and forth in a torrent of wheeling and dealing, along with, in some cases, highly unprofessional comments. In one 2018 email, an associate dean and director of admissions, Kirk Brennan, mocked an applicant's grammar and joked that he was "good enough to shag balls for the tennis team anyway." (The applicant's admission was conditional based on his spring semester grades.) To which Tim Brunold, USC's admission dean, joked, "You said balls."

In another exchange in 2014, Donna Heinel and Ron Orr, both of USC's athletic department, and Sarah Peyron Murphy, director of development for USC's Marshall School of Business, discussed a walk-on recruit to the water polo team whose family the university had been cultivating a relationship with over the past year. The email chain began with Heinel writing that she had received approval through the athletic admissions subcommittee for the student to be let in as a water polo recruit. But the family—identified as "a high level prospect with 1–5M potential"—had also been having conversations directly with the business school, and jockeying ensued as to where those potential millions would be headed. After Murphy wrote that discussions with the family have "included several conversations about [their] desire to support Marshall," she said she was "100% in support of a donor-centered strategy" that also included sports, seeing as the family's "passion for athletics will likely play a significant role in their shared experience with the University."

Heinel then wrote Orr: "If this is not working out the way you planned, I can have Admissions pull the approval. Let me know. Tell them it was a backdoor development case of Marshall that I was not aware of."

Orr responded from his iPhone: "Really sucks don't pull we will guilt them."

Haden himself offered up lists of his own VIP candidates, showing one way he lured in wealthy families—though sources close to him say that he did not have the power to make a final decision on a candidate. In an email from 2016 with the subject line "special interest to Pat Haden," Heinel sent USC's two top admissions officers Haden's "list of recommendations for admission to USC." Included was a spreadsheet with more than thirty names of applicants, along with their GPAs, test scores, and "notes," such as: "dad well known ortho surgeon"; "pledged 1 million"; "Personal Friend"; "Father is MLB owner"; and "realtor in Aspen." In many cases, the students' scores were well below the regular admission standards for nontagged students.

❧

In a photograph of the Springfield College women's swim team, taken in 1983, Donna Heinel is in the back row on the far end. The only swimmer who is not wearing one of those glossy, satiny team jackets from the era of all things glossy and satiny, Heinel is wearing just her team swimsuit. She's also the only member of the team not looking into the camera and smiling. Instead, she's staring off into the distance with a blank look.

The photograph was taken Heinel's senior year at Springfield, where she'd been an All-American swimmer and a standout in free-style and the one-hundred-meter individual medley. "She was one of the best swimmers, if not the best, at Springfield College," said Mary Ellen Olcese, the head women's swim coach at Springfield, a Division III school, when Heinel was there. "As an athlete, she was a really hard worker. She was a main stalwart of the team."

But out of the pool, Olcese said, she kept a distance from her peers. "She was not a warm, fuzzy person. She was not the person everyone clung to. She was a good teammate, but she took to herself."

John Bransfield, who coached diving at Springfield then, said, "Donna was a very independent human being. She was extremely dynamic. She walked her own walk."

Heinel has admitted to having her own struggles growing up, telling an LGBTQ panel in 2013 that when she came out as gay to her parents, she didn't have a relationship with her family for two and a half years. As a result, she said, "I've been a loner for most of my life. Because from early on, and that reaction from my parents. I've just been someone that just, I do what I want to do when I want to do it."

After graduating from Springfield with a degree in physical education, Heinel pursued coaching, volunteering first for Olcese at Springfield and then landing a job at the University of

Massachusetts as the women's water polo head coach and assistant coach for women's swimming. In 2003, she switched gears into sports administration and arrived at USC, where she started as an assistant athletic coordinator.

Tall and wiry, with short-cropped blond hair and a thin, chiseled face, Heinel arrived at the office every morning at seven and kept her nose to the grindstone. She was someone who got the job done efficiently and without complaint or drama. "She was a pretty hard worker, pretty serious and in a rush," said Myron Dembo, who was Donna Heinel's academic supervisor when she completed her doctor of education degree at USC in 2006. "She didn't have time to schmooze." Indeed, Heinel was intensely private, never sharing information about her personal life with colleagues—she lived with her partner and their two children—in part because she didn't feel the atmosphere at USC was very gay-friendly. At the time, most gay student athletes at USC didn't come out to their teammates, and the general attitude within the athletic department was don't ask, don't tell.

But with the arrival of AD Pat Haden, who had a gay son and with whom Heinel quickly developed a rapport, that changed. A spotlight was placed on LGBTQ issues, and Heinel would lead the charge within athletics, opening up a discussion about gay student athletes and organizing a Pride T-shirt day for student athletes in honor of National Coming Out Day. Heinel has said that when she first met Haden, "He said, 'I want you and your partner to come on the plane to Hawaii'"—where USC was playing a football game. "At that particular time, I had two children," she said. "One was three; the other was just a little over one. And I hadn't even been acknowledged for having two children. So the fact that he said that to me made me know that everything was going to be okay."

Haden's arrival changed things for Heinel in other ways, too. A vocal proponent of Title IX and women's sports, one of Haden's first moves as athletic director was to promote Heinel to the position of "senior woman administrator," significantly broadening the scope of her responsibility at USC. Sources say Haden was impressed with Heinel's work ethic and commitment. "To Pat, Donna was someone who got shit done," said one.

With her promotion Heinel effectively had two jobs: overseeing women's sports and continuing in her previous role as director of admissions and eligibility. In her latter role, she communicated with coaches and gathered a prospective recruit's athletic and academic profiles, which she then presented to the athletic admissions sub-committee. The committee, which met every other Thursday and was made up of members of the admissions department and other faculty, would review the materials and, a few days later, either give a student a green light or deny them admission. Heinel had previously shared the admissions job with a peer, Brandon Martin, but when he left in 2013, he was not replaced and Heinel controlled the whole process with no oversight.

"She was the gatekeeper," said former women's cross-country head coach Tom Walsh. "Once Carol [Dougherty, Heinel's predecessor in the SWA job] and Brandon left, it seemed like there were very few people" in Heinel's sphere. "She was it. She became an island."

Coaches reacted to this with a collective groan. Heinel had a reputation for being "a hard-ass," said Walsh, when it came to vetting candidates that coaches presented to her. "She was tough as nails," he told me. "Coaches were pulling their hair out. 'What do we have to do to get somebody admitted?'" Walsh said that USC water polo coach Jovan Vavic, who was known for his temper and foul language, would go especially crazy when Heinel denied him recruits for his national championship–winning team.

When Brandon Martin was around, coaches would sometimes go over Heinel's head and ask him to help them push recruits through. But once he left, there was no one else to turn to. Walsh recalled one particularly excruciating case when he was recruiting a Latvian runner. Walsh repeatedly presented Heinel with the student-athlete's materials—her high school transcript, test scores, running stats, et cetera. "There was always something more I needed to do," he said. Meanwhile, the months were dragging on, and the runner, whose first choice was USC, had been left in limbo as to her admission. At one point, Heinel demanded that Walsh submit *original* art from her art portfolio—she was planning to be an art major—as opposed to copies of the work. Walsh was able to wrangle them, only to be told there was still missing information. He was so frustrated, given that she was a good student and a top-ranked runner, that a meeting was called with him, Heinel, Haden, and Ron Allice, the head track-and-field coach.

In the meeting, Walsh said that Haden asked Heinel, "What else do we need to do to get this girl in? She's a good student. She's a good athlete," causing Heinel to back off. But by the time Walsh got the green light and got in touch with the runner, she'd already committed to the University of Florida.

"She'd had enough of waiting," Walsh said. "She became an All-American and one of the best runners in the NCAA. It kind of hurts to see that."

This portrait of Heinel as a stickler for rules is in stark contrast with other aspects of her behavior at USC, where she was taking advantage of the athletic department's free and easy ways. In 2008, she'd started her own independent side business, Clear the Clearinghouse, where she advised high school coaches, counselors, and administrators on NCAA rules for athletes. She charged up to $700 a year for a subscription to her services, along with holding two-hour workshops that cost $100 to attend. The workshops were held on the USC campus at the Galen Center, the university's on-campus sports arena, despite the fact that Clear the Clearinghouse was totally separate from the university. It was also a for-profit business for Heinel, but she reportedly sent notices advertising her workshops from her USC work email and from that of an assistant.

The arrangement was a blatant conflict of interest, but no one seemed to notice. Myron Dembo told me, "As a professor, I've done consulting work, but never in a million years would I do consulting work on campus, where I bring people from off campus on campus and then charge them."

"Only at USC," sighed one department veteran, rolling their eyes.

Heinel's lawyer, Nina Marino, has said that Donna Heinel didn't meet Rick Singer until 2015, when she was brought into a meeting in Pat Haden's office and found Singer there. Haden presented him as someone that she should work with to bring in development funds. Marino has said that the charges against Heinel "come as a complete shock. Anyone who knows Donna Heinel knows she is a woman of integrity and ethics with a strong moral compass."

With his connection to Heinel, Singer moved beyond the fringe world of coaches and into the university administration itself. While coaches could lie and present false papers to their higher-ups in athletics and admissions, their power was ultimately limited. Coaches at USC, as cross-country coach Tom Walsh demonstrated, were subject to Heinel's verdict. Indeed, Heinel wasn't just one step closer for Singer to the most sensitive point in athletic admissions—passing off recruited candidates to admissions officers. She *was* the point in the system. After she made her case, no one followed up to cross-check a student's athletic credentials—not in the admissions department or the athletic departments. In a January 2015 email, Singer would tell Hodge, who the year before had begun the side-door process at USC for his third child, a son who was being sold as a football player even though he'd played only one season in high school: "Admissions just needs something to work with to show he is an athlete. They do not follow up after Donna presents."

Furthermore, unlike Gordon Ernst or other coaches, Donna Heinel controlled budgets at USC, and so she could accept payments from families, an incredibly helpful tool for Rick Singer, both in the way he could pitch his services (as a donation to USC) as well as an alternative to a direct bribe to an individual. Starting with Hodge's son, Singer began asking families he was helping get into USC to write checks to the school's Women's Athletic Board, an account that Heinel controlled.

Heinel's name by now was showing up frequently in Singer's email chains, and in some cases she was communicating directly with his clients. "Thanks so much for your time yesterday," Hodge wrote Heinel in one email. "We are preparing [my son's] 'sports resume' as you requested and should be ready to send it on to you early next week." Heinel wrote back, "Great, looking forward to it...you should concentrate on his primary sport with accolades and achievement." (Hodge's son was also being presented as a competitive tennis player, another lie.) Later, when Laura Janke—who was now creating all athletic profiles for Singer, regardless of the sport—emailed Heinel two athletic profiles for the boy, Heinel replied with the athletic profile of a different student with a note that said "an example of football." She included handwritten notes on the football profile and said that the photograph should be exchanged for a "better picture" that was "more athletic." Hodge would end up paying Singer $250,000 (half to the Key, half to Singer), along with a $75,000 payment to Heinel's Women's Athletic Board.

According to Hodge's lawyers, Singer maintained the line that the money Hodge was paying to USC was a legitimate donation, a line that seemed all the more credible when Hodge received a letter from university president Max Nikias, thanking him for his contribution and saying that he hoped Hodge's son would decide to join his older sister at USC. (Even though, by this point, Hodge had already directly paid money to Ernst to get his older daughter into Georgetown, so he was aware of how Singer operated.) Hodge also received an invitation to a private dinner at Nikias's house, where Hodge and his wife were seated directly next to the president and his wife. At the dinner, Hodge was invited to attend a USC football game in Nikias's private box. "Singer minimized the uncomfortable and illegal aspects of the process for Doug, and Doug took comfort in Singer's assurances that his payments were helping not only his own children, but also the educational institutions where his children were seeking admission, and, through [Singer's charity], children from disadvantaged backgrounds," Hodge's lawyers wrote.

But Singer didn't always need Heinel to work his side door at USC. According to the prosecution in the Varsity Blues case, in 2013, he worked directly with USC's water polo coach, Jovan Vavic, to get the son of John B. Wilson, a former Staples executive in Hyannis Port, Massachusetts, into USC as a water polo recruit. Vavic was one of USC's most famed coaches. An acerbic Yugoslavian, known for cursing at players, his tough-love tactics got results. His men's and women's teams had won sixteen national championships since 1995, making him the winningest coach in USC history. Water polo was an ideal sport for Singer to manipulate, seeing as there is no cap on how many players

Members of the Lincolnwood All-Stars, a traveling baseball team that Rick Singer (second row, third from the left) played on while growing up in the Chicago suburbs. *Credit: Mike Wolfe*

Rick Singer (right) shone as quarterback of the ragtag flag football team "Etc." at Trinity University in Texas. Described by teammates as a "strategist," he led Etc. to an upset championship victory over a team of fraternity guys. *Credit: Trinity University Mirage, 1986; Coates Library Special Collections & Archives, Trinity University (San Antonio, Texas)*

Rick Singer makes a dive for the Trinity University baseball team. Trinity provided the perfect environment for Singer to thrive as an athlete as it transitioned from a Division I to Division III school. *Credit: The Trinitonian, April 19, 1984; Coates Library Special Collections & Archives, Trinity University (San Antonio, Texas)*

Even for a formal photo of the Alpha Epsilon Pi fraternity at the University of Arizona, Rick Singer (bottom row, center) opted for athletic gear. "He was going to wear what he wore," said frat brother Mike Wolfe. "He was wearing shorts, running shoes, T-shirts. That was it." *Credit: University of Arizona Yearbook, 1980; University of Arizona Libraries, Special Collections.*

Rick Singer working with a family at his first college counseling company, Future Stars. "His fee was negligible," said one former student, Kim Perry. "It was a hundred times cheaper than getting braces." *Courtesy of The Sacramento Bee*

As the head basketball coach at Encina High School in Sacramento in the late 1980s, Rick Singer made waves from the sidelines. "It was the Bobby Knight style of coaching," said Pete LeBlanc, a *Sacramento Bee* sportswriter at the time. "Very high expectations. A lot of yelling and screaming." *Courtesy of The Sacramento Bee*

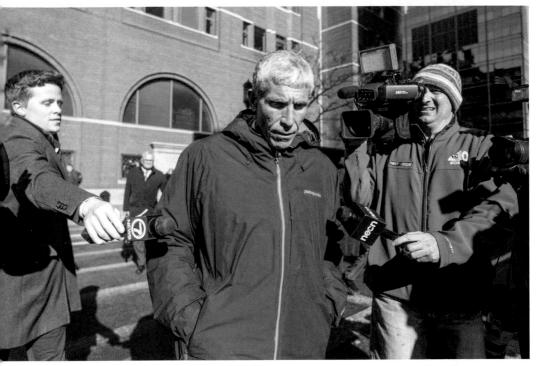

The ringleader of the "biggest college admissions fraud of all time," William "Rick" Singer, outside the John Joseph Moakley Federal Courthouse in Boston on March 12, 2019. *Credit: Scott Eisen/Stringer via Getty Images*

Actress Lori Loughlin serenely enters the Boston federal courthouse in April of 2019 after signing autographs for fans. A year later, she and her husband, Mossimo Giannulli (pictured left) would plead guilty to conspiring to get their two daughters into the University of Southern California as fake crew recruits. *Credit: Boston Globe via Getty Images*

Actress Felicity Huffman and husband William H. Macy minutes before Huffman's sentencing hearing in September of 2019. Huffman spent eleven days in a minimum-security federal prison near San Francisco. *Credit: Boston Globe via Getty Images*

Los Angeles entrepreneur Jane Buckingham, pictured here in Boston in May of 2019, was told by Rick Singer that her son Jack was "not getting in anywhere."
Credit: Bloomberg via Getty Images

Former University of Southern California women's soccer coach Ali Khosroshahin is doused with water after his team won the NCAA National Championship in 2007—USC women's soccer's first-ever title. *Credit: NCAA Photos via Getty Images*

Gordon "Gordie" Ernst, the former tennis coach at Georgetown University, leaves his arraignment at Boston Federal Court in March of 2019. Ernst allegedly accepted $2.7 million from Rick Singer for admitting non-tennis players as Georgetown recruits. *Credit: Scott Eisen/Stringer via Getty Images*

Vavic could recruit. Although the NCAA mandates that the sport can have only sixteen players in a championship tournament, it doesn't stipulate how big the team itself can be. Vavic's roster could get as high as fifty, with many of the players designated as water boys or practice players (i.e., they never saw game time), who were nonetheless thrilled to be training under a legend.

Wilson's son, a student at Menlo School in Atherton, California, actually was a water polo player, but Singer allegedly falsified his credentials and improved his swimming times. In one email exchange, Wilson wrote: "Would the other kids know [my son] was a bench warmer side door person?" Singer then communicated directly with Vavic, who said he'd present the boy to USC's subcommittee for athletic admissions along with his "top walkons." After the boy was admitted, Wilson wired $100,000 to Singer's charity, $100,000 to his for-profit organization, and $20,000 to Singer personally. Singer in turn wrote a $100,000 check to "USC Men's Water Polo," a fund that Vavic controlled.

Stephen Larson, Vavic's lawyer, denies that the water polo coach accepted any bribes from Singer or that he falsely presented any candidates for admission to USC. He said Vavic had been introduced to Singer by someone at the university as far back as 2007 and that Singer had brought Vavic several student athletes who went on to do very well as water polo players at USC. If those students happened to come from families of means, all the better. In one email, Singer wrote to Vavic that the Wilson "family is ready to help."

"It should not be any surprise to anybody that USC placed tremendous pressure on all of their coaches to fundraise and to recruit students whose parents were able to support USC," Larson told the *Los Angeles Times*. "That was no secret. That was the directive for all the programs and all the athletic departments."

Wilson's lawyers have submitted documents saying that Wilson—who is fighting the charges against him—believed the money he donated would go to an underfunded program like water polo. They say Wilson thought the entire $200,000 was going to USC and that Singer "stole half." As evidence that Wilson was unaware of any bribing, they included the transcript of a phone call with Singer later on, when Wilson is talking to him about getting his two daughters into college via the side door. "We get the girls in, it's a done deal," Singer said, "and you're gonna take care of your part of it, you're gonna make the payments to the schools and the—to the coaches."

"Uh, uh, help me understand the logistics?" Wilson responded. "I thought I make the payment to you and you make the payment to the school."

"Correct," Singer said. "That's correct."

"Oh, you said *I* make the payment to the schools."

USC quickly became the Holy Grail of Singer's side-door scheme, the university he temptingly dangled in front of parents, walking them through how it all worked with breezy confidence and startling candor. There were no holes at USC, nothing left to chance. It was a surefire system that he had built and now was shamelessly exploiting. As he would tell one parent (who ended up declining the side-door offer): "Let's say if it's USC, then I'll probably use athletics to help them get in, and I'll go to one of the coaches, because we've already done six at USC already. I'll go to one of the coaches who has a guaranteed spot in a sport, and ask them if they'll give me that spot. And in turn we will help their program, and then the kid gets in. We apply usually early, and then the kid gets in early action if it's a place like USC. They don't hear until March twenty-fifth, but I hear months before.

"So what I normally have to do," he continued, "is I have to create a profile of that kid in that particular sport. And then the athletic liaison takes that person to admissions when they have what they call subcommittee meetings, which happen usually every other Thursday at most schools. And then they walk the kid through with whatever sport it is. And they make decisions right then and there if the kids are getting in, or they may say, 'I need to see one more set of grades' or 'I need to see a progress report and then we'll admit.'

"And it's done. Families don't pay anything until after it's done. I take the risk, and I take the responsibility."

But however slick his game had gotten, and however skillfully he'd wired USC by this point, Rick Singer was still angling for one more connection at the school, one that would be the real finishing touch: an in with Pat Haden. To have the athletic director embrace him, or at least take his calls and hear his pleas for candidates, would make his life that much easier. A good word from Haden, after all, could tremendously influence the chance of a student being admitted to USC.

According to the *Los Angeles Times*, Singer aggressively courted Haden, arranging to have coffee with him at the Los Angeles Country Club, where Haden was a member. In June of 2015, Haden agreed to the meeting because of an ulterior motive—the person who had arranged the get-together was Chuck Kenworthy, a close advisor to Patrick Soon-Shiong, a Chinese billionaire (and, later, the white-knight owner of the *Times*), who'd used Singer as a counselor when his daughter was applying to college (he said Singer had given his daughter "great advice"). Haden was eager to make inroads with Soon-Shiong so he could pitch him on buying a series of luxury suites that he was selling as part of USC's $270 million upgrade to the LA Coliseum. If having coffee with Singer would facilitate an introduction to Soon-Shiong, Haden was game.

The coffee lasted all of ten minutes, with Singer doing most of the talking—dropping names, promoting himself, and talking up how wealthy his clients were. Pat Haden and John McKay Jr., who was also there, excused themselves in the midst of Singer's torrent, saying they had another meeting. McKay told the *Times*, of the pitch: "That was of zero interest to us. We didn't need Rick Singer. In a million years, no way we would have taken that meeting if it wasn't for Chuck Kenworthy and Patrick Soon-Shiong." (Soon-Shiong has not been implicated in the Varsity Blues case.)

Nonetheless, after the meeting, Haden wrote an email to Kenworthy saying, "WOW!! Thanks for the introduction to Rick. Fascinating guy. I really look forward to seeing him again soon. Thx!!!"

Singer again connected with Haden in July at Haden's office at USC, where Singer asked him for help getting the daughter of one of his Texas clients into USC. She had been denied admission and had unsuccessfully appealed the decision, but Singer was making one last push. The next day, the *Times* reported, he wrote an email to Haden, saying: "Pat thank you very much for the special time you spent with me yesterday. You are doing an amazing job at USC." He then followed up with another email, in which he sent Haden the girl's transcript and test scores.

Haden then forwarded the email to Heinel, asking her if the athletic department could be helpful. Heinel responded with an inquiry about Singer. She wondered if he was "in good graces" with USC.

"I have no idea," Haden replied. "Do you know him?"

Heinel's response was vague. She said she remembered Singer as being "a guy that counseled a person" that was applying to USC as an athlete. "Not sure though," she wrote. (According to the prosecution, by this time Heinel had already been communicating extensively with Singer and Hodge about getting Hodge's two children into USC.)

Despite his earlier enthusiastic words to Kenworthy, Haden then told Heinel that he had "a red flag up" about Singer. "I am being careful with him," he said.

Singer, meanwhile, kept pestering Haden with follow-up emails about the girl from Texas. When Haden wrote him and said, "Rick, I am told it is too late to make something happen," Singer kept up the barrage. He asked Haden if he would meet with the girl's parents, whom he said had already given $100,000 to USC and were "incredibly successful folks in the technology space in the Bay Area."

A month later, Singer again emailed, saying the family was a "strong investor" in a professional basketball team. "Could you please provide dates for a potential meeting?" he wrote.

Haden ignored him.

USC's athletic director might have been blowing him off, but Singer's relationships with Heinel and other coaches were making the rest of the school friendly territory. With those connections intact, Singer upped his networking game in LA, drawing on every contact he had to infiltrate places where he could hobnob with the city's wealthiest residents. One of those contacts was Mark Hauser, who ran a group of hedge funds in Cincinnati and LA. According to legal documents, Singer's charity had invested in Hauser's company, Hauser Private Equity. Perhaps in exchange, Hauser—who was paying Singer $40,000 to have Mark Riddell "proctor" his daughter's ACT exam—began recommending Singer around LA, and bringing him to the Bel-Air Country Club, where Hauser was a member. Hauser had another valuable point of entry for Singer. He was the chairman of the board of Marymount High School, the independent Catholic school that his daughter attended. Peter

Dameris, another indicted parent in the Varsity Blues scandal, was also on the Marymount board. Dameris used Singer to get his son, who attended Loyola High School, into Georgetown as a fake tennis recruit. (Both Hauser and Dameris have pled guilty.)

It was through Hauser that Mossimo Giannulli first heard about Rick Singer. Giannulli, a fashion designer and the husband of *Full House* actress Lori Loughlin, was a die-hard Trojan even though he wasn't technically a USC alum. Their two daughters were at Marymount, and Giannulli had their future on his mind when Hauser mentioned Singer and touted him as *the* college admissions guy.

When Singer met with the Giannullis, he lived up to his reputation. He seemed incredibly knowledgeable and exuded an "I got this" attitude that made the couple feel at ease, according to a source. He also seemed extremely busy, giving him yet more cred—he was clearly someone who was in high demand. Soon a bevy of tutors from Singer's company started arriving at the couple's home to work with the girls.

The first warning sign that tutoring might not be enough, however, came in the spring of 2016, when a college counselor at Marymount suggested to Giannulli that their eldest daughter, Isabella, apply to Arizona State University. Following the meeting, an enraged Giannulli fired off an email to Singer: "I have some concerns and want to fully understand the game plan and make sure we have a roadmap for success as it relates to [Bella] and getting her into a school other than ASU!"

Singer wrote back: "If you want SC I have the game plan ready to go into motion. Call me to discuss."

CHAPTER 8

Buckley Blues

At the Buckley School, Adam Semprevivo was known as a jock, to the extent that there were such things as jocks at Buckley, which is not known for its sports prowess. He played on the basketball team and got good grades, but he wasn't a so-called AP kid, who loaded up on advanced placement and honors classes and was gunning for valedictorian. Until Rick Singer became Adam's independent college counselor, his standing at Buckley would have been enough for him to sail on to a solid college or university—all the more so when Adam transferred to Campbell Hall his junior year, where he had a weighted 4.0 GPA. But once Singer entered the picture, it wasn't nearly enough.

Buckley, which is located on eighteen rolling acres near the gated community of Mulholland Estates in Sherman Oaks, was historically shrugged off as a "valley school" that would take anyone who would pay. While Harvard-Westlake was the favored school of old-money (by LA standards) oil tycoons like the Gettys, along with a more conservative strand of entertainment industry elite, Buckley welcomed a more colorful population of showbiz kids, wealthy Persians, and other rich folks from Beverly Hills and Burbank. The characters that populate *Less*

Than Zero, Bret Easton Ellis's seminal portrait of the coke-fueled, club-hopping eighties LA teen scene, were based on his Buckley classmates.

Over time, social stratifications loosened, and Harvard-Westlake, along with other snooty peers like Brentwood School, are now chock-full of flashy entertainment scions and tech kids. But Buckley still has a reputation for drawing from the glitziest ends of the showbiz register. A Kardashian has never graced the campus of Harvard-Westlake; two of them attended Buckley (Kim and Rob), as did Michael Jackson's kids, along with Paris Hilton—whom it is difficult to imagine surviving a semester of Harvard-Westlake's onerous curriculum.

As at all elite high schools in LA, status and name brands are flaunted across campus, but at Buckley the showcasing is a tad more flagrant. Ninety-thousand-dollar student cars in the parking lot are not unheard-of, and one former student said that Cartier love bracelets, a "bougie bag," and Chanel flats are "the Buckley starter pack." Even asking someone to the prom is an elaborate production meant to impress. Over-the-top "promposals" are a Buckley tradition, whereby a student publicly asks another student to go to the dance with them. These can take place at a school assembly, or in the hallway, but generally they involve a great deal of spectacle—flowers, gifts, signs—and draw a flash mob of spectators. One year, a Buckley boy's promposal was to surprise his would-be date with a new car.

"If you thrive in an environment where your value to your peers is how much money you have, it's the place to go," said Marie, a recent Buckley graduate. (Students' names in this chapter have been changed.)

Buckley parents acknowledge this with rolling eyes—"You go to Parents' Night, and there are women in six-inch stilettos walking around to classrooms," said one—but they say there's a healthy population of kids who are self-aware about their affluent trappings and go out of their way to shun them. "I think there's a lot of kids who want to not have anything to do with that," said this parent. "It grosses them out, and they're getting the message from their peers that this is not where you want to lay your foundation— on 'rich.' You want to lay it on 'I'm funny. I'm charming. I'm gay.' Whatever it is. Money should not be the thing."

Nor is academics the sole measure of a student's identity at Buckley. Most families say the reason they chose the school is precisely because it's not as much of a pressure cooker as other private schools. Their kids aren't always obsessing about grades and are encouraged to do more than stick their nose in a book. "My kid was accepted into Harvard-Westlake, but it's so institutional," said the parent. "It seemed like the wrong choice."

Nonetheless, the focus on students' success, particularly in terms of where they go after high school, borders on the extreme at Buckley. "There's this really commonly held belief that your value and the accumulation of everything you've put your efforts into at Buckley, it all just comes down to where you go to school," said Marie. "Like, you are where you go to college."

Adding fuel to the fire was the sense among some parents that Harvard-Westlake and Marlborough had better track records of placing students in top colleges. "The environment was like, 'Well, Barbara [Wagner, Marlborough's former head of school] just picks up the phone to Stanford and says, 'These girls are coming to Stanford this year,'" said one former administrator. "Does Buckley have those kinds of connections to Stanford?"

Of course, no school administrator, no matter how powerful, tells a college which students will be enrolling. But the desperation felt by Buckley parents, combined with their emphasis on status and keeping up appearances, gave Rick Singer the opening he needed. And Adam Semprevivo's father, Stephen, became Singer's first test case, epitomizing the type of status-obsessed Buckley parent that Singer could most ably exploit. A successful senior executive and entrepreneur who had earned a reputation as a turnaround wizard for ailing companies, Semprevivo was credited with the revived fortunes of GetSmart.com, an online mortgage shopping company; the recruitment firm Korn Ferry Futurestep; and Machinima, one of the biggest early players in the YouTube space that created video content for gamers, where he helped diversify its revenue. Machinima sold itself to Warner Bros. in 2016 for a reported $100 million.

An intense man with a thin, angular face and a salt-and-pepper goatee, Semprevivo first attended Harvard University via a program for high school students, where he took university-level classes in genetics and marine biology. He aced both. "Based on that experience," he has said, "I knew [Harvard] was where I wanted to go to college." He would end up getting both an undergraduate degree and an MBA from Harvard.

He let people know it, too. Semprevivo was known to mention his alma mater so frequently that even friends of his two sons were aware of where he'd gotten his degrees. "He was always talking about Harvard," said one. "He was one of those guys."

According to legal documents, it wasn't just ego, but it was also Semprevivo's own experience that made him feel so strongly about where his sons earned their college degrees. A criminologist report that was submitted in Semprevivo's Varsity Blues case states, "Harvard had played such a key role early in Stephen's career that he understood, perhaps better than most people, how seminal the choice of a university can be."

Further, Semprevivo felt his older son lacked confidence and needed a "boost" to thrive, according to the report. Adam had begun suffering from depression and severe bouts of self-doubt. His father wanted to help him—fix him, in a way—and the way he thought he could do that was to send him to an outstanding four-year institution. But while Adam's grades and SAT score—the first time he took it he got an 1820 out of 2400 (the scale at the time), which was in the eighty-third percentile—were good *enough*, they were not up to the standards of Harvard or even top universities of lesser prestige. Semprevivo's fear that Adam would not have the same opportunities as he had, thanks to his Harvard degrees, led him to seek out Rick Singer.

Singer first met with the Semprevivos at their Bel-Air home, a Tuscan-style villa with views of the surrounding canyon and a slice of the Pacific off in the distance. The house had four bedrooms, six bathrooms, and an infinity pool with a cascading waterfall. Out front, there was a basketball hoop not far from a three-car garage. Semprevivo had always supported his sons' athletic interests and had coached over a dozen of his kids' Little League and junior basketball teams.

In the fall of 2014, Singer visited the house and sat down with Adam, Stephen, and Adam's mother, Rita, who worked in luxury real estate. (She has not been charged in the Varsity Blues case.) The consultant did his usual thing. He dropped names, postured, and talked endlessly. By this point, his bragging had reached new levels of fabrication. He told one parent that he'd been LeBron James's AAU basketball coach, had been an assistant to Bobby Knight at Indiana, and had become a "surrogate big brother" to Steve Jobs's son when Jobs was dying of cancer. But Stephen Semprevivo, a consultant himself who often had to make quick appraisals of others, overlooked those red flags because, he said, "he seemed to know his business very well, and seemed professional at first."

Singer had also come recommended from family friends Mark and Renée Paul, and had by that time built up a reputation at Buckley as being the go-to guy for college counseling. He was cozy with members of Buckley's board and would soon be working with some of them, including Devin Sloane, who would also become entangled in the Varsity Blues scandal and whose son was two years younger than Adam. Singer further had the stamp of approval from the financial world, and talked to the Semprevivos about how many of his clients had come through financial management firms like Morgan Stanley, Oppenheimer, and UBS, where he regularly gave presentations—the blue-chip seal of approval for a serious business-man like Semprevivo.

What would ensue over the next two years, based on Sem-previvo's detailed sentencing memo, offers an up-close look at how Singer had worked out a formula for determining how and to whom to pitch the side door. It also provides a psycho-logical assessment of him and his "antisocial personality traits," as characterized by Richard Romanoff, a forensic psychologist who conducted a psychological assessment of Semprevivo that is included in court documents. Romanoff wrote that people like Singer "often try to seduce and ingratiate themselves with people around them for their own gain." They "can be charismatic and at least superficially charming. They tend to embellish the truth as it suits them, and they lie easily to get what they want, or to get themselves out of trouble."

But first came the charm offensive. Singer offered himself up to the Semprevivos as a nose-to-tail aide-de-camp, someone who couldn't do enough for his clients, and who was the epitome of solicitous grace and service. After setting Adam up over Skype with his Sacramento employee Mikaela Sanford, who input all of his high school transcripts and test scores, and created a profile for him in the Key's system, Singer lined up an SAT tutor for the boy. "You want that in home or via Skype?" he said in an email to Semprevivo. "Do you want once a week, twice? Big difference in the cost—50-100 Skype an hour to 150-300 an hour at home. Your thoughts?"

And there was more. Singer set up a college tour for the family back east, and even got Adam a summer job with California congresswoman Karen Bass, where Adam pounded away at data entry. Singer, who was charging the family a total fee of $7,000 for his help, began meeting personally with Adam once a month at the family's home. During his visits, he interspersed his own bloviating—how he knew how the donations process at Harvard worked, who his big-name clients were—with an onslaught of calculated flattery. Semprevivo and his wife, he said, did such amazing philanthropic work, and their business and real estate investments were so impressive. Only later would Semprevivo look back and realize that this was all part of Singer's game, that he was actually sussing out the family's financial situation, all while ingratiating himself into their home and lives.

But in the meantime, he fell for it.

☙

For many years there was a sign affixed to the Buckley School that read: COLLEGE BEGINS AT TWO. The saying belonged to Isabelle Buckley, who founded the K–12 school in 1933. She would later pen a book bearing the mantra as a title. Buckley's intention wasn't to scare parents or have them practicing long division with their toddlers in between nap times. Rather, she sought to stress that even the youngest of children can learn to think independently and push their creative limits. A progressive Midwesterner who'd studied education in Australia, Buckley had noticed that on that continent children were reading by the time they were five. She sought to mold American youngsters in the same fashion.

Yet as Buckley evolved over the years from an unorthodox educational experiment combining traditional academic rigor with free-wheeling artistic expression into a reliable vehicle to funnel students into the nation's most prestigious colleges and universities, its founder's words took on a less idealistic meaning. For many parents, college prep did, quite literally, start the minute their children enrolled in the school. According to one former administrator, parents of children as young as kindergarten would inquire whether the school would "still have a good relationship with Harvard" by the time the student was in high school. There was also "a lot of concern about math classes being rigorous enough for their child to be respected by Stanford."

Buckley, meanwhile, fed into the frenzy by kicking off discussions about college admissions very early in a student's education and openly presenting itself as a ticket to a prestigious degree. Like most independent schools, Buckley advertises its matriculation statistics on its website, and each year the college counseling department gives a presentation to the school's board of trustees on how Buckley is faring with college admissions. The college counseling office is lined with flags from colleges and universities, with prominence given to Ivy League schools. According to a former student, when college application time approached, students were advised to take classes they would succeed in. If an AP class might lead to a B or, God forbid, a C, they were encouraged to drop it quickly. One student was told to audit a class rather than risk the chance of getting a grade that wouldn't look good to college admissions officers. "Because it's all about optics in LA," said one source. "I think for a lot of LA schools, not just Buckley, frankly, their brand is 'How many kids do we get into schools that you want your children to go to?' It's not 'Where can I get my child the best education?'"

According to Hank, a former Buckley student, college "is brought up in lower school" there. "It's like, 'When you get to high school you're going to prepare for college.' Middle school's all about 'Hey, we have to prepare you for high school, because then everything counts. And ninth grade counts...' The whole thing revolved around college."

Pressure mounted during senior year as students frantically sent out applications, in some cases to as many thirty schools, the former students said. One year, the night before acceptances to an Ivy League school that nearly a dozen Buckley kids had applied to went out, texts were flying. "People would say, 'We think you're going to get in. We won't hate you if you do,'" Hank said. "It was almost like they were trying to cover their skin but at the same time diss you. It was one of those environments that was like, 'Wow, this is insanely toxic.' It was very competitive, and the competition was driven by the parents at the school, not the kids."

Underlying their anxiety was the realization that many students at Buckley, which has a low percentage of African American and Latino kids, fit a profile that is increasingly out of vogue with admissions officers. "I remember kids saying, 'I'm going to get my DNA tested so hopefully I show up one-sixteenth Native American," said Hank. "It was mostly jokes, but it reflected a culture that we all knew. Me, as a straight white male in the upper class—that was a detriment. People would say, 'You have to make sure your application is incredible,' and all this other stuff. 'You have to compensate for that.' That was openly discussed."

Administrators at Buckley were aware of the dilemma; they had gotten feedback from colleges that some of their students were one-dimensional, according to a source, and in some cases struggled to perceive the world beyond their bubble of privilege. Parents had complained that their kids' college applications asked things like "Describe an experience where you felt 'other,'" and their kid wasn't sure how to answer. To align Buckley more with the movement in higher education toward diversity, the school had worked to augment their offerings in order to expose students to contemporary social issues. A diversity, equity, and inclusion program had been established, along with special weeks devoted to diversity, where meetings and panels on social justice themes were organized. One event, a series called "Social Justice Symposia," encouraged students to "lean into discomfort." But the attempts often felt forced and more emblematic than anything else. For a Kwanzaa assembly, a Buckley staff member asked a student, who was half-Black, to participate, without bothering to ask her if she actually celebrated Kwanzaa—she didn't. "There'd be assemblies that tried to be impactful," said Marie, "but when you're presenting to an audience of which probably eighty percent are white students, it's like, 'We get it. But isn't it a greater issue that the crowd is majority white?'"

Buckley's efforts were stymied by parents who simultaneously wanted the school to move into a more progressive lane while also being terrified that it might go too far and wind up like a more hippy-dippy—in the eyes of Buckley parents—school like Crossroads. "There was a feeling that parents didn't want Buckley to make their kids feel bad about being rich," said one source.

᠅

Everything with Adam Semprevivo was going smoothly. He was studying for the SAT, narrowing down his college choices. It was going so smoothly that his father didn't want to interfere with the work that Rick Singer was doing with his son. So it came as a shock when, in January, Singer emailed Semprevivo saying that "Adam needs to spend more time studying if he wants to create a significant improvement in his [SAT] score." He also proclaimed that the schools they'd laid out for Adam to apply to were now "a stretch." Boston College, Georgetown, Vanderbilt, and UCLA, among others, were suddenly deemed out of reach.

Thus began Singer's "pivot," as Stephen Semprevivo's sentencing memo described it, when the coach began planting seeds of doubt in him about his son's abilities. He said Adam needed more help, particularly with his SAT prep, and questioned the strength of his GPA. Singer, who Semprevivo said ran "hot and cold," was now decidedly the latter. He made Semprevivo feel that if he didn't heed his advice, he would be abandoning his son's future. "I was concerned and felt bad since Adam had been putting a good amount of time and effort into studying," he said. "Unfortunately, I was falling for Singer's method. Instead of doubting Singer, I doubted Adam."

"The greatest danger" is when individuals like Singer "turn," forensic psychologist Richard Romanoff said in his assessment. "They verbally cut people down with a cruel disregard for feelings," he wrote, "using their sharpened instinct for what hurts their victims most. They often accumulate knowledge early on during 'good' periods to know how to most effectively harm their targets with an eye toward exploiting the situation most effectively later on. Some such people become threatening, or even openly violent, as needed to achieve their ends."

Singer wasn't violent, but by the summer of 2015, he was forcefully applying more pressure to the situation, making both father and son distressed, according to the sentencing memo. He started aggressively pushing Georgetown as the only school Adam should apply to, even though after Adam had gone on his college tours, his heart was set on Vanderbilt. On Saturday, August 8, Adam was clearly grappling with his own desires and those of his college counselor. In an email with the subject line "Georgetown vs Vandy," Adam asked him which school had a stronger business program and which would lead to more job offers after graduation. To which Singer wrote: "Georgetown is in a location that is favored by most because of the business opportunities. Its degree is more widely accepted nationally. Vandy is good nationally but not to the same level."

An hour later, Adam replied: "Ok thanks. I'm going to go with Georgetown as my number one and Vanderbilt as my number two."

Unbeknownst to any of the Semprevivos, of course, Singer had a reason for pushing Georgetown. It had Gordon Ernst. And with Adam now on board with the school, Singer could move in for the kill. In a meeting that same month, he told Semprevivo that he'd helped families in the past get into universities by having them make donations to athletic programs. He described it as a "booster" program in which the athletic teams would use the funds to hire coaches and fill in budget gaps. According to the defense memo, "Stephen, who had donated to Harvard, didn't think too much of it at the time."

In their next meeting, Singer was more explicit, saying that Semprevivo would need to donate $400,000 to Singer's charity, which he would then pass on to Georgetown. He said the donation would be tax-exempt and would go to holes in Georgetown's athletic budget. For good measure, he reiterated how much help Adam needed with his SAT and grades.

"That was a new piece," Semprevivo told Romanoff of the

$400,000 figure. Each time he met with Singer, he said, there was something new. "First it was the booster factor, then the charity," Semprevivo added. "Everything Rick did was calculated and he was very defensive. You couldn't question him. He had an air about him that just demanded that you trust him. I didn't feel comfortable but I didn't talk to anyone about it, either."

But Singer reassured Semprevivo that there were no "issues" going through the charity, that it was a legitimate organization. He said that by going this route, Adam would get "an extra push," which Semprevivo now believed his son needed in order to get accepted.

On August 19, only eleven days after Adam had decided on Georgetown, Singer emailed the Semprevivos a letter he'd written in Adam's voice, presenting himself as a standout tennis player. He instructed Adam to email it to Ernst, which Adam did later that day. The letter falsely suggests that Adam and Ernst had already had discussions about being recruited and that he knew Ernst on a personal level; at the end of the note, he refers to Ernst's summer home in Cape Cod. The note read:

Dear Coach Ernst

I wanted to update you on my summer doings. After your suggestion I have played very well with terrific success in Doubles this summer and played quite well in singles too.

I am looking forward to having a chance to play for you. Our conversations have inspired me to try to dominate my competition this summer.

Senior year is about to start and you can count on me to achieve great grades.

Thanks for the chance to play for you and Georgetown University. Safe travels back from Cape Cod.

Adam Semprevivo

The next day, Ernst forwarded the email to a member of Georgetown's admissions staff, who responded that it "looks fine." Ernst then emailed the admissions officer to "confirm" that he had used three of his allocated admissions "spots" on the tennis team—one for Adam and, unbeknownst to the admissions officer, two for other Singer clients, including the daughter of Elizabeth and Manuel Henriquez, a Silicon Valley financier; and the son of Peter Dameris, the LA-based CEO of ASGN, an information technology company—and that he still had one to fill.

In some cases, Ernst wasn't even going through Singer anymore. In May of 2015, just a few months before Adam Semprevivo fired off his disingenuous email to the Georgetown tennis coach, Amin C. Khoury, an investment executive with homes in Palm Beach, Florida, and Mashpee, Massachusetts, flew from Florida to Cape Cod to pay Ernst $200,000. According to federal prosecutors, the coach had just gotten Khoury's daughter into Georgetown as a fake tennis recruit. The transaction hadn't been set up by Singer but by a tennis recruiter in Massachusetts who has not been identified. (Khoury's lawyer has said he will plead not guilty to the charges.)

However he was operating, Ernst was making serious money now. From his Singer admits alone, the coach wound up pocketing $950,000 between September of 2015 and November of 2016—by the time the Varsity Blues scandal hit the headlines in 2019, Ernst had raked in $2.7 million. Friends took note when Ernst suddenly upgraded his country club membership from the Edgemoor Club (nice enough, but no golf) to the much tonier Chevy Chase Country Club, whose initiation fee is nearly $100,000. "I remember thinking, 'Whoa. Chevy Chase,'" said one friend. Ernst also purchased a condo on Cape Cod in 2015 for $530,000, just a few years after he and his wife had bought a five-bedroom, $1.6 million home in Maryland.

At Georgetown, Ernst was still a beloved coach on campus, but some at least sensed that he'd given up the fight in terms of trying to improve the team's resources. When the university razed the existing tennis courts in order to make room for the new athletic facility, one former player recalls "going into his office and saying, 'This is ridiculous. Why are we losing our courts? Why can't they be built somewhere else on campus?'" The effect was even more devastating for Ernst, as he would no longer be able to run his summer tennis camp, which was a significant part of his income. (He also made money on the side teaching private lessons to VIPs like President Obama's daughters, a fact he liked to toss out.)

"He'd just say, 'Well, we just have to take what we can and do our best.' He was more trying to manage the team. We'd be a little bit frustrated by it. We'd joke about the fact that we couldn't get courts at Yates when we were the tennis team."

This player empathized with Ernst but also wondered why he didn't fight harder with the athletic department. He seemed to almost roll over. "Sometimes the mentality seemed definitely to not want to rock the boat."

Other players disagree with this characterization and say that Ernst was still committed to doing the best he could for his players, both on and off the court. He'd check in on their academics, oblige if they needed a recommendation for an internship, and push them to play their best. Yet, as always with Ernst, there were oddities. After Georgetown's women's team lost the first round of the Big East tournament to Seaton Hall in 2015, there was an opportunity to play a consolation match—not for any trophies or points, but to practice against competitors and prepare for the next season. But Ernst told his players to just go home. "Any opportunity to really try to improve the team and get better, play more—those weren't really seized upon," said the former player.

Meanwhile, back in LA, Adam Semprevivo was being finessed on paper into Ernst's next tennis star. Singer had always talked to Stephen Semprevivo about packaging Adam as a scholar athlete in order to help him get into college. He had once emailed the name of two crew coaches in Los Angeles, with the idea that Adam could learn erg technique from them, presumably to present him as a rower (a sport he'd never participated in) on his college applications. Nothing ever came of it, but it's evident that even before the tennis scam there were discussions about falsely presenting Adam as something that he wasn't. Ironically, the son of Peter Dameris actually was a competitive rower in high school, but Singer instructed him to not discuss crew when he had an interview with a Georgetown graduate as part of the admissions process.

With Adam Semprevivo, the email to Ernst was "the opening move in the fraud scheme," according to the prosecution. One that both Stephen and Adam knew was "a sham." Stephen himself admitted that at this point he understood what he was doing was "unethical" and knew he had relinquished too much control to Singer over his son's college application process, according to his sentencing memo, but he said that he felt powerless. When he called him to discuss this and to try to reassert his own control, he said Singer lashed out. "The train has left the station," he told Semprevivo. "I felt I was in a situation that I couldn't back out of," Semprevivo later said. "It made me very uneasy."

Nonetheless, he plowed ahead with the plan. In October, Singer emailed father and son an essay he had written in Adam's voice for Georgetown's application that began, "When I walk into a room, people will normally look up and make a comment about my height—I'm 6'5"—and ask me if I play basketball. With a smile, I nod my head, but also insist that the sport I put the most energy into is tennis." Adam's Georgetown application would also falsely state that he'd played tennis all four years in high school and was ranked in both singles and doubles, was a "CIF Scholar Athlete" and an "Academic All American" in tennis and basketball, and that he'd made the "Nike Federation All Academic Athletic team." These embellishments were added by Singer. Semprevivo and his son were unaware until after the application was submitted.

According to the defense memo, Semprevivo was, in fact, experiencing uneasiness about his actions, causing Singer to begin "bullying" him and asking him if he was "fully committed" to the plan. He also began threatening him, Semprevivo added, saying things like "It won't go well if we don't follow through," suggesting that he might sabotage Adam's admission if his dad made trouble.

"Rick became much more aggressive and negative," Semprevivo told Romanoff. "More than anything, I didn't want to let Adam down...I felt tremendous pressure about interfering with a process that Rick claimed couldn't be stopped. I was concerned and afraid for Adam about what Rick might do if we didn't go forward with his plan."

Singer added stress to the situation by being "furtive" and "prone to rushing others to get his way," the memo said. "That was the way Rick operated," Semprevivo explained. "He was adamant that everything be done yesterday."

Meanwhile, Singer made it clear that the side door was "the only shot Adam had" at Georgetown.

In November, Adam—who has said he had no idea about his father's scheming with Singer—received a likely letter from Georgetown that said he had more than a 95 percent chance of admission based on the review that had been conducted by Ernst. When Adam was formally accepted the following April, Semprevivo received an invoice from the Key Worldwide Foundation for $400,000. Singer followed up with a phone call, in which he demanded that Semprevivo pay promptly. He said he didn't want to have to "chase Stephen down" for the money. The call made Semprevivo feel all the more threatened. "That was a scary thing to hear him say," he told Romanoff. "So I felt trapped, that I couldn't back out.

"Rick had a volatile personality, I was afraid of him," he went on. "I kept thinking, what would happen if he erupted, if we pulled out? What would happen to Adam? Would he be able to get into any school? I didn't know."

He wrote the check.

Not long afterward, Rita Semprevivo posted a photograph on Facebook showing her, her husband, and their two sons all smiling and wearing matching Georgetown T-shirts, with the comment: "DC bound…Super Proud…Go Hoyas."

❧

Months before Adam Semprevivo started classes at Georgetown in the fall, Rick Singer was already laying the groundwork for his next big side-door scheme with another Buckley family. In April of 2016, he sat down with three buddies who were on the school's board together: Brian Werdesheim, Adam Bass, and

Devin Sloane. The meeting had been organized by Werdesheim and Bass, who already knew Singer, with the purpose of introducing him to Sloane, whose eldest son was in his sophomore year at Buckley and was starting to think about college.

Werdesheim, in particular, was a Singer devotee, and had been working with him as far back as 2009, offering him up as a perk to his clients at Oppenheimer's Summa Group for years. He claimed to have introduced Singer to former Saint Louis Rams owner Chip Rosenbloom, who hired Singer after hearing him speak at an Oppenheimer event. After the Varsity Blues scandal broke, however, Rosenbloom issued a statement saying, "We have never been clients of Mr. Werdesheim, and we have had no business relationship with Oppenheimer for over 15 years. Most importantly, like many others, we only used Mr. Singer for his legitimate college counseling services."

When Werdesheim had joined the Buckley board that spring, he waxed on about Rick Singer to his fellow board members, making a special introduction to Valeria Balfour, the board's chair. The trio then reportedly had lunch together to discuss having Singer come speak to the board, as Buckley was looking to shift its messaging. Werdesheim has said he didn't pursue the idea because "Rick's insights were less relevant." There was even talk of bringing him on as a consultant to the college counseling department, seeing as he had such a great track record getting kids into good schools. (This, too, never came to pass.) Werdesheim would also host private financial events for Buckley parents and have Singer speak as a kind of "sideshow," one source told me. In Werdesheim, an affable guy's guy who happens to be a graduate of USC, Singer had found another perfect target—a highly connected wealth executive who also was a father at one of LA's most prestigious private schools. Werdesheim's tentacles extended even further—one of his employees at Summa Group, Qiuxue Yang, had introduced a Chinese family to Singer, who was packaging their daughter to Yale as a soccer recruit. The scheme would be his biggest side-door scheme yet: The family would pay him $1.2 million.

As one source put it, "Rick worked that board like a Stradivarius. Brian was the way in."

Werdesheim's two children weren't yet old enough to need Singer's assistance, but Sloane was concerned about his son, Matteo, feeling that the admissions process was far more complicated than it had been when Sloane had applied to college, and that Matteo might need more assistance beyond what Buckley could offer. According to a source, Sloane had always been protective of Matteo, the eldest of his four children, who had struggled at Buckley when he'd enrolled in eighth grade, having come from an Italian school system and not being 100 percent fluent in English. Matteo once sat on a panel of first-generation immigrants at the school and talked about how his initial year at the school had been difficult. But he'd adjusted and gone on to be a solid student. In high school, he was popular and bubbly. He was a "soccer kid" who played on the team and did funny things like, during one Spirit Week, take his shirt off and whip it around his head. He had also already taken a smattering of AP classes. "He was smart," said one classmate. "I never would have thought he needed help getting into college."

Nonetheless, Devin Sloane, a feisty blusterer for whom nothing seemed to move fast enough—during Buckley board meetings, he was always wanting to get on to the next thing—seemed to worry about his son's future prospects. After Matteo participated in a leadership program in environment sciences and engineering at Yale one summer, Sloane remarked casually in conversation that while Matteo had had a great experience and learned a lot, it was unlikely that his son would ever get into Yale. "There was a nervousness" that Sloane had about his son, said a source who overheard the comment.

Sloane's own route to college had been defined by hard work and self-reliance. He was raised by his mother, a former professional ice-skater, and his stepfather, who'd gone to medical school. During high school, Sloane started his own car-detailing business and worked construction jobs. After transferring into USC from nearby Chapman University, he continued to juggle his responsibilities, working the night shift at a financial news agency and then showing up for classes after he'd caught a few hours of sleep in his car. His senior year, he invented a toy that allowed you to paint on fabric. He sold it to a toy company and used his proceeds to buy a multiservice retail gas station.

Sloane's stepfather had been verbally abusive and disengaged, but he'd introduced Sloane to Eastern religion, and Sloane had grown up making pilgrimages to an Indian ashram to study with the spiritual guru Sathya Sai Baba. When Sloane was thirty-one, Sai Baba told him who his wife would be: Cristina Candiani, the twenty-five-year-old daughter of an Italian oil executive. They married. The couple started off in Los Angeles, but then in 2005 they moved to Italy, where Sloane worked for his father-in-law's business. Eight years and three children later (their youngest wasn't born yet), they returned to LA, where Sloane got into the wastewater treatment business, giving him a reputation as a socially responsible environmental warrior. His shining credentials and philanthropy work—he and Cristina funded Indian orphanages and were sponsors of the Special Olympics in LA in 2015—made the family rising stars at Buckley, as did their generosity toward the school. Soon after his kids were accepted, Sloane wrote a check for $125,000 to Buckley, and he eventually worked his way up to the million-dollar-donor level, earning him a bronze plaque at the school. When Adam Bass, the president and CEO of the large LA law firm Buchalter, recommended Sloane to the board, he accepted. (Cristina has not been charged in the Varsity Blues case.)

Flaunting money in the form of donations to the school is a popular sport at the school, whose buildings, and even classrooms, bear the names of generous families. Pamphlets at concerts and dance performances are slathered with the names of families who have contributed, and the annual Buckley Fair is as much about getting the family name displayed in a prominent location as raising money for the school.

In May, Singer was invited over to Sloane's Bel-Air home to sit down with him, Cristina, and Matteo. The $3.4 million Spanish Revival house was packed with the Sloanes' nineteenth-century-style art collection as well as relics from Sai Baba. But Singer had no interest in talking art or religion. He got right down to business, delivering the same pitch he'd given to the Semprevivos, throwing in some old-school folksy instructions to Matteo—study hard, don't stay out late, no drugs—which Cristina, especially, appreciated, and offering the same price for his services: $7,000 plus hourly expenses for SAT tutors. The Sloanes were impressed.

A month later, Singer started going over to their house every third Sunday to work with Matteo. This time, Singer moved in more aggressively with his charity angle, finding common ground with Sloane's own philanthropy, to start sowing the seeds for a deeper connection between them. Singer talked up his organization and how it helped needy kids who didn't have access to an expensive education. Sloane, in turn, shared his own work helping kids through the Special Olympics and UNICEF. Singer then pressed on, saying that he'd be spending a lot of personal time with Matteo over the next year and a half—something he said he didn't do with all clients—and that he'd be working his relationships with college admissions departments to help Matteo gain acceptance. In exchange for this, he said that he expected Sloane to make a $200,000 donation to his charity. At this point, there was no mention of any universities in particular, or any sports angle; it was just pure charm offensive.

Matteo later told the *Wall Street Journal*, Singer "would kiss up to my dad." He went on to say that during this time he was on "the college essay train" at Buckley, working with teachers on his college application essays. He was also involved in extracurriculars and sports and was taking some AP classes—all while he prepped for the SAT and worked with Singer.

Singer's change of tune happened several months later, in the spring of 2017. Suddenly, Matteo was no longer looking like a strong college candidate. Suddenly, he needed to be "more interesting." Singer said that one way to do this would be to position him as a water polo player. Sloane was confused, since Matteo had never played water polo, but Singer pressed on, saying it didn't matter, that he could be coached, and explaining that water polo teams had forty players, not all of whom competed. Matteo could practice with the team or even be an ambassador for the team, seeing as he spoke three languages.

According to the prosecution in the Varsity Blues case, by this time Singer had already brought up the side door with Sloane, emailing him that if Matteo applied to Georgetown through that method he didn't need to earn "all A's" at Buckley. He'd also told Sloane not to worry that Matteo was dropping out of soccer, because Singer would "create a story for him." And in a January email, he flat-out asked Sloane if he was "ready to commit to the notion of the financial side door."

All the while, Singer was pushing USC on the Sloanes. Even though Matteo said he wasn't interested in applying there and was instead planning to tour schools back east, Singer kept selling USC as the best place for him to go, playing on the fact that Sloane was an alumnus and that Cristina wanted Matteo to stay close to home. Singer told her that if Matteo went to school on the East Coast, he'd probably meet a girlfriend there, and that would be that—no more Matteo. Singer went further, setting up a tour at USC. This cinched the deal. Matteo fell in love with the campus, and the school became his first choice.

By June, whatever misgivings Sloane had had about Singer's side-door tactics were gone. He'd agreed to sell Matteo as a water polo recruit and ordered water polo gear for his son on Amazon. He then had Matteo pose in the family pool wearing it and throwing a ball, for an action shot. Sloane then emailed the photographs to a graphic designer so they could be manipulated to look like Matteo was in an actual water polo match. After the graphic designer tweaked the image, Sloane responded: "Wow! You nailed it!!!" Sloane then emailed the image to Singer and asked: "Does this work??"

"Yes but a little high out of the water—no one gets that high," he responded.

Sloane and the graphic designer then went back and forth; at one point, the graphic designer said that it would be hard to manipulate the image further "without looking 100% fake." The designer then sent a new photo to Sloane, which he forwarded on to Singer, who deemed it "perfect."

In September, Sloane went to the Hotel Bel-Air, where Singer was giving his "CEO and Master Coach" college admissions spiel to Oppenheimer clients. Hearing him speak validated in Sloane's mind that Singer was the real deal. He was helping all of these afflu- ent, successful bigwigs. Nothing about him seemed illegitimate.

The following month, Donna Heinel, in USC's athletic depart- ment, presented Matteo's athletic profile to the athletic admissions subcommittee. Among its numerous fictions was that Matteo had been a "Perimeter Player" for the "Italian Junior National Team" and the "LA Water Polo" team. When Matteo was then conditionally accepted to USC, Singer instructed Sloane to write a $50,000 check to USC Women's Athletics. He said that once Matteo was accepted in the spring, Sloane should send a $200,000 check to the Key Worldwide Foundation. But then in January, two months before Matteo was officially accepted, Steven Masera sent Sloane an invoice asking for the payment. Sloane emailed Singer, asking him if anything had changed in their plan. Singer replied: "We are getting everyone ready—I am trying to get money in so there is no delay as [U]SC will call the markers in very soon thereafter."

In March, Matteo was officially accepted by the school. Sloane was thrilled, writing to Singer and cc'ing his son: "We got to celebrate two times. The second being official." Then he wrote only to Singer, thanking him for his "hard work and incredible strategic thinking." He told him he was "in transit to Hawaii so is it OK if we process payment when we return?" On April 11, Sloane wired $200,000 to KWF.

It had all gone so smoothly, so free of a hitch—except now a college counselor at Buckley was asking questions. After Matteo was admitted to USC, Julie Taylor-Vaz, a highly respected counselor who'd worked at Stanford as an admissions officer and ran Buckley's college admissions department, spoke with Kirk Brennan, an associate dean and director of admissions at USC, who mentioned Matteo's recruitment. Taylor-Vaz was perplexed. Buckley, she said, didn't *have* a water polo team. The confusion was relayed to Donna Heinel, who let Rick Singer know. He then wrote to Sloane to warn him about Buckley's admissions team: "They know about USC." He went on to explain that "[his] folks at USC" were going to restate that Matteo had played water polo in Italy in order to cover up for the fact that there was no high school team.

"Any concerns?" Sloane wrote back. Then, three minutes later, he sent another email, venting to Singer: "The more I think about this, it is outrageous! They have no business or legal right considering all the students privacy issues to be calling and challenging/questioning Matteo's application."

Sloane was so outraged that some time afterward, he showed up at the Buckley School and confronted Taylor-Vaz about her questioning of Matteo's application, insisting that Matteo played water polo for an Italian team. It wasn't uncommon behavior at Buckley, where "parents treat the college counselors like servants who have done something wrong," according to a source.

For Taylor-Vaz, it was like *Groundhog Day*. A few months earlier, on Thursday, December 7, 2017, she'd been on a routine check-in, or "advocacy" call with Tulane admissions to see how things were looking for the Buckley kids who'd applied early. Wildfires were raging around the city, and Buckley was technically shut down, but Taylor-Vaz had come into her office to get through some calls, given how soon early admissions decisions would be made. As first reported by *Vanity Fair*, the admissions officer from Tulane expressed amazement about one Buckley student in particular. Could Taylor-Vaz please tell them more about Mary Bass, an African American first-generation student with great test scores? (Her name has been changed.) Taylor-Vaz knew Mary, but she was neither African American nor first-generation. She was the daughter of Buckley School board member Adam Bass.

After Taylor-Vaz hung up, she got on a conference call with her colleagues at Buckley to discuss what to do next, according to a source with knowledge of the call. There was concern about how a falsified application might reflect on the school and its other students' applications—that colleges would start to doubt any application with Buckley's name on it. She and her colleagues wanted to handle the situation carefully.

Buckley decided to look into whether Mary's other early applications, to Georgetown and Loyola Marymount, had misinformation. Joe Blassberg, then an associate director of college counseling at Buckley, then reached out to Georgetown. On his call, it was revealed that Mary's Georgetown application had the same fictions about her ethnicity and her parents' education level, but it went a step further—it positioned her as a tennis recruit. When Georgetown learned that the application was false and that Mary was not in fact a tennis player, they said they'd look into it on their end. (Adam Bass has not been implicated in the Varsity Blues case.)

It's not clear exactly what transpired next, but Ernst seems to have then contacted Rick Singer to alert him that Georgetown was asking questions, because later that day, Singer called up Mary and told her that if Georgetown asked her if she was a tennis player, she should say that she was, according to a statement that the Bass family later released. Mary refused, and she and her parents tried to get into Mary's Common App, only to discover that they'd been locked out. After getting the password from Mikaela Sanford and logging in, they saw the lies that had been submitted. Adam Bass then called James Busby, who was then Buckley's head of school, saying something was wrong with Mary's application.

According to a source close to the Bass family, they were "not aware of a Dec. 7th phone call between Buckley and Tulane officials regarding their daughter's application," and they first learned about issues related to Singer when he called on December 8.

The Basses began working with Buckley that very weekend to start writing letters to send out to schools Mary had applied to in order to apologize and set the facts straight. Until then, the Buckley admissions team had no idea that Rick Singer was her independent counselor, or that he had filled out her applications using her password. The Basses had never shared that information. When the Singer connection was revealed, the school's reaction was: *Fuck*.

Buckley had already had a disturbing run-in with Singer. A year or so earlier, he had falsified another student's college application by going into his Common App and filling it out himself. When the student had tried to get into the account to work on his personal essay, he found he was locked out because Singer had changed the password. When Taylor-Vaz confronted Singer, he copped to it, but he said that it was "standard practice" for his company, seeing as they had so many applications to keep track of. He apologized, and the problem seemed to go away. But the incident prompted Buckley to send a letter to parents, warning them that they should be wary of Singer and that if any independent college counselor asked for their child's password and log-in information for college applications, they should not give it to them. Buckley was not in the mindset of telling parents *not* to hire outside counselors, figuring that was a lost cause, but the school strongly suggested relying on their in-house team, or to at least be open about it should they choose to hire someone else.

Within days of the news about Mary Bass's fake application, Georgetown put Ernst on leave and opened up an investigation into the coach with outside counsel. The school was also concerned about the credentials of another student being recruited by Ernst. (Per the investigation, Georgetown "established a new policy concerning the recruitment of student athletes" and "implemented audits to check whether recruited athletes are on team rosters," according to a statement made by the university. Ernst was asked to resign in July of 2018.) Singer's excuse to the Basses was that someone on his staff had put false information in Mary's application; he was sorry. But he had jeopardized her shot at her early action schools—Georgetown and Tulane did not admit her.

Meanwhile, after Devin Sloane erupted at Taylor-Vaz for daring to question his son's water polo credentials, Donna Heinel emailed Kirk Brennan in the USC admissions department, saying that Matteo played water polo for a private club in LA. During the summer, she said, he played for "the youth junior team in Italy."

"I don't know if the people at Buckley are unaware of his participation," she wrote.

Brennan replied that he'd pass the info along to Buckley, noting that the school "seemed unusually skeptical."

Singer then emailed Sloane a script to use should Buckley raise any more questions. He instructed him to keep up the indignation—"WHY are they questioning??"—and say that the Sloanes had developed a "close relationship" with USC's water polo coach, Jovan Vavic, and his wife, Lisa, ever "since Matteo has participated in Water Polo in the summers while we were in Italy." Vavic, Sloane was to explain, spent his summers overseas, training and recruiting players.

❦

The duplicity didn't end there. A few months later, Sloane told Singer on a phone call that when a member of USC's advancement office called him, wondering about his curious donation to women's athletics, he had told them, "Well, you know, my mom, my mother was an Olympic athlete and she just passed away last year."

"You're the greatest," Singer said.

The ruse worked, and Matteo sailed into USC, entering the class of 2022 that fall. But by that time, Buckley had other, bigger headwinds to deal with. Word had gotten out that Adam Bass, along with five other board members, had petitioned the head of school to change their children's grades. (Mary's C plus in math had been changed to a B minus.) When word leaked to the school community in February of 2018, there was an uproar. Students skipped class in protest and organized a school-wide sit-in. Some kids noticed that Mary had stopped showing up for school. A town hall meeting was called, in which board members and James Busby answered questions from indignant students in the school auditorium. Ultimately, Busby was forced to resign, although an investigation into the matter found that he had not done anything wrong and that the grade changes were warranted. Buckley was in flames.

But Singer, having gotten what he needed from the school, had already moved on.

CHAPTER 9

Don't Cheat

Y ou're not getting in anywhere."
Rick Singer had pivoted. It was the spring of 2018, and he had been working with Jack Buckingham, the son of youth branding expert and LA socialite Jane Buckingham, for a year now to help turn him into a more attractive college applicant.

Jack had been a sophomore at the prestigious Brentwood School when Singer first came into the family's life a year earlier at the suggestion of a fellow parent who had used him. Tall and reedy, with blond hair that matched his mother's, Jack was the goalie for the Brentwood soccer team. He was popular and funny, but not necessarily an academic giant, particularly at a school where kids were killing themselves to maintain their 4.5 GPAs. Brentwood has a reputation for being slightly less rigid and academically demanding than Harvard-Westlake (its head of school goes by Dr. Mike), but it is even more of an upper-crust bastion for power players. US Treasury Secretary Steve Mnuchin's kids go there, and among Brentwood's board members are Calista Flockhart and Lance Milken, son of billionaire Michael Milken, the former junk bond king. "It's the poor man's Harvard-Westlake, except no one there is poor," remarked one Harvard-Westlake parent. Another

LA parent said the wealth factor at the school is "stratospheric," half joking that families without private jets need not apply. The school earned notoriety in 2016 after a group of mostly white students posted a Snapchat video of themselves partying on an LA billionaire's yacht, singing "Dump Dump," a rap song by A$AP Ferg that's replete with instances of the N-word. After other students at Brentwood posted it online, the video went viral.

At Brentwood, Buckingham believed that Jack's grades were a problem, and she worried what his transcript would look like to college admissions officers. Buckingham, who'd attended Duke, wasn't hell-bent on Jack going to an elite school. Indeed, she often joked to friends that her kids (she also had a younger daughter, Lilia) were "never going to Harvard." But she wanted him to go to college, and when he said he was interested in Southern Methodist University and USC, she was determined to do all she could to help him apply. (This narrative is based on off-the-record conversations with sources close to Buckingham.)

At Brentwood, as at all private high schools in LA, there was a panic to line up an independent college counselor. As early as a student's freshman year, parents started worrying that all the independent counselors would be taken if they didn't move quickly. The chatter among Brentwood parents was that the school's own team of newly hired college counselors advocated hard for top students and bottom students, but that if your kid was somewhere in the middle, they'd be lost in the shuffle. Therefore, parents believed they needed to bring on their own champion and strategist for their child. Buckingham had been at one of Jack's soccer games when a friend asked her which college counselor she'd hired. She was surprised. "What? I thought we didn't have to do that until junior year," she said. "Oh, no," the woman said, informing her that sophomore year was actually considered late. The woman then gave her Singer's name, saying that other friends were using him and raving. She shared Singer's contact information with Buckingham on her iPhone.

Buckingham had been delighted when Singer first arrived at their home and immediately gelled with her son. Jack, like most high school students, wasn't thrilled about having a new tutor in his life, but Singer swept in and immediately began talking sports with Jack, who was a basketball fan. The two of them began ticking off basketball stats, and, at one point, Singer casually mentioned that he was part owner of the Sacramento Kings. It was a lie, but no one knew that, and it made the whole scenario seem all the more too good to be true.

As Buckingham listened to Singer and her son chat it up in the living room, she marveled at how lucky she'd been to find this college counselor, whom she agreed to talk to only because he was willing to come to her house in Beverly Hills for their initial meeting. She'd been given the name of another college counselor, but his office was in Brentwood, and there was no way Buckingham was going to deal with LA traffic at three in the afternoon on a weekday, let alone try to drag a son along with her who was less than eager to proceed with this whole college counseling thing.

Blond and birdlike, with a wide smile that conveys alternating layers of empathy and performance, Buckingham could easily be confused for a Real Housewife of Beverly Hills, something even she joked about in her self-deprecating way. She was a hugger and an air-kisser, a thrower of galas, baby showers, and fundraisers, someone who understood the power of seeing and being seen, and whose own brand, according to a friend, had always been "perfection." Even more so than others in a city defined by gloss and sheen, Buckingham seemed to have it all. The company she'd founded had been bought by a Hollywood talent agency powerhouse. Her

$7 million mansion was filled with impressive contemporary art. Her kids were creative and successful: Lilia was a huge Instagram star, who'd written a novel with *Pretty Little Liars* author Sara Shepard about teen influencers. And until recently, she'd been flanked by an equally captivating husband, Marcus Buckingham, a hunky Brit and a successful motivational speaker and best-selling author. To their friends, Jane and Marcus had been the ultimate power couple. They were more than good-looking and rich. They were idea people who were thoughtful and creative. "They discussed trends and how the world works and all of that," said a friend.

Among her pals, many of whom were the wives of producers and agents, or producers and agents themselves, Buckingham was the one who knew where to get the best facial and the best handbag, and which was the "best" elementary school in town. ("When you have a child, you *have* to go to the Center," she'd told one friend when both of Buckingham's own children were enrolled there.) She also had a social radar that paid dividends in the Hollywood circles she ran in. "Jane will always know the right people in the room," said another friend. "When she walks into a room she knows the two people she needs to talk to before leaving." But she was also a hardworking CEO as well as a caring and loyal friend, whose main fault was caring too much for those around her, most notably her children, whom she'd always doted on. This was in part because Buckingham's own experience growing up had been so turbulent. She'd been raised by a single working mother in New York City who'd barely paid the bills, and who died suddenly after Buckingham graduated from college. Although she attended an elite private high school, Horace Mann, she and her brother were often called into the head of school's office and told that if her mother didn't pay their tuition, they wouldn't be allowed to come back.

"Because her mother hadn't been there a lot, Jane needed to be this successful career woman, but she also wanted to be this very hands-on mom," said another source. "I think she did a pretty good job of that. Obviously, she wasn't perfect."

Buckingham had been obsessed with adolescent behavior since she'd been in high school, when she wrote a book called *Teens Speak Out*, in which she polled her peers for their thoughts on sex, women in the workplace, and other issues. After studying at Duke, she got into advertising, and went on to combine her new skills in market research with her passion, creating the trend-forecasting company Youth Intelligence, which published the newsletter the *Cassandra Report*. In 2003, the company was bought by Creative Artists Agency (CAA) in a headline-grabbing acquisition that catapulted Buckingham into the heart of Hollywood business and social circles. She now lived in LA and had started writing advice books for teens, the Modern Girl's Guide series, in which she jauntily doled out tips for, in the case of *The Modern Girl's Guide to Sticky Situations*, "surviving headaches, pickles, jams and everyday emergencies." The books were adapted for a series on the now-defunct Style network, polishing her entertainment industry cred even further. In 2009, she founded Trendera, a youth marketing and consumer insights company, and was working with movie studios and producers, telling them how their franchises needed to be tweaked in order to more authentically reflect teen culture, or why a certain actor wasn't popular anymore. Before Jack had enrolled there, the Brentwood School had even hired her to help them improve their messaging.

As the culture's obsession with millennials escalated, Buckingham rode the wave, enlightening the world on a subject she'd been studying for decades. In 2016, she gave a lecture on millennial entitlement, saying, "It's not their fault—it's their parents—because that's what happens when you give them a gold star for going to the potty and a trophy for not participating, and telling them they are fantastic every day of their life.

"Now, ten years later," she went on, "we are mad at them. We made our beds. We have to lie in it."

But for all of the togetherness and authority she exuded when it came to the topic of kids, Buckingham felt extreme insecurity and parental guilt about her own, especially Jack. As a child, he'd developed a stammer, which she believed was due to her always working so much. When she moved to LA from New York, she was grinding full-time at CAA and writing a book. Her assistant had to remind her to leave her desk to take lunches. This was LA, not New York, after all—schmoozing was part of the job. Always conscious of her own childhood, Buckingham did her best to be a present mother, to be the one doing pickup and drop-off, but it wasn't always possible, and she feared that her son suffered as a result. After hearing teachers comment about Jack, and eventually Lilia's, learning differences—the latter was showing signs of number dyslexia—Buckingham had them both tested by a neuropsychologist when Jack was in seventh grade. As a result, both were granted accommodations. In Jack's case, he was able to get extended time on tests if he wanted it and was able to use a keyboard in class, seeing as his handwriting was atrocious due to fine motor issues.

By the time Jack was in high school and college applications started hovering in the near distance, more disruption set in. Marcus announced he was leaving in 2016, setting the stage for an ugly divorce. After Marcus moved out, he retained joint custody but saw the kids infrequently, according to legal documents and sources close to Buckingham—Jack and Lilia slept in her room with her for two months as the family tried to reorient and find its bearings. Jack started having trouble in school. His grades tanked.

(Marcus Buckingham, who has not been charged in the Varsity Blues case, declined to comment.)

And then in walked Singer. Suddenly, there was a coach-slash–parental figure who could help control at least one piece of disarray in Buckingham's life. He could talk to Jack, oversee his schoolwork, help him get things on track. In that first meeting, Singer talked guy-to-guy to Jack, being at once motivational and tough, in an I'm-holding-you-accountable way. It was exactly what he needed, Buckingham thought.

"Jack," Singer said. "Let's talk about your grades. Are you gonna get this B to a B plus? Or can we get an A minus? What about this? Can we get this up?

"I'm gonna check in with you every month," he went on. "We're gonna see where these grades are. We're gonna get them up. Your mom can't do it for you. No one can do it for you—only you can."

He also brought up the idea of having Jack say he wanted to be a manager of a sports team as a way to give him a boost in college admissions. Every team needed a manager, he said, and seeing as Jack loved sports, was an athlete himself, and was so good with stats, he'd be a perfect candidate. Buckingham was impressed—she'd never considered this before, and when Singer later asked her to send her an "action shot" of her son playing soccer in order to help him apply as a manager, she acquiesced. (Later, it would be suggested that this photo was presented so that she could package Jack as a soccer recruit, but a source close to Buckingham said that was never discussed with Singer.)

Between Singer's knowledge and savvy about college admissions and his connection with Jack, Buckingham couldn't help herself. She gushed to him: "You are my hero. You are my savior. Tell me what to do, I'll do it. Thank you."

After he left, Buckingham asked her son what he thought, bracing for the worst. She was hooked, but was he? "He's a cool guy," Jack said. "I'm happy to work with him."

⚜

By the time Jane Buckingham met Rick Singer in 2017, word-of-mouth buzz about the college counselor had spread among parents at virtually every private high school in Los Angeles. It was the Sacramento effect, only times ten. Here was a much bigger, much richer, and much more desperate community of parents, who cared deeply about status and keeping up with the Joneses, both in terms of hiring the "best" college tutor and sending their kids to the best schools. LA's wealthiest pockets were also cesspools of insecurity about parenting. These were families who had been hiring tutors and outsourcing instruction in so many subjects for so long—the personal lacrosse coach, the Spanish tutor—parents were often loath to trust themselves when it came to advising their children. They were used to having an expert do it. Enter into this environment Singer, who had not just made inroads at Buckley, but also at Harvard-Westlake, Marlborough, Marymount, Brentwood, Crossroads, and Loyola High School. (Not all of his dealings were illegal at these schools.)

Interspersed in the chatter of how amazing Singer was, however, were increasing comments that he was "sleazy" or "scuzzy"—that he'd do or say strange things, in one case asking a family to say that their child was African American on the (white) student's college application. (They refused.) Buckingham raised an eyebrow when she looked at Jack's Common App one day and saw that Singer had written in that Jack had volunteered for A

Soldier's Child Foundation. Jack had done plenty of volunteering at nonprofits—it was something his mother had encouraged him to do—but not for A Soldier's Child. She alerted someone at the Key, assuming they'd mistakenly input the information, thinking Jack's application belonged to someone else, but then never gave it another thought. Indeed, for the most part, families shrugged off any warning signs or irregularities on Singer's part and continued to work with him, chalking it up to his overzealousness getting the most of him, and figuring that he was nonetheless the best college counselor they could find.

There were families who'd meet with him and instantly be turned off by his arrogance, and that was that. They'd hire someone else. One family who hired him let him go after he berated their child to the point of tears every time they met, telling her how much harder she needed to be working. But for those who fell for Singer's magic, it was just that: magic.

In some cases those who fell hardest were, like Buckingham, mothers. These women were by nature caretakers, doters, and worriers. They were also often highly distressed by the demands of modern parenting and modern parental judgment: the endless choices, the many ways they could be seen as doing it "wrong" by their peers, whether by selecting the less-liked dance studio on Yelp for their eight-year-old or feeding their toddler nonorganic strawberries in public. Fathers, of course, can feel these stresses, too, but by and large it is mothers who are the ones sweating the details and the ever-shifting zeitgeist when it comes to child-rearing. Wait, soymilk, not almond milk? Play-based or academic preschool? Soccer at age three or five? The stress begins as soon as the child is born, or even earlier, actually—pregnancy is perhaps the most plagued period of self-doubt and anxiety of all—but it continues on, through elementary school, middle school, and high school, explaining why parenting gurus like Betsy Brown Braun have "baby groups" that continue on for twenty years.

Unlike the fathers that Singer preyed on, these mothers were less impressed by his ties to financial institutions or the fact that he said he had connections at Harvard or claimed to have been hired by the Obamas. What they found in him, what seduced them, was that he was a caretaker of the highest order, someone to whom they could offload some of the burden they were so tired of carrying when it came to their child. He could orchestrate all the details that had piled up sixteen, seventeen years into a kid's life. Not to mention, he was available twenty-four/seven—on text, on email, by phone—and was willing to chat. He was ultimately a friend, a family member of sorts, someone they could trust and feel comfortable with. Unlike everyone else making demands of them—teachers, coaches, colleagues, partners—he allowed them to breathe.

Elizabeth Henriquez, the Silicon Valley parent who paid Singer $400,000 to have two daughters fake their way into college, wrote this in a letter following her arrest: "I am preoccupied by the question: was I a good mother? And how can I be a good mother going forward?" Henriquez, who pled guilty and was sentenced, blamed her actions on her "deep, unconditional love for her daughters," a love that had become "warped" under Singer's influence. Elizabeth's husband, Manuel, was also charged and pled guilty but has not yet been sentenced.

This idea of overprotective mothers, vulnerable mothers, and most especially "good mothers," a phrase that actress Felicity Huffman would also muse upon, is rarely applied to fathers, or at least does not carry the same connotations. Mothers, it is assumed, *are* good, simply by nature. They are paragons of moral rectitude, nurturing love, and solicitude. They give, they love, they protect, and they deflect. But as Huffman noted, there is an unrealistic ideal at work with this image, a sense that mothers aren't allowed to be human and make mistakes. Fathers can go rogue, have a few too many drinks, stay out late. All will be forgiven, and such behavior is, by the way, expected. But not mothers. Forget imperfection. What about when a mother's love indeed becomes warped? When it's too much? When it goes in not-good directions?

In the case of mothers' stress over where a child was going to college, it wasn't always about making sure a child got into the "right" school in order to protect social standing, though in some cases there was that. But often it was more about protecting the child from discomfort and disappointment, something the obsessive and, especially, the deeply insecure mother can't bear. As in: The child desperately wants to attend College X, and thus the mother feels compelled to make that happen for him or her. Mothers could even display a kind of codependency with their children, so deep and connective was their relationship. A former private-school administrator said that mothers would often talk about college admissions as though it were a communal act. As in: "We got into Brown!" or "We're applying to NYU."

Not that fathers are not guilty—one mother told me of a father who opened up his daughter's admission letter from his alma mater, Yale (back when notices arrived by mail) and was crying when the girl walked in. She had been rejected. "So, one, he opened her letter," the mother said. "And two, he took away her chance to react."

Singer quickly sussed out mothers' insecurities and leaned into them. In the case of Jane Buckingham, he would often praise her parenting, saying: "It's clear you're such a *great* mom. You love your kids, and your kids love you." Other times, he played on the fact that she was an attractive, newly single woman, chatting her up in a way that was borderline flirtatious.

❦

Around the same time Buckingham was giving lectures on millennials, Felicity Huffman was making a name for herself off camera as a counterintuitive DGAF mom expert, through her website, called What the Flicka? (Flicka was Huffman's nickname growing up.) She'd started the site in 2012, just after her hit show *Desperate Housewives*—for which she won an Emmy—went off the air, and Huffman realized how many women out there sympathized with her character on the show, Lynette Scavo, a harried working mother. Why not cater to that crowd and give herself a new marketing platform, not to mention a place where she could vent and wax on about her own real-life parenting woes?

Huffman had always been open about how anxious she was as the parent of two girls, whom she'd had with her husband and fellow actor William H. Macy. Both of their daughters were diagnosed early on with learning disabilities, which only fed her concern. As she would write in a legal document, "From the moment my children were born I worried that they got me as a Mother. I so desperately wanted to do it right and was so deathly afraid of doing it wrong. My own fears and lack of confidence, combined with a daughter who has learning disabilities often made me insecure and highly anxious from the beginning."

Macy wrote to the judge in her case that his wife "has not carried being a mom easily. She's struggled to find the balance between what the experts say and her common sense."

Felicity and Macy's eldest daughter, Sophia, in particular, caused concern. When Sophia was four, "she couldn't even walk across a lawn in bare feet without flipping out," Huffman wrote in her letter to the judge. "Tags in her shirt would cause a 20-minute meltdown. She didn't know how to physically play with other kids, and most often she couldn't sleep."

Sophia was eventually diagnosed with sensory modulation issues, meaning she either over- or under-responded to her environment and couldn't regulate her emotions. After being tested by a neuropsychologist, she received accommodations at her schools.

Like Buckingham, Huffman was a working mother who felt the simultaneous, and overwhelming, desire to be a hands-on parent. Her own parents divorced when she was very young, but she's said that her mother, who acted in plays before she had kids, was always supportive of her and attended every play she ever starred in, starting when she was a kid growing up in Aspen, Colorado. Her mother was also away a lot, however, and Huffman has said she was raised by her six sisters; she also has a brother. Huffman's family had money—her maternal grandfather helped found the investment banking firm Morgan Stanley, and her father was a partner there. She was able to attend boarding school in Vermont, followed by a brief stint at the Buckley School in LA, and then went on to finish high school at the Interlochen Arts Academy in Michigan.

While studying theater at NYU, she fell in with a troupe of actors working with playwright David Mamet, including Macy, who was teaching acting workshops for Mamet. The group would go on to found Atlantic Theater Company, and Huffman and Macy would become artistic and actual partners for life. From the start, the two made for a yin-and-yang coupling. Macy, who'd met Mamet while attending Goddard College, a small progressive school in Vermont, was the easygoing hippy, while Huffman was the "type

A perfectionist," according to an actor who knew them in New York. After they got together, Macy stopped smoking pot, or smoked less of it, and fell in step with his new girlfriend. To Huffman, Macy was the older, wiser mentor—a "god," she's said, who was more experienced in his craft and directed her in a play.

By the mid-1990s, they'd married, and Macy's Hollywood career took off with a starring role in the Coen brothers' film *Fargo*. The couple was now living in LA, both pursuing movies and TV projects. For Huffman, success was gradual. She starred in some *Frasier* episodes, and was cast on the acclaimed but short-lived Aaron Sorkin series *Sports Night* on ABC. Then, in 2004, *Housewives* debuted, and everything changed. "I was shooting long hours, much more than thirty, forty hours a week," she has said. "Then you'd have publicity on weekends. I never had a weekend off. Those were some very tense times, some real fun times." But the flip side, she said, was that she was "drowning in motherhood."

Indeed, every one of the film and TV projects she'd worked on since having children was fraught with "a lot of mommy guilt," she said in an interview with the Television Academy. Filming *Transamerica* in 2004, for which Huffman received an Oscar nomination, meant flying to New York for a month of rehearsal and leaving her two children, who were under the age of four, at home. Her audition for *Housewives* had meant leaving the house at five o'clock in the afternoon while her daughters were in the bathtub. "I said, 'I have to pull myself together,'" she said. "The kids are crying because I'm leaving."

Her feelings seeped into the show's writer's room. "I think it was in season two, the scene where [Lynette] is on the soccer field after she's been taking Ritalin to try and keep up with being a mother, keep up with kids. She has a breakdown, and she's surrounded by her friends," Huffman said. "She talks about, 'I feel like a bad mother. I feel like my kids would be better off without me.'

"That all came from me. I was like, 'This is what it feels like for me to be a mom. I feel sorry for my kids to have me as a mother.'"

On What the Flicka? website, Huffman played with this sentiment, turning self-pity into self-lacerating humor. "My first step in setting us free would be to make the phrase 'Good Mother' synonymous with 'Mother Fucker,'" she wrote in June 2016. "Because that's what we are doing to ourselves, and letting others do to us, being vicious and despicable. We are fucking ourselves."

She presented herself as a fellow survivor in the mothering game, an imperfect warrior willing to reveal her lapses and infractions, someone mothers everywhere could sit down with and wearily raise their glass of wine with, celebrating the act of just getting by. "If our kids are alive and decent citizens at 18," she once posted, "we all deserve a fucking medal."

In another post, she admitted, "I have made so many mistakes as a parent it actually makes me nauseous to think about it."

The site hawked items such as mugs imprinted with I CAN'T ADULT TODAY and NOT NOT WINE, as well as background images for phones that said GOOD ENOUGH MOM. Books such as *The Blessing of a B Minus* were touted, cautioning against overparenting and holding children to impossible ideals.

But however much she sold a WTF attitude toward mothering online, in real life she was hardly winging it. Macy has said that she constantly sought out parenting experts, both in friends whose children she admired and professionals. After reading the book *The Blessing of a Skinned Knee*, she tracked down its author, Wendy Mogel, and began consulting with her over the course of several years. And when Sophia enrolled at the Los Angeles

County High School for the Arts (LACHSA), a public performing arts school in downtown LA, Huffman and Macy were highly visible and involved parents, using their clout to help fundraise for the school, which is tuition-free and depends on parental involvement. It also depends on donations, and Huffman and Macy gave $20,000 to the foundation that supports the school—other donors have included Frank Gehry, Paul Thomas Anderson, as well as Sony and Disney. Macy starred in a video promoting the school, and he and Huffman even hosted a party for LACHSA kids one night at their $3.8 million home in the Hollywood Hills. Popeyes chicken was delivered, and Macy was the cool dad, playing guitar along with a couple of guitar students, and joking around with everyone. "You guys better watch out—people are starting to get crazy!" he'd say playfully. Huffman, meanwhile, watchfully stood by the door, screening to make sure no non-LACHSA kids were coming in. "She was intense," said one person who was at the gathering. "She made it clear she didn't want anyone who wasn't from the school attending."

LACHSA may not cultivate the academic intensity of, say, Harvard-Westlake, but it has its own culture of extreme competitiveness. Much like the seminal arts–high school movie *Fame*, while kids might break into song and dance during lunch, they're also killing themselves to prepare for senior-year auditions. There are an abundance of stage parents, who try to wrangle their kids into starring roles in school productions, hoping that their time served at the school bake sale will pay off. A privilege divide exists between families who can afford voice, dance, and acting tutors, to keep their child ahead of the game, and families who can't. Students, meanwhile, are all eyeing the same set of elite arts schools: Juilliard, Yale School of Drama, Carnegie Mellon, and CalArts, which are the equivalent of the Ivy League in the performing arts world. The result is a "dog eat dog" culture, said one former LACHSA student.

Unifieds, where colleges set up shop in a hotel one day in the spring and have seniors come to audition, are especially stressful. "I know people who auditioned up to literally twenty-three times," the former student said. "They were so scared they weren't going to get into a college right after high school. It's a huge status thing in the arts, because it's not so much like 'Oh, my grades aren't good enough' or 'Who I am isn't good enough.' It's 'My talent isn't good enough.'"

Another graduate, Camilo Estrada, said the school added to the pressure by having a wall where seniors could elect to put their college acceptance letters. "It was a corkboard thing where kids could pin up schools they'd gotten into," he said. "I remember thinking, oh my God, someone got in here? Maybe I should apply there. It was definitely a pressure."

Sophia Macy didn't need to ride her parents' coattails at LACHSA. A member of the school's theater department, she landed many prominent roles in school productions, including the lead in *Spring Awakening*, and the role of Mary Jane in a one-act Spider-Man play. Students who knew her said who her parents were had nothing to do with her success; she had real talent.

But to get her through the college admissions process, her mother hired Rick Singer in the fall of 2016, when Sophia was a sophomore, after a friend told her he was the best college counselor in California. Part of Huffman's impulse to hire someone was that LACHSA's own college counseling department was overburdened: The school had just two counselors for more than six hundred students, according to Huffman's sentencing memo. Huffman didn't want to risk it with Sophia, given her learning disabilities and the fact that her PSAT score had not been promising, according to legal documents. She'd barely cracked 1000; a perfect score is 1520. Sophia hadn't taken her ADHD medicine the day she took the PSAT, and neither she nor Huffman had given the test much thought—it was, by definition, a "practice test," after all—so they figured Sophia would do better on the SAT with some level of preparation. She hadn't even gotten extra time on the test, though she qualified for it. Still, Huffman wanted to cover all her bases.

Things started off with Singer as they always did. He hooked Sophia up with SAT tutors and began helping her map out her college plan as he let it be known how well he understood college admissions. A year in, he had so won over Huffman that she entrusted him with the academic future of her younger daughter, Georgia, who was starting high school at Westridge School, a private, all-girls school in Pasadena. He even met with administrators at Georgia's school to advocate for an education program for her that took into account her learning disabilities. He had become Huffman's most trusted educational advisor.

Everything thrummed along smoothly for a year. Then, in August of 2017, he began to change his tune. In a meeting with Huffman, he said that Sophia really needed to improve her test scores. He was worried. He said she needed a math tutor to work with her twice a week. He also lectured Huffman on the dire state of college admissions, with all those legacies, athletes, and donors' kids out there. He did not point out that Huffman and Macy were parents with pull: accomplished and famous thespians who volunteered their time and helped fundraise at their kids' schools and presumably would do the same for any college their children attended. He did not remind them of their ability to make a donation to a college and turn their children into VIP candidates.

All Huffman heard was Singer. And when he gave his doomsday

speech, nothing else factored in. When he said that even if a school posted an admissions rate of 10 percent, for someone like Sophia it was more like 2 or 3 percent, Huffman went cold.

Sophia had her heart set on Juilliard, which doesn't require standardized test scores, but Singer brushed this aside. Yes, her audition was important, he said, but her talent wouldn't be enough, and other schools Sophia was interested in would need to see better test scores to even consider her. She would need, he said, between 1250 and 1350 on the SAT; without that score, Sophia would be rejected, no matter how good her audition was.

Having planted the seeds of dread and pushed them firmly down in the dirt, Singer then offered a solution. He said he had a way to "level the playing field." Huffman, who was taking notes on her iPad during the meeting, began to type.

❧

Back at the Buckinghams', Rick Singer was showing up once every month to meet with Jack for an hour throughout his junior year. Whenever he came, he'd chat Jane Buckingham up, asking her how she was, what was going on with work, and in turn telling her about all the good work his foundation was doing. He said he was building playgrounds for underprivileged kids that he'd get companies like Nike to sponsor all over the country. At one point, he called her from Boston, saying he was building a playground there.

Once, he mentioned a strategy called "the side door," but the way he described it was vague and didn't sound illegal, according to a source close to Buckingham. The side door, he said, was how he got kids into colleges using his relationships. "I know these coaches, and I know these administrators," he said. "They like me, and they get my kids in." Buckingham listened but didn't pay much attention to it, nor did she think it made much sense. Later, she was comparing notes on him with a friend who was using him, and they were trying to decode things he'd said. "Do you understand this side-door thing?" Buckingham asked. The friend didn't, nor did the friend understand other confusing and vague comments he'd made. Singer, they assumed, was only being Singer.

But around April of Jack's junior year, Singer was in no way fuzzy about what he was saying. Jack, he said, was in trouble. His grades hadn't gotten as high as he'd hoped they would, and college—not just *a* college, but all colleges—was looking iffy. Jack had toured SMU in Dallas and loved it, on top of which it had a sports management program. That was his first choice, and he planned to apply early decision. (The plan to have Jack talk up his interest in being a team manager had disappeared into the ether, however, even though Buckingham asked him about it a few times—yet another way in which Singer could be flaky.) But Jack also liked the idea of staying closer to home, to be with his mother and sister, especially because of the divorce, so he was also considering USC.

But Singer was hearing none of it. He'd turned off the niceties. Now he was harsh, even mean. "You're not getting into SMU," he told Jack. "Or USC. You're not getting in anywhere."

"This is a real problem," he said.

Jack had taken the ACT twice on his own and placed in the ninety-second and ninety-fourth percentile. His GPA was around a 3.3. He was not, in fact, in disastrous standing for the midtier schools he was looking at. Perhaps they weren't a slam dunk, and USC might have been a stretch, given how tough it was to get in, but he did not fit the profile of a lost cause. Yet that's exactly the picture that Singer painted.

Buckingham was now afraid. A whole new wave of guilt washed over her: She'd ruined her kids' lives because of the divorce, she thought, and now Jack's future was going to be taken away from him. She also felt ashamed for not having better connections. So many other parents knew board members at USC or other higher-ups who had enough clout to mean something, should they advocate for a kid. Buckingham knew people at USC's journalism school, and they'd helped set up a tour, but they weren't the kind of people who could get a kid in.

These thoughts were completely unfounded, they made no sense, but feelings, as they say, are real. It was a moment where she should have turned to someone and asked for help, or at the very least, advice. She desperately needed a sounding board. But she felt there was none. By this point, Marcus and Jane were no longer speaking, according to a source close to Jane. Whenever she tried to talk to him about the kids, he shut her down. If she said, "Jack's grades are in trouble," he'd respond, "I'll talk about it with Jack." If she said, "Lilia's having trouble with" whatever it was, he'd say, "I'll talk to Lilia about it." When she emailed him asking advice about college—"Should Jack apply early to USC?"—Marcus didn't respond.

And so she leaned in harder with Singer, who suddenly said: "I can get his ACT score up."

In what would later be seen as a hugely ironic impulse, in May, when one of Buckingham's kids came home from school and told her about another student who'd been cheating in class but hadn't gotten caught, Buckingham took to Instagram, where she often posted positive, life-affirming messages, and wrote in all-caps: DON'T CHEAT.

CHAPTER 10

Nailing a Score

No one worked harder at IMG Academy than Mark Riddell. Now head of the school's SAT and ACT test-prep division, Riddell hustled nonstop, from seven in the morning, when test review classes for students began, until nine at night, when they wrapped up. The former Harvard tennis player and SAT whiz kid was a whir of positivity and productivity. Always cheerful and solicitous—and spiffily decked out in country-club casual—if Riddell spotted someone across campus carrying something heavy, he'd wave and run over to give them a hand. In the morning, as the college-aged tutors who worked for him were doing their best to gain consciousness over coffee before class, Riddell was already buzzing. "All right! Let's do this! Let's get some SAT done!" he'd enthuse. Later, when tutors were in the midst of sessions with students, Riddell would pop his head in the classroom to check in on things. "Do you need me to make copies of anything for you? Everything good?" he'd say. Then he'd give a thumbs-up or say, "Super-duper!" and move on.

By 2016, Riddell no longer had any outward ties to Rick Singer, who was long gone from IMG's Bradenton, Florida, campus. But after the Pendleton School closed in 2012 and IMG took its academics in-house, Riddell became IMG's standardized-test-prep guru. (Scott Treibly, who'd worked alongside Riddell as Singer's other tutor at IMG, had left in 2014 and become an independent college counselor for student athletes in Sarasota.) Riddell's job at IMG meant running classes throughout the day to help the school's student athletes bump up their scores in order to make them more appealing to college recruiters. Unlike at the Pendleton School, standardized test prep was no longer an opt-in service that families paid for; it was now part of tuition. But even so, not all kids showed up for class. In fact, attendance was, at best, 50 percent, according to former tutors. In some cases, only a handful of kids would show up or, at times, none. Kids were tired, after all, from practicing their sport for half the day and then balancing that with their regular course load and enforced study halls in the evening. There was also an assumption among many of them that test scores weren't going to get them into college, anyway; instead, either their athletic ability or their parents' connections would. There were some exceptions—students who were genuinely interested in doing the work and learning how to ace a standardized test—but for the most part, the tutors said that Riddell was dealing with an apathetic constituency.

According to an IMG Academy source, about a quarter of the school's senior class of about three hundred students take advantage of the school's test-prep courses. This person said that classes become more popular closer to standardized test dates, but then wane because "students are procrastinators like the rest of us sometimes. So when it gets closer to the test date, they're going to do what they can to brush up on" the test. "But there's a smaller percentage that might do it over the course of the whole semester."

Test-prep courses are given in the evening, "which makes it hard," the IMG Academy source said. "If you're getting up somewhere between 6:30 and seven a.m.; eating breakfast; you're in your first class by 7:40 a.m.; you go to school till 12:15 p.m.; you get out; you've got forty-five minutes to eat, get changed, maybe get a treatment; practice starts at 1:30 p.m. and goes to 5:30, six o'clock. You've got to take a shower, eat, be back at study hall at 7:30 pm. There's not a lot of time to be a teenager.

"So if you're going into test prep at 7:30 p.m., you've already had a pretty rigorous twelve- to thirteen-hour day going. That's a lot. That's hard to do."

Riddell still seemed committed to his job and interested in helping kids. He still tirelessly sat with them, going over question after question. He dutifully made Xerox copies of SAT and ACT practice tests. "Other teachers would complain about how much we used the copier, because we were in there so much," said Dylan Gygax, a tutor who said copying could go on for three to four hours, and that Riddell often pitched in. "Copying is what we did."

But as time went on, his peers couldn't help but notice that his job—or something—was taking a toll on him. It wasn't just the long days and the kids that needed to be hounded to show up for class, but the political minefield that came with tutoring kids from wealthy, demanding families and working for an institution invested in keeping those parents happy. There were parents who insisted that Riddell personally tutor their child, seeing as he was known as the top SAT guy at IMG as well as a Harvard grad, adding more work to Riddell's already-overflowing plate. There were others who held him personally accountable for their kids' progress, or lack thereof. During the summer, IMG ran three-week sports camps where kids could come and practice with coaches.

Some also enrolled in daily three-and-a-half-hour test-prep classes. Students took an ACT or SAT practice test on the first day of class, worked on the sections that needed improvement over the course of three weeks, and then took a final practice test at the end of the session. The goal was to raise a student's score by two hundred points, another pressure on Riddell.

One summer, Riddell had a student who couldn't be made to pay attention in class. As a result, his score actually dropped by the end of the session. The boy's father had been calling Riddell constantly to check in on his progress, and Riddell had been assuring him that the student was doing fine. So when Gygax, who'd been running the boy's class, informed Riddell that he was in fact doing poorly, Riddell was visibly unnerved. "You could tell he was upset," said Gygax. "He was under pressure from the higher-ups to justify the existence of the program, and he was gonna have to hear shit from a parent."

One tutor who worked at IMG in 2016 said that around that time, Riddell opened up more and said that he was interested in starting an MBA program but that he wasn't sure how he'd do it due to his work schedule. "It sounded like he didn't want to do this tutoring, SAT-teaching thing anymore. He was applying to schools and was talking about how difficult it was to find time to do the applications," the tutor told me. "He said he mainly wanted to do [grad school] online, because he just didn't have the time to go to a classroom.

"It definitely seemed like he was tired of doing what he was doing," this person went on. "I think it made sense to me at the time, because he was just working so much."

Riddell had entertained the idea of starting his own college prep company, and had registered the domain name RiddellCollege Prep.com, according to the *Tampa Bay Times*. In 2014, he also incorporated a company called Prometheus International Education along with a business partner, but it never came to fruition.

But beyond a growing beleaguerment with test prep, his colleagues said there seemed to be something else going on with Riddell. Tutors noticed that he would mysteriously disappear, never explaining where he was and never giving anyone a heads-up. A tutor would simply receive a text ten minutes before Riddell had said he'd come in to help them prepare for a class, saying, "Hey, I'm out of town." When he'd returned a day or so later, he would vaguely imply that he'd had to go somewhere for work, but he didn't say anything more. No one asked any questions, because Riddell never invited true engagement with the people he worked with.

His always-on personality helped to create a distance from those around him. He rarely talked about his personal life, other than to say that he was married to an investment banker, with whom he was expecting a child, and that he'd gone to Harvard. In one of the rare displays of personal taste, on his office bookshelf at IMG, stacked in among rows and rows of SAT- and ACT-prep books, there were novels by Ayn Rand.

"Mark was always charismatic, always smiling," said another former tutor. "It was impossible for him to be in a bad mood or to express that in any way. But it was to the point where I don't think I ever really believed that the emotion he was showing was truly how he felt. It almost was forced twenty-four/seven."

❧

Unbeknownst to anyone at IMG at the time, Mark Riddell's strange absences were tied to Rick Singer. All the while he was Xeroxing copies of standardized tests and drilling kids on advanced vocabulary and rational equations, Riddell was leading a double life as Singer's "guy"—as Singer referred to Riddell in conversations—flying around the country to take standardized tests for his clients. Riddell was the primary player in Singer's second side-door scheme—the first being the creation of fake athletic profiles to slip students through college admissions. This was the test-cheating side door, wherein Singer had Riddell take a standardized test for a student, sit next to them and help them while they took it, or correct their answers afterward, in many cases without the student having any idea. Singer orchestrated it so the students would not put their answers down on the actual Scantron form, the official test, but on a separate answer sheet. That way, Riddell could later "bubble in all the answers, and we wouldn't have erase marks," Singer said in court. "The kids still had to write their own essay in their own handwriting, so that was the only legitimate part of the test that the kids actually did." After the student and their family left, Riddell would fill out the actual test over the course of several hours.

The cheating almost always took place at two test-taking sites that Singer controlled, in LA and Houston. He would instruct parents to concoct a reason to be in one of those cities—a bar mitzvah, he suggested to one family, or a wedding—and arrange to have their child take the test there. He told them to show up at seven forty-five in the morning. Riddell typically flew in the night before.

In Houston, Singer's connection was Lisa "Niki" Williams— "my gal in Houston," as he called her—an assistant teacher at Jack Yates High School, where she also administered SAT and ACT tests. He had been introduced to her by Martin Fox, who ran a tennis academy in Houston, and whom Singer paid $50,000 for the connection, according to legal documents. Fox also introduced

Singer to Michael Center, the men's tennis coach at the University of Texas at Austin. (Williams, Center, and Fox have all pled guilty in the Varisty Blues case.) In LA, Singer relied on Igor Dvorskiy, the Ukrainian director of West Hollywood College Preparatory School, a small pre-K–12 independent school founded by Dvorskiy's mother. The school has about one hundred students, most of whom are Russian, and bills itself as a place that is "preparing young minds for the future." Singer paid Williams and Dvorskiy $10,000 for every test-taking student he sent their way, according to the prosecution. In exchange, Williams and Dvorskiy would allow Riddell to proctor the test for the student at their school but then fill out the ACT or SAT paperwork claiming that they, in fact, had proctored the test, or in some cases, one of their colleagues. They would also lie and say that the test had been taken over multiple days. (Dvorskiy has pled guilty to charges.)

Riddell, who has also pled guilty, didn't have access to answers on the test; he was simply so good at taking the ACT and SAT that he could "nail a score," according to Singer, who also said: "I would already tell him the score that we wanted to get, and Mark would get that score exactly." For kids who'd never taken the ACT or the SAT before, Singer instructed Riddell to obtain a perfect or near-perfect score. But for kids who'd already taken a test, he told him to not get too high a score, as the discrepancy might raise red flags with the ACT or the College Board. He paid Riddell about $10,000 per test, but he took credit for the results himself. "I can make scores happen," he bragged to one parent. "And nobody on the planet can get scores to happen."

According to legal documents, Riddell participated in more than half a dozen of these scenarios since at least as far back as 2011. That was the year he impersonated the son of David Sidoo, a Canadian businessman and former professional Canadian football player. Riddell posed as the boy by using a fake ID, and took the SAT for him, boosting his score by 210 points to a 1670 out of 2400. (Singer instructed Riddell to not obtain too high a score because it would draw scrutiny.) He also took the boy's high school graduation exam for him. A year later Riddell took the SAT for Sidoo's younger son, earning him a score of 2280 on the test. Included in Singer's services was writing a college essay for that son, which claimed that he'd done volunteer work with Los Angeles gangs. "Can we lessen the interaction with the gangs," Sidoo wrote Singer after he looked over the draft. "Guns...? That's scary stuff." David Sidoo, who paid Singer $200,000, has pled guilty to charges in the case.

Another case involved the daughter of Elizabeth and Manuel Henriquez, a Silicon Valley venture capitalist, whose SAT score Riddell pumped up 320 points to a 1900 (again, out of 2400) when he sat next to the girl in 2015 and doctored her answers. After the test, Riddell gloated with the girl and her mother about how they'd gotten away with it, according to legal documents. This was one of the few instances when Riddell took the test at a student's (private) high school. It was arranged when Riddell emailed the girl's guidance counselor saying that his wife had just had a newborn. "I would really appreciate the opportunity to proctor the test bc I'm applying to grad schools and I could quite frankly use the work," he added.

The next year, when it was time for the Henriquezes' younger daughter to take the ACT—Singer had told her mother the girl was "too stupid" to take the test on her own—Riddell sat with her and another Singer client, the daughter of Laguna Beach real estate mogul Robert Flaxman, and helped them take the test at the test center in Houston. (Singer had told Flaxman that without an improved test score, his daughter was getting in "nowhere.") But

Riddell was careful to have the girls input different answers, so as not to raise concerns with the ACT. Henriquez's daughter wound up scoring a 30 out of 36 on the test, which the Henriquezes then deemed not good enough, so another Singer "proctor" cheated on a subsequent ACT for the girl, as well as SAT subject tests. Flaxman's daughter's score rose to a 28 from a 20. The Henriquezes ended up paying Singer and his charity $400,000 for the test cheating and the fake tennis application—Singer reduced his rate after Manuel Henriquez helped him get a client into Northeastern University. Flaxman's bill was $75,000.

Central to Singer's scheme was to get kids authorized for special accommodations in the form of extra time on the tests. With this allowance, they would be able to take the exam alone and over the course of multiple days, either at their high school or at a special site, as opposed to at one of the crowded testing centers where kids normally take the ACT or the SAT in one sitting. Separating kids out from the herd allowed Singer and his cohorts to work in the shadows—the shadows he himself had devised—and orchestrate fraud undetected. He would tell one parent, "It's the home run of home runs." Some of his students had already been granted accommodations at their high school, having been tested in the past for learning disabilities. These kids were almost always granted extra time on the SAT or ACT when they applied for it, seeing as they had proven documentation of a learning issue. But sometimes, Singer told parents whose children had no such history to request extra time, by having a neuropsychologist evaluate them—he would offer to let them use doctors he relied on, who would play along and say the student had issues—and write a report saying they had ADHD, for instance. In one case, he instructed Gordon Caplan, then the co-chairman of the white-shoe Manhattan law firm Willkie Farr & Gallagher, to have his daughter see a neuropsychologist and to tell the girl to go in and "be stupid."

"The goal is to be slow," he added, "to be not as bright."

Once extra time had been granted, Singer would instruct families to arrange to have their child take the test at one of his sites. As he explained to Caplan: "So here's the first thing we need to do. We need to get your daughter tested for a learning difference. Here's why. If she gets tested for a learning difference, and let's say it's my person that does it, or whoever you want to do it, I need that person to get her one hundred percent extended time over multiple days.

"So what that means is, we'll have to show that there's some discrepancies in her learning, which there's gotta be anyways. And if she gets one hundred percent...then, I own two schools. I can have her test at one of my schools, and I can guarantee her a score. If it's ACT, I can guarantee her a score in the thirties. And if it's the SAT, I can guarantee her a score in the fourteen hundreds. Now, all of a sudden, her test score does not become an issue with all the colleges. Because she's strong enough."

But, Singer emphasized, "You gotta get the extended time first."

Caplan admitted to paying Singer $75,000 to help his daughter ace the ACT.

❦

The concept of "extended time," and the number of kids both at private and public schools who receive it, has exploded in recent years. According to a *Wall Street Journal* survey, the number of students with a so-called 504 plan more than tripled between 2000 and 2016. Named after a section of the Rehabilitation Act of 1973, 504s—which are federally funded—are granted to students at public schools who have learning disabilities, offering them things like extra time on tests, front-row seating in a classroom, and, in some cases, the ability to take tests orally as opposed to in writing. These students can also qualify for an individualized educational plan (IEP), which provides services, such as specialized instruction, that are not covered under a 504. At private schools, there is no public data on how many kids receive accommodations, but anecdotal evidence suggests that the trend is similar, if not more extreme.

"It's so common," independent college counselor Jen Kaifesh told me. "And in the last couple of years, it's gotten insane. At a couple schools on the west side [of Los Angeles], I don't have a single kid that doesn't have extended time." She said in some cases, there are legitimate learning disabilities, such as dyslexia, but she's also seen parents say their children suffer from more gray-area afflictions, such as anxiety and OCD. "I've even seen eating disorders play into it, depression," she said. "It's always tough because when people say, 'My kid has test-taking anxiety,' okay, I know this is a legitimate thing, but also, who doesn't on some level?"

The dramatic uptick in accommodations cases has been driven by the anxiety surrounding college admissions, as families see a way to gain a leg up and take advantage of a system that is fairly easy to game. It's no secret that once students receive accommodations at their high school, they almost always receive them for standardized tests. "There are exceptions," the ACT told the *Washington Post* in 2019, when a student who has accommodations at high school doesn't qualify for them for the ACT. "But they are rare."

They're even rarer for SAT test takers. Starting in 2017, the College Board, which administers the SAT, stopped making its own assessment of a student and now simply relies on a high school's designation. Kids who receive accommodations at their high school, and use them, automatically get extra time to take the SAT. This has led to a huge number of students being "grandfathered in" to getting extra time on the SAT, said Oren Boxer, a clinical neuropsychologist in LA, who tests children and adolescents for learning disabilities. The College Board saw accommodation requests jump 200 percent from the 2010–11 school year to the 2017–18 school year.

Boxer said he sees his share of families who state expressly that they're interested in accommodations for their child, and he often has to disappoint them. "Sometimes, I'll stop it on the phone," he said. "If a family says, 'Well, my child's really anxious. They have test anxiety. Can we do some testing to verify that, and can I get her accommodations?' I typically say, 'That's really hard to prove. Especially if your child isn't in therapy, isn't being followed by a psychiatrist, and teachers aren't seeing it.' I'll say, 'You may be wasting your money with me if you come in and do this, because we may get to the end and there won't be anything to support that recommendation.'"

Boxer has even seen kids try to cheat on the exam he gives to test for learning disabilities, pretending not to understand things. In some cases, if families don't wind up with the recommendation they've been hoping for, they find another doctor to do the assessment.

Kathy Pelzer, a former public-school counselor in a well-to-do area of Southern California, said the craze for accommodations in high school is absolutely driven by students (and their parents) who are "positioning themselves to get extra time on the SAT or ACT." She said that when she left high school counseling in 2010 to work as a licensed therapist, there were very few kids who had

504s at her school, Capistrano Valley High School. Yet when she returned five years later, the landscape had completely changed. "I couldn't believe the numbers of kids on 504s," she said. "I was asking a lot of the counselors I was working with [what had happened], and they said, 'Oh, it's because they want to get extra time on the SAT.' It was pretty much out of control."

At both private and public schools, receiving accommodations generally comes down to money. Just getting tested by a neuropsychologist can cost thousands of dollars. Boxer, whose offices are in two of the wealthiest enclaves in LA—Pasadena and the Pacific Palisades—charges $7,500 for his two-day exam. Some neuropsychologists charge as much as $10,000.

At private schools, obtaining a report from someone like Boxer is often all that's required to qualify a student for accommodations, making the process far simpler than at public schools. "At a private school, all you need is money and someone willing to say, 'Oh, sure. Your kid has anxiety,'" said Gina Kornfeind, a pediatric social worker at UCLA who has a daughter with a learning disability who received accommodations at a private high school. "Kids at private schools are at full advantage."

A college counselor at a private high school echoed this, adding that part of why the process is so seamless is that parents have tremendous influence at institutions where they're shelling out $40,000 a year. "If you're the school psychologist and you say no to an affluent family who's gone out and gotten an independent assessment from a neuropsych? They're going to ask for you to be fired. They're gonna say, 'How dare you? This person should be gone.' So we've created a culture where now most people are going to get extended time," this counselor said. "From top to bottom, I'd say the system is broken."

At public schools, students must prove that a "major life

activity" has been impacted by their disability, meaning that it's harder to get a 504 because a kid is suddenly getting Cs and claims to be stressed-out, said Pelzer. Unlike at private schools, there are layers of approvals and conversations that must take place—with teachers, school principals, and counselors—before an accommodations plan is put in place. But even so, families with means can get their way. And if a family requests accommodations but is denied, they can hire lawyers to appeal the decision, an ugly battle that few schools want to fight. "It happens at a lot of districts: Schools will just say, 'Let's give it to them.' They don't want to deal with a fight. They don't want to deal with parents," said Pelzer. "That's where the problems start happening."

The role of money in obtaining accommodations is made clear in data, which is available only for public schools. According to the *Wall Street Journal* survey that showed the number of 504 plans doubling, the majority of the increases were in wealthy areas of the country. In Los Angeles County, the school with the highest number of 504s is Palisades Charter High School, a.k.a. Pali High, which is located in the Pacific Palisades. Residents include Steven Spielberg and J. J. Abrams, and the median home price is $2.4 million. Situated on a hill overlooking the ocean, with a sparkling aquatic center, Pali High is 52 percent white. Fewer than 30 percent of its students qualify for free or reduced-price lunch. Compare this to El Monte High School, on the other side of the city, where almost 85 percent of the students are Latino or Hispanic. More than 95 percent of students there qualify for free or reduced-price lunch. At Pali High, 8.5 percent of students have a 504. At El Monte, only 0.1 percent do, as a report in the news site *LAist* pointed out.

"It's unfortunate," says Boxer, "because so many kids in public schools [who are not in affluent areas] are just missed, because, first of all, the parents just don't have the education or the information to know that these services are available."

❧

In the fall of 2018, the buzz around Brentwood School was that Jack Buckingham, who was now a senior, had gotten "amazing" accommodations for the ACT. Jack told friends that he'd taken the ACT over the summer at his house, where his *mother* had proctored him. He said he could barely believe it himself, and now kids were asking their college counselors if they'd be able to get such an awesome arrangement. "Jack got this and this and this," they were saying. The buzz even reached parents at the school. Said one: "I thought that sounded weird, but then again Jane is someone who can figure out ways to do things." That parent shrugged it off.

Jack, who was not charged in the Varsity Blues scandal, had been granted extra time to take the ACT before he started working with Rick Singer, as he had already received accommodations at his high school for his learning disabilities. But the very unorthodox scenario in which he took the test at home had been orchestrated by Singer, not long after he sent Jane Buckingham into panic mode, saying that her son wasn't going to be able to get into any colleges. After then tossing out his lifeline—"I can get his ACT score up"—he was at first vague about how, exactly, he could do that. But Buckingham was in such a state of despair over her divorce that she preferred it to remain fuzzy. Deep down, she knew that whatever Singer was proposing was completely unethical, but in her mind, the less she understood, the better.

Here was a solution to a problem, and Buckingham had always prided herself in being a problem solver.

The scheme revolved around Jack's need to retake the ACT, which Singer had said was necessary to do before his senior year started. But he had also said the ACT wasn't offered in LA over the summer, so Jack would need to take it in Houston, at Niki Williams's high school. That was fine for Buckingham. They had family friends there and could combine a trip to visit them with taking the ACT. By early July, Singer was more explicit about how all this would go down. In a phone call, he said that she and Jack would meet Williams in front of the high school at eight in the morning; then they'd walk across the street to take the test at another location, because the school was being remodeled.

"Okay," Buckingham kept saying on the phone. "Okay."

Singer told her they'd then meet Mark Riddell in a classroom. "Niki will take care of the rest," he said.

"Amazing," Buckingham said. "And is it okay if he takes it all in one day?" (Jack had been granted two through his accommodations.)

Singer said yes, because Riddell was flying in from Florida only for the day, but that they'd tell the ACT Jack had taken it over two days.

"Got it, got it," Buckingham said.

But a few weeks later, there was a problem. Jack had been scheduled to have sinus surgery after he returned. But a few days before he was set to go to Houston, he'd come down with an infection, and the doctor said the surgery had to be delayed. The doctor also said that Jack couldn't fly. Buckingham panicked. No, Jack had to be on a plane, had to be in Houston that weekend, she told the doctor. Making matters worse, Marcus was already annoyed over the surgery, which he deemed "elective" and which coincided with a vacation he was taking in Europe. He'd already agreed to come home early for the surgery. Moving the dates around would only cause more acrimony with her ex.

Determined to find a win-win in the mess, she asked Singer over the phone: "So my question is, there is no way for [Jack] to not go [to Houston] and it still to be done, I assume?"

She then offered her own solution: "Can you give me a test for him to take at home that we proctor him, that I proctor him?"

"Okay, yeah, I guess we could do something like that," Singer said, but he added that he'd have to run it by Williams.

Later that day, he called Buckingham back and said it was a go. Williams had told him she would send her a copy of the ACT for Jack to take. Singer told Buckingham that Williams had called the plan "crazy," but that he'd assured her that he'd been "doing this forever."

"Yeah. I know this is craziness, I know it is," Buckingham said. "And then I need you to get him into USC, and then I need you to cure cancer and [make peace] in the Middle East."

"I can do that," Singer joked back. "I can do that if you can figure out a way to boot your husband out so that he treats you well..."

"That's impossible, that's impossible," she said. "But, you know, peace in the Middle East. You know, Harvard, the rest of it. I have faith in you."

The next day, he asked Buckingham for a sample of Jack's handwriting, so that Riddell could match it on the ACT. Seeing as Jack had taken the test twice before, the handwriting would need to look the same.

On July 14, Riddell took the ACT in a hotel room in Houston. He earned Jack a 35 out of 36, raising his score by five points and landing him in the ninety-ninth percentile. Three days later, Jack took an ACT practice test at his house, while his mother stood by.

He believed he was taking an actual test. Buckingham even took a video of him on her iPhone answering questions, so that it seemed entirely legitimate, and then sent the completed test to Singer.

Sources close to Buckingham said she had no idea Riddell had taken another test in Houston, and that she thought Singer or one of his employees would correct the answers on Jack's test and then send it to the ACT. She knew it was wrong and unethical, but she was also trying hard not to think too much about it; trying to keep the details vague and not ask too many questions. More than anything, she wanted to help her son. Her main thought was: "If there's something I can do, I should do it." Worst-case scenario, the ACT would find out that Jack's score hadn't been legitimately achieved, and they'd toss it out—end of story.

When Singer said that Buckingham needed to donate $50,000 to his charity in exchange for his services, she similarly didn't investigate, and justified it in pay-it-forward terms. She'd done something bad, and now she was going to put money toward something good: all those playgrounds Singer said he was building all over the country. It was the same as when she gave a speech and took the payment and donated it to a charity, or when her kids misbehaved and she made them go spend some time volunteering at one of the many nonprofits she was involved in. In her mind, paying the $50,000 (tax-deductible, as Singer informed her) was putting good out in the world to compensate for what she'd done.

✌§

Six months before Jack Buckingham took his at-home ACT, Felicity Huffman was driving her oldest daughter, Sophia, to West Hollywood College Preparatory School to take the SAT. It was a twenty-minute drive from their home, and Sophia was seated next to Huffman in the car. Like most teenagers, Sophia was nervous about taking the test. She asked her mom if, after she was done, they could go out for ice cream.

Huffman tried to assure her daughter that everything would be fine, but her mind was elsewhere. As she steered the car down the winding canyon roads, she was plagued by the thought that she was doing something very wrong.

Turn the car around, she told herself, according to a letter she wrote to the judge. *Turn the car around. Just turn it around.*

Huffman drove on.

Eventually, she pulled up at the drab beige-colored building at the corner of Fountain Avenue and Crescent Heights Boulevard. The school, which looked more like a concrete block that shared space with a synagogue, was less than a mile from the Sunset Strip and glamorous hangouts like the Chateau Marmont. But there was nothing glamorous about the prep school, which advertised itself by way of a large white sign leaning against one of its walls, with the school's phone number written in large blue print.

Waiting inside the building was Mark Riddell, who'd flown in from Tampa the night before to proctor Sophia's test. He would receive $10,000 for the job. Sophia had no clue he was not a legitimate proctor and that, by the time she and her mother were having ice cream, he'd be correcting her answers and then handing the test over to Igor Dvorskiy, who would send it in to the ACT. Aside from the weird, desolate building, everything seemed normal.

Huffman was now formally entering into Rick Singer's side-door scheme—but only after months of deliberation. When Singer had first proposed cheating on the SAT at the meeting at her home in August of 2017, Huffman had dutifully taken notes on what he said, but that was it. As he described how he could "level the playing field" for Sophia, Huffman typed into her laptop: "Control the outcome of the SAT—15 grand—get a proctor in the room with her and she gets the answer she needs to get. At the end of the test—the proctor is making sure. 75 grand guy will make the scores perfect." Singer had assured Huffman that he had done this with many other families.

He had also said that if Sophia's scores went up too much— she'd already taken the PSAT and gotten around 1000 of 1600—it would arouse suspicion with the College Board. Huffman wrote: "If we start taking it multiple time—college board will only allow you a certain amount of increase—between tests—they would investigate you." As per this logic, he said that it would be better for Huffman's younger daughter, Georgia, to skip the PSAT altogether and go straight to having Singer set up an SAT for her. "If we decide to do it—don't do PSAT—just do SAT in October," Huffman wrote. Singer's final point, one that he insisted on, was that Sophia needed to get 100 percent extended time on the SAT so that she could purportedly take it over two days at a site that he controlled.

Huffman would write to a judge that after listening to Singer, "I was shocked that such a thing existed. And after he made the initial suggestion, it remained on the table. I couldn't make up my mind for six weeks. I kept going back and forth while avoiding a final decision."

Sophia had been seeing a neuropsychologist for her learning disabilities since she was eight and was retested every three years, as is recommended, in order to continue obtaining accommodations at school. In fact, Huffman had taken Sophia to be retested earlier that year, in June, and she had requalified for extra time.

A few days after meeting with Singer, Huffman called up Sophia's neuropsychologist and told the doctor to contact the College Board to make sure that Sophia would receive extended time on the SAT. She still wasn't committed to Singer's plan; she wanted to make sure Sophia had extra time on the test whether or not he was involved. In fact, at that point, the only thing Huffman had agreed to do, based on Singer's advice, was to hire a new math tutor for Sophia.

The mental and moral dilemma that Huffman was experiencing is brought to light in her letter. "I honestly didn't and don't care about my daughter going to a prestigious college," Huffman wrote. "I just wanted to give her a shot at being considered for a program where her acting talent would be the deciding factor...In my mind I knew that her success or failure in theater or film wouldn't depend on her math skills. I didn't want my daughter to be prevented from getting a shot at auditioning and doing what she loves because she can't do math." All she wanted to do, she said, was give her daughter "a fair shot."

Sophia still had her heart set on Juilliard. But she would be applying to other schools as well, and Huffman was concerned that a bad SAT score would hurt her chances of getting in to those universities, that her shot would be taken away.

Huffman was weighing all of this when, in October, the College Board notified Sophia that she had been approved for 100 percent extra time on the SAT. Huffman forwarded the email with this news on to Singer and a counselor at the Los Angeles County High School for the Arts.

"Hurray! She got it," Huffman wrote.

When the high school counselor wrote Huffman back, she said that Sophia could take the SAT over two days in December at LACHSA and that the counselor would proctor the test. Huffman then forwarded that email to Singer, adding: "Ruh Ro! Looks like LACHSA wants to provide own proctor."

Singer responded: "We will speak about it."

According to her legal defense, Huffman was still confused as to what she should do. And so she called Singer up to discuss the options: Should Sophia take the test on her own with the extended time she'd been granted, or should he orchestrate things to ensure a good score? But there was no discussion to be had. Singer repeated his fear-mongering themes. The work Sophia had been doing on test prep wasn't enough, he said, even with the extended time. She was going to be rejected by schools unless Huffman relied on him.

Accustomed to relying on experts, especially in the perplexing world of parenting, and so fearful of Sophia having her dreams dashed, Huffman made her choice. Later in the day, Singer emailed, asking: "Are we doing this on our own or with my help?"

"With your help," Huffman replied.

CHAPTER 11

Moss Baby

On April 12, 2018, a very perturbed Mossimo Giannulli strode onto the Marymount High School campus, where his youngest daughter, Olivia, was a senior. He wanted to have a word with her college counselor, Philip "PJ" Petrone, who had raised questions about Olivia's application to USC in a conversation with an admissions officer there. Giannulli, who'd struck a $28 million licensing deal with Target for his eponymous line of casual wear, wasn't a typical Marymount parent, nor was his wife, actress Lori Loughlin. Perennially tanned and dressed in crisp, colorful button-downs and Italian footwear (sans socks), Giannulli stood out at Marymount, whose celebrity quotient was low for an LA private school. Not that the Giannullis were a major presence there. They were rarely spotted at its popular events, like the father-daughter dance or the annual barbecue, but they were big donors to the school and their name showed up in Marymount's annual reports.

But news of the phone call with USC warranted an appearance. During Petrone's routine check-in call about Marymount applicants to USC in March, the university admissions officer had mentioned that Olivia had been "flagged" as a walk-on recruit to

USC's women's rowing team. Petrone was confused. Olivia was a famed YouTube and Instagram influencer known as Olivia Jade, with over 1.4 million followers; her "video vlogging schedule," as he would write in his notes, kept her busy. Olivia herself, who was known to her friends at Marymount as OG—a nod to the slang term *original gangster*, as well as her actual initials—admitted this to fans in one video post. "I'm also, literally, never at school" to the point "that I think my class . . . maybe they forget I go there," she said distractedly as she applied beauty cream to her flawless cheeks.

PJ Petrone was slightly built and preppy, with wavy dark hair that fell to his shoulders. Marymount parents thought of him as a "family man." He was known for helping students find "the right fit" in a college, as opposed to a big name; he might suggest that a student apply to Sarah Lawrence or Reed instead of Boston College or Penn. He had a reserved demeanor and would never outright tell parents or students that he disagreed with their choices, but he would calmly walk them through his thought process, like a parent soothingly explaining to a toddler why Pop-Tarts were actually not the best choice for dinner. "He would check your expectations," said Gabby Johnson, who graduated from Marymount in 2014. "If a student came in saying, 'I want to go to this school,'" and it was an obvious reach, "he'd be honest or try to be realistic. He was nice about it, but also kind of stern."

Given the demands of Olivia's internet gig, Petrone was doubtful that she did crew. Marymount, after all, was an incredibly small community, where "everyone knows who's doing what," according to one former Marymount parent. "Everyone knows what kid is doing equestrian on the side," that parent said. Although Marymount did not have an official crew team, if enough girls were interested in the sport in a particular year, the school would drum up an ad hoc team to represent Marymount at races.

People at Marymount also knew which girls rowed for private clubs, as it was a serious commitment that often meant showing up for morning classes after practicing at dawn. On the call with USC, the admissions officer then brought up Olivia's older sister, Isabella, who had been admitted to USC a year earlier as a crew recruit. Petrone told the officer that that there might be some connection with the outside college counselor that the Giannullis had been working with. The USC admissions officer said they would look into it with the athletics department.

That outside counselor was, of course, Rick Singer, who was notorious among Marymount's college counseling staff, and not just for inaccuracies that were popping up on applications. Students at Marymount who used him rarely met with their high school counselors, as he had instructed them. "They took the whole process outside," one source said. And when the school counselors, who are required to write recommendations for students, gave the students surveys to fill out so that they could be more informed about them, "Singer's kids would fill out five of the fifty questions," the source said.

Singer kids, who were predominantly from überwealthy families ("the private-airplane crowd," noted one parent), were also known for not showing up or being sick on the days they had a class called Human Development. The class met every two weeks and part of its curriculum was to walk students through the college application process and standardized testing. The class also discussed things like stress management, "emotional awareness," and "practicing self-compassion," according to the Marymount website. On the days Singer's students did attend, they'd often put their feet up on their desks or otherwise make their disinterest clear.

A month after Petrone's check-in call with USC, on April 11, the admissions officer called back and asked for the name of the independent college counselor that the Giannullis were working with. Petrone said his name was Rick Singer. The admissions officer started to connect the dots, and said that another client of Singer's who had applied from the Bay Area had submitted false athletic credentials, for a sport the student didn't play.

The next day, Giannulli—who goes by Moss—arrived at Marymount to confront Petrone. Despite its Bel-Air address, Marymount, which is an all-girls Catholic school, has a low-key vibe. Its old Mission-style buildings are a far cry from the state-of-the-art facilities at Buckley or Brentwood School, and in lieu of a valet parking attendant out front, there is a statue of a robed Jesus opening his arms to welcome a student body that is a mix of affluent locals and scholarship students who commute long stretches from less monied areas of the city and its outskirts. For a private school, Marymount is decidedly normal and down-to-earth. This culture, combined with its less cutthroat academic reputation, can be met with eye-rolling condescension in LA parenting circles. One mother disdainfully dismissed the school as a "distant third" behind its all-girls rivals Marlborough and the Archer School. But Marymount parents generally seek the school exactly because of its indifference to social standing. "Marymount's culture is, 'Oh, your mother's on a TV show? Big fucking deal,'" said Ross Johnson, a crisis management publicist whose two daughters (including Gabby) attended the school. "There's no velvet rope or greenroom or Hollywood bullshit hierarchy. You can't buy status at the school."

This made Marymount an odd place for Bella and Olivia to enroll after completing middle school at Marlborough, other than the fact that the school was less of an academic grind and was right next to their home—literally. The Giannullis' $28 million Mediterranean-style mansion abutted Marymount's parking lot. The home was also adjacent to the Bel-Air Country Club, and the

Giannullis would often take a golf cart over to the exclusive club. Fellow club members teeing off at sunset could spot the cardinal-and-gold USC flag that proudly flew on the family's property.

Petrone was sitting in his office when he received a call from the front desk that Giannulli wanted to speak with him. Petrone hadn't seen Giannulli since two years earlier, when he'd had his first meeting with the Giannullis to discuss Olivia's college plans. As he walked downstairs to greet him, he guessed Giannulli's sudden appearance on campus had something to do with the call with USC the day before. His suspicion was confirmed when Petrone casually asked, as they made their way back to his office, if Giannulli had walked or driven over to Marymount that day.

"What does it matter?" Giannulli said curtly.

When Petrone said he was just trying to make small talk, Giannulli shot back: "Let's not."

❧

Despite the flag that fluttered above his home, Mossimo Giannulli hadn't graduated from USC. In fact, he'd never even enrolled. But in the mid-eighties, he took a few classes there and joined the Beta Theta Pi fraternity, where he stood out as being more fashionably dressed than his shorts-and-flip-flop-wearing frat brothers. "He always looked like he was trying to be Valentino," said one of his former frat brothers. Giannulli's sense of style extended to interior design: One day, he decided to redecorate his room in the frat house in white tiles, so that it had a Studio 54 vibe. "He was all about image," said the source. "He drove around in this VW dune-buggy thing that had a striped top. He definitely liked attention." He was unique in other ways, too. While his peers were busy concocting elaborate pledge pranks (such as dumping a load of manure on the frat house from a helicopter) or doing keg hand-stands on the lawn, Giannulli used the money his dad was sending him for tuition to plant the seeds for his future clothing empire. "He made sweatshirts for the girls' sororities and brought back those neon colors," the former frat brother said. "He did interest-ing graphics draped all around, rather than just on the front. All the girls loved them and bought them. He started selling them to other colleges, and that kind of jump-started his business."

But his time at USC came to an end when members of the frat found out he wasn't technically a USC student and kicked him out of the house. Giannulli's stint as a faux Trojan was over.

His relationship with USC might have been tangential, but he'd always had "a passion" for the school, according to a source close to him. That passion went into overdrive when it was time for his daughters to apply to college. As for Lori Loughlin, sources say she wasn't in any way obsessed with where her daughters would go to school and admitted to not knowing much about the college landscape. But she "wanted them to have the college experience," according to one source. She herself had never attended college, having had a TV career in place by the time she was sixteen, as a regular on the soap opera *The Edge of Night*. At twenty-four, she was cast in the long-running sitcom *Full House*, cementing her image in American culture as the Olsen twins' sweet and squeaky-clean aunt Becky. Both Olivia and Bella had followed in their mother's showbiz footsteps to varying degrees. Bella had dabbled in acting, and Olivia was a celebrity in her own right, albeit in the context of twenty-first-century stardom. A doe-eyed brunette with a strain of celebrity-kid world weariness, she reportedly made between $10,000 and $15,000 for video posts of her packing for a trip or applying makeup before going out, thanks to sponsorship deals with beauty brands like Sephora. Loughlin was close with her daughters and seemed to revel in having them as red-carpet sidekicks. In one of Olivia's videos, she and her mother appear sitting together on the edge of a bed, giggling like schoolgirls as Olivia quizzes her on contemporary slang terms like *fire* and *thot*. "'Thot'?" Loughlin says in exaggerated disbelief. "I *thot* I knew that one!" At one point, she turns to her daughter and congratulates her on "all [her] success."

By the time Giannulli was sitting down with Petrone, their older daughter was already enrolled at USC, thanks to Singer, whom the family had hired in order to get "her into a school other than ASU," as Giannulli had remarked in disgust. Singer had packaged Bella as a crew recruit after telling the Giannullis that Bella's academic qualifications were at or "just below" USC's admissions standards—in other words, that without his help and scheming, she was never getting in. He failed to remind them that they had their own connections at USC and presumably could have used them to help get their daughters in, not to mention that Giannulli was often contacted by development officers—who didn't seem to care that he wasn't technically an alum—looking for donations. Instead, Singer told them that their only option was the side-door track. Giannulli and Loughlin ultimately agreed to the plan, and in September 2016, when Singer instructed them to send him a photo of Bella on a rowing machine "in workout clothes like a real athlete" so that he could create a "coxswain portfolio for her," Giannulli complied. Coxswains, who are generally petite, do not row, but they sit in the stern of the boat and steer, as well as guide rowers through workouts and races.

Singer had long been pushing crew as an entrance ticket to colleges, even to families he worked with legitimately. The sport, especially for women, had exploded in the 1990s on college campuses, thanks to Title IX's requirement that the number of women's athletic scholarships equal that of men's. For schools looking to balance their football team numbers (programs are allowed eighty-five scholarships annually) with those of women's sports, crew was seen as the great equalizer. A large Division I women's crew team could have over forty-seven members, and to qualify, all that was required was endurance and strength; a high school soccer player or track star could be turned into a skilled rower in six months. (Coxswains didn't even need athletic ability; they just had to be small enough to squeeze into the front of a boat.) "A lot of walk-ons do really well who have high-level backgrounds in other sports, but are not good enough to compete in those sports at the collegiate level," said Montana Butsch, founder of the Chicago Training Center, which offers free rowing instruction to inner-city youth. "A really good high school volley-ball player might not make the college team, but because they're tall and fit and are willing to grind, they're teachable. In eighteen months they could turn around and be a really good rower."

This phenomenon, combined with Title IX, opened up the floodgates for women's rowing walk-ons. In 1990, there were 305 female rowers at twelve US colleges, most of them on some form of scholarship, according to an NCAA report. In 2018, that number jumped to 7,277 female rowing slots at 145 schools.

Singer was early to realize this, and he brought it up to the families he worked with. Eric Webb, an advertising executive in Peoria, Illinois, said that when Singer was helping his daughter—who was a competitive cheerleader and gymnast—on her college applications, he asked her: "Do you have any interest in rowing? Because that can help you get into schools where grades alone, and your brand alone, might not be able to get you in." The comment prompted Webb to go out and buy an erg for his daughter to prac-tice on, but in the end she applied to colleges as a regular student.

In the photo that Giannulli sent to Singer, Bella is wearing a gray T-shirt and black Nikes, pulling on the erg in a bare room filled with workout equipment. Singer forwarded the photo to Laura Janke, who created a fake athletic profile that said Bella was a coxswain for MAC Rowing, a team in LA, that she'd rowed in the famed Head of the Charles Regatta, and that she had taken home a gold medal at the San Diego Crew Classic. On the side, Bella was purportedly the captain and starting midfielder for a club soccer team, as well as a member of Marymount's soccer team. All of this was patently false.

Singer sent another email to Janke, saying, "Donna asked for a picture of [Bella] in a boat. Is there a coxswain photo we can use that is tough to see the face?"

On October 27, Donna Heinel presented Bella as a rowing recruit, and she was conditionally approved for acceptance. Two days later, Singer emailed Giannulli: "Please send $50K payment to the person below[:] Donna Heinel, Senior Womens Associate Athletic Director[,] c/o of USC Athletics." Giannulli wrote back that he'd have his business manager FedEx the check. He also asked if it was okay to discuss Isabella's conditional acceptance with USC athletic director Pat Haden, whom he knew and would be going with to Augusta, Georgia, in a couple weeks for the Masters golf tournament. "Best to keep [Haden] out of it," Singer wrote back. "When I met with him a year ago about [Bella] he felt you were good for a million plus."

Giannulli replied: "HAH!!"

Meanwhile, Giannulli was rebuffing assistance from a USC development officer, who had emailed him around this time offering to set up a "1:1 opportunity for [Bella], customized tour of campus for the family, and/or classroom visit." The development officer added, "I'd also be happy to flag her application."

"Thanks so much, I think we are squared away," Giannulli replied. He then forwarded the email to Loughlin, writing: "The nicest I've been at blowing off somebody."

In the spring of 2017, when Bella was formally accepted to USC— causing her Marymount peers to raise eyebrows and assume her parents' connections were at play—bookkeeper Steven Masera sent Giannulli an invoice from the Key Worldwide Foundation for $200,000. The money was wired, and Giannulli received a statement saying "no goods or services were exchanged." (Earlier, he had asked, "For accounting purposes would I categorize this as a donation?" Singer had replied, "Yes.") He then wrote a grateful email to Singer, cc'ing Loughlin, with the subject line "Trojan happiness." He wrote another email to his accountant, forwarding the $200,000 invoice. "Good news my daughter…is in SC," Giannulli wrote. "Bad [news] is I had to work the system."

According to documents submitted by Giannulli and Loughlin's attorneys after they were charged, the couple believed that Singer was facilitating a "legitimate" donation to USC women's athletics. In other words, they were paying to play (i.e., working the system) at a university where that practice was common, but not in a way that was any different from donating a library wing in order to ease a student's admittance to a school. After all, they had been making sizable donations to schools ever since their children were little, and were accustomed to being straight-out asked for money. Was this really any different? They believed that the $50,000 check that Singer had them write to USC was, in fact, going to USC, and not to Donna Heinel or a rogue coach. As for the $200,000, they initially stated that this also was a donation in exchange for services—even better, it was for a charity—but not a bribe to pay anyone off. "At trial," wrote their attorney Sean Berkowitz, who led the Department of Justice prosecution of Enron executives,

"Giannulli and Loughlin will help establish their innocence by showing that they understood both sets of payments to be legitimate donations and did not understand or intend that either sets of payments would be used to directly or indirectly bribe Heinel."

(Despite these initial denials about being involved in the college admissions scandal, and their initial not-guilty pleas, in May of 2020 the Giannullis changed their stance. Loughlin pled guilty to conspiracy to commit wire and mail fraud. Giannulli pled guilty to conspiracy to commit wire and family fraud, and honest services wire and mail fraud.)

When it came time for their youngest daughter, Olivia, to apply to college, the Giannullis pursued the same side-door crew route at USC. "Yes USC for [Olivia]!" Loughlin exuberantly emailed Singer when he asked the couple if they wanted to repeat the steps.

The decision seems to have been made solely by her parents— Olivia had openly told her fans that she had no interest in college, and she certainly didn't need a degree for professional success, having already achieved it with her internet business. Nonetheless, Singer whipped up an athletic profile, presenting her as an accomplished coxswain who'd competed in the Head of the Charles, the San Diego Crew Classic, and the USRowing Southwest Regional Junior Championships, where she was purportedly awarded bronze and silver medals. Meanwhile, despite her protestations about college, her parents got Olivia, too, to pose on an ergometer. In the photo, which Giannulli sent to Singer to use for the profile, Olivia is fashionably dressed, wearing trendy leggings and a white tank top as she balances on the erg.

After Heinel presented her athletic profile to the athletic admissions subcommittee in November of 2017, Olivia got the green light. When Singer alerted the Giannullis via email, Loughlin wrote back, "This is wonderful news!" along with a high-five emoji.

Singer wrote back: "Please continue to keep hush hush till March."

"Yes of course," Loughlin responded.

But even if the Giannullis weren't talking, suspicion was being raised at Marymount. It was around this time that PJ Petrone had the call with USC admissions and was told that Olivia had been flagged as a crew recruit. He then questioned Olivia about it, and asked her about her sister's crew credentials. Word got back to Loughlin, who once referred to Petrone as "our little friend" at Marymount in an email to Singer. She also texted Olivia, warning her that telling Petrone that USC was her first choice might be "a flag for the weasel to meddle" and to not "say too much to that man." Giannulli added: "Fuck him," and remarked that Petrone was a "nosy bastard."

As Giannulli walked into Petrone's office—a light and airy room with a New Englandy nautical vibe, in keeping with Marymount's Sailor mascot—he was visibly angry, according to notes that Petrone took down after the meeting. Accustomed to dealing with celebrity minions and yay-sayers and blasting through velvet ropes, Giannulli demanded to know what Petrone was telling USC about his daughters and why he was trying to ruin their opportunities there.

He then asked Petrone what he had said to USC about Bella the previous year. Petrone said he'd been told she was a crew recruit by USC, and that he'd said he had no knowledge of her being on a crew team but that he did not contest the decision. Giannulli then wanted to know if Petrone had said Bella wasn't a good admit for USC—she was thriving there, he added.

Petrone said he was happy to hear that, and that he'd never said she was a "bad candidate"—he just didn't know she did crew. By this point, Giannulli's voice had gotten so loud that the codirector of college counseling came by and shut the door to Petrone's office.

Giannulli then moved on to Olivia: What had Petrone said to USC? He worried that they would now rescind her admission. Petrone said he'd had a similar routine call with USC admissions a few weeks earlier: He had been told that Olivia had also been recruited for crew, and he said he didn't know she was a rower.

"She's a coxswain," Giannulli retorted, saying that she was on a private club team. (The club that Singer had come up with for Olivia, the LA Marina Club, does not exist.)

"I was unaware of that," Petrone said, and assured Giannulli that he would pass that information on to USC.

Giannulli then went into "an agitated stream of consciousness," saying how annoyed he'd been that Petrone hadn't been able to combine Bella's GPA from Marlborough with her GPA at Marymount. (Combining GPAs from separate schools is not standard practice; high schools that students attend send their transcripts to colleges separately.)

"I let that go," Giannulli said, "but I'm astounded that you endangered Olivia's admission to USC this year!

"She'd be crushed by this if she ever knew!" he went on. "Do you have any idea who Olivia *is*?"

Petrone said he was well aware of Oliva's YouTube channel and that if Giannulli could read the letter of recommendation he'd written on her behalf, he'd see that he'd portrayed her as a "guru in her field with a bright future" and that any school would be happy to have her.

Giannulli was unmoved. "I still don't get it," he said. "You're their college counselor. You're supposed to help them.

"I know lots of people," Giannulli pressed on, saying that he'd "delivered" some high-profile "admits" to USC that Petrone had been able to put on Marymount's profile. Why, Giannulli asked, would Petrone want to "negate that by talking to USC negatively about his daughters," the notes say.

Petrone said that he'd done no such thing. In fact, he thought to himself but didn't say out loud (because he didn't want things to escalate further) that *Singer* had put them in jeopardy by falsely presenting them as athletes.

"It's my job to ensure there is integrity in this process," Petrone said calmly, meaning the college admissions process. "I have my professional reputation, as well as that of Marymount, and of every past and future graduate on the line when I make a statement."

Giannulli listened and then asked: "What are you going to do now?"

Petrone said he would call up his contact at USC and tell them that Giannulli had told him that Olivia was a coxswain for a private club.

Seemingly satisfied, Giannulli stood up, shook Petrone's hand, and walked out.

Petrone relayed the encounter to Marymount's head of school, Jacqueline Landry, who then reached out to Giannulli to assure him that Marymount would not interfere with Olivia's application. Petrone also checked in with Marymount's head of athletics to see if there were any records of either of the Giannulli girls being rowers. There were none.

Later that day, Petrone offered even more assurance in an email to Giannulli: "I wanted to provide you with an update on the status of Olivia's admission offer to USC. First and foremost, they have <u>no</u> intention of rescinding [her] admission and were surprised to hear that was even a concern for you and your family. You can verify that with [the USC senior assistant director of admissions]...if you would like. I also shared with [the USC senior assistant director of admissions] that you had visited this morning and affirmed for me that Olivia is truly a coxswain."

Giannulli responded, cc'ing Loughlin: "Thank you very much." He then forwarded Petrone's email to Singer and another parent involved in Singer's scheme, writing, "Here we go..."

The next day, Giannulli texted Singer and the other parent, asking: "Any conversations?"

"All quiet," Singer replied.

But as waters were being calmed at Marymount, across town at USC, Donna Heinel was freaking out. She'd recently put out the fire over Matteo Sloane's water polo recruitment after Julie Taylor-Vaz, Buckley's director of college counseling, had called up admissions and questioned whether Sloane actually played the sport. Now here was another pesky high school counselor making waves. Having been alerted about the altercation between Giannulli and Petrone earlier that day, she left Singer a panicked voicemail: "I just want to make sure that, you know, I don't want the—the parents getting angry and creating any type of disturbance at the school. I just want to make sure those students...if questioned at the school that they respond in a[n] appropriate way that they are walk-on candidates for their respective sports. They're looking forward to trying out for the team and making the team when they get here. Okay? That's what I just want to make sure of.

"So," she added, "I just don't want anybody going into [Buckley] or [Marymount], you know, yelling at counselors. That'll shut everything—that'll shut everything down."

Donna Heinel had more reason than ever to be invested in Rick Singer's side-door system. He had recently started paying her $20,000 a month, a consulting retainer fee that prosecutors say was a sham. What it really was, they allege, was money in exchange for getting his clients' kids into USC as fake athletes. And the numbers were adding up. By 2018, Heinel had paved the way for over two dozen Singer "athletes" to enroll at USC, many of whom had never played the sports they were being recruited for; a few had even been falsely presented as athletes for high-profile teams like football (one as a long snapper) and men's basketball. This flood of kids was lining USC's coffers—between 2014 and 2018, Singer's clients paid more than $1.3 million to university accounts controlled by Heinel.

Meanwhile, water polo coach Jovan Vavic received a total of $250,000 from Singer in payments to a USC bank account that funded his teams. The prosecution alleges here, too, that the money was in exchange for getting Singer's clients into USC as water polo recruits. Singer explained to one parent that "What Jovan usually does is, I subsidize his staff salaries…I put two of his staff members on my books as contractors…And then I pay them throughout the year." It was a simple quid pro quo. "'Cause he's the guy giving up the spot [on the team]," Singer said. (Both Vavic and Heinel have pled not guilty and will fight these charges at trial.)

Heinel's value to Singer wasn't just as a facilitator, but as a fixer within USC's athletic department. She was someone he casually mentioned in conversation with clients, touting her as his sidekick gatekeeper to the school: "What happens is Donna tells me she's in, we're good," Singer told Napa Valley vintner Agustin Huneeus Jr., who has pled guilty to using the side door to get his daughter into USC. "And then she gets a letter from admissions, which'll say in there she's been admitted, conditionally admitted, she needs to do her NCAA clearinghouse, she needs to send her transcripts to the NC clearinghouse, blah, blah, blah, blah..." But Heinel was by now doing much more than just presenting fake athletes. When a member of the admissions department asked Heinel why the daughter of casino magnate Gamal Abdelaziz was a no-show at basketball workouts even though she'd been recruited for the team, Heinel claimed the girl had plantar fasciitis, saying she'd been injured over the summer and would be out for six to eight months. When another Singer applicant who was being packaged as a fake women's water polo recruit had an incomplete on her high school transcript, Heinel assured him she'd "white out" the incriminating detail. Abdelaziz has pled not guilty to charges against him. His attorney Brian Kelley wrote in a motion: "Although the government will certainly attempt to prove that Mr. Abdelaziz knew his donation was a bribe, Mr. Abdelaziz... 'was not told about the nature of the payments and did not infer the payments were corrupt from the circumstances.'"

At times, other Singer cohorts ran interference. When Singer set things in motion for Lauren Isackson, the daughter of Bay Area real estate mogul Bruce Isackson and his wife, Davina, to apply to USC as a soccer recruit, there was a snafu; her application wound up in the regular admissions pile, not Heinel's. This "clerical error" botched the plan, and so Singer instructed Khosroshahin— who was now coaching a junior club team in Orange County—to have the application sent to Jorge Salcedo, the men's soccer coach at UCLA, who had been brought into Singer's circle of rogue coaches. Salcedo then forwarded it on to the UCLA women's soccer coach and the application was presented to UCLA's student-athlete admissions committee. (Bruce and Davina Isackson, and Salcedo, have all pled guilty to charges.) Lauren, who had never played competitive soccer in high school—she was into horseback riding—was accepted, and Singer sent a check for $100,000 to a sports marketing company that Salcedo controlled. (Khosroshahin earned $25,000 for his liaison services.) UCLA mandates that all recruits play on the team for at least the first year, so Lauren was forced to practice for a season as a midfielder on the school's nationally ranked team. On her UCLA team web page, Lauren listed her "greatest athletic thrill" as "becoming the champion of her horseback riding division two years in a row."

Having missed out on Trojan happiness the first time, the Isacksons then arranged to have Singer get their younger daughter into USC as a rowing recruit, even though, like her sister, she was more of a horse person. "Another crew girl," he wrote to Heinel when he forwarded the girl's transcripts and test scores. The athletic profile that he concocted said she'd been a "varsity 8 stroke" for the Redwood Scullers in Northern California. The team does exist, but as its name suggests, it rows sculls, or two- or four-seat boats, not sweep boats, which have eight rowers— which anyone familiar with the sport would immediately know. The younger Isackson also took the ACT at the West Hollywood test center with Mark Riddell. In exchange for all this, Bruce Isackson transferred a total of over $600,000 in Facebook stock to Singer's charity.

Indeed, by 2018, Singer's empire of coaches was rapidly expanding. Khosroshahin had also introduced him to Bill Ferguson, USC's men's volleyball coach until 2015, when he moved on to Wake Forest University. When a Singer kid was wait-listed at the North Carolina school in 2017, Ferguson allegedly agreed to designate her as a volleyball recruit in exchange for $50,000 worth of payments from the Key Worldwide Foundation to athletic accounts at Wake Forest, and a $50,000 payment to a private volleyball camp that Ferguson ran. (Ferguson is fighting the charges.) And Singer had paid Michael Center, then the men's tennis coach at the University of Texas at Austin, $100,000—in a hotel parking lot—to get a wealthy client's son into UT as a tennis recruit. The boy withdrew from the team soon after he enrolled. His father made a donation to KWF of over $500,000 in stock. Center pled guilty and was sentenced to six months in prison.

Someone else Khosroshahin introduced Singer to was Rudy Meredith, the Yale women's soccer coach. Meredith was another beleaguered coach whose team had been suffering losses and who seemed disillusioned by his job. In 2017, Singer was introduced to a Chinese family that had recently moved to Southern California, through Qiuxue Yang, who worked for Brian Werdesheim at Oppenheimer. The family was looking for someone to help their daughter, Sherry Guo, apply to college. Guo's parents—who have not been identified—did not speak English and were naive as to how college admissions worked in the United States. Guo's lawyer, James Spertus, has said that Guo, who was a strong student and accomplished artist, had had her heart set on Oxford and Columbia, but Singer had pushed hard on Yale, saying he could guarantee her admission there. Another source said that Singer then frightened Guo by saying that she would never get into Oxford, and that he knew someone on the board of the school that would ensure that she was not accepted.

When the family conceded to Yale, Singer sent her résumé and personal statement on to Meredith, telling him that he would "revise" her portfolio—which showcased her artwork—to focus on "soccer." He then created a fake athletic profile and forwarded it on to the coach. After Meredith, who has pled guilty to charges against him, designated Guo as a soccer recruit—and facilitated her admission as an early decision applicant even though the deadline for applying early had passed—Singer sent him a check for $400,000. Guo's family paid him $1.2 million in several installments, marking his biggest side-door payday to date. Guo's attorney told the *New York Times*, "The amount alone shows that he was preying on the Chinese community. The donation was made to help underprivileged youth. [Guo's parents] were not aware that the money went to Meredith. They did not know that he was going to use that money for a bribe. There is no evidence of that whatsoever." Neither Guo nor her parents have been charged in the Varsity Blues scandal. In March of 2019, when the scandal broke, Yale rescinded the admission of Guo, who was enrolled there.

But Singer's biggest new gateway coach worked for a university he'd been trying desperately to infiltrate for years: Stanford. Since at least 2009, Singer had been trying to make inroads at the school, approaching seven coaches there about potential "recruits" to their sports. None of them bit until, in the fall of 2016, he called up Stanford's sailing coach, John Vandemoer, on his cell phone.

Long considered the Harvard of the West, Stanford's profile was burnished exponentially by the tech boom and the multiple start-up gods that it seemingly mass-produced, most famously Google cofounders Sergey Brin and Larry Page. To Californians, particularly the wealthy Northern Californians whom Singer was targeting, Stanford was better than Harvard. It was their own backyard Cambridge, which, besides bestowing a pedigree on its graduates, was considered a rocket ship to a job at Apple or an IPO-bound start-up. If Harvard and its Ivy peers were still very much about old money and connections and a job at Goldman Sachs, Stanford had a more modern, meritocratic sheen to it, which was hugely appealing to Silicon Valley's nouveau billionaires. The school's überselective admissions rate made it all the more of a brass ring.

Abby Falik, founder and CEO of Global Citizen Year, a nonprofit that places high school graduates who are taking a gap year before college in impoverished communities around the world, where they work on projects in health, the environment, and education, said that "the Stanford influence" is pervasive in the Bay Area. "I'll give presentations at Palo Alto High School, which is within sight of the Stanford campus, and my guess is that half of the kids at that school have a parent that went to Stanford, either undergrad or graduate. I'm making that number up, but that's my guess," she said. "But the people who are raising kids there—there's basically only one college in their sights or in their worldview."

In Silicon Valley, she said, "There's such a mafia of people who carry the Stanford degree"—Falik is one of them—"and it's opened up opportunities."

When Singer first contacted him, John Vandemoer was a preppy thirty-eight-year-old who had been sailing since he was a kid on Cape Cod. Groomed on the East Coast, he'd gone on to sail for St. George's School in Rhode Island and Hobart and William Smith Colleges in New York before turning to coaching, first as an assistant at St. Mary's College in Maryland and then as head coach at the US Naval Academy. Even his wife was a sailor; she competed in the 2012 Olympics.

Vandemoer was driving back from sailing practice when the college counselor called. The conversation was brief. Singer introduced himself and said he was interested in talking about recruiting athletes to Stanford's sailing program—Vandemoer coached both the men's and women's teams. He presented himself just like any recruiter would, and Vandemoer readily agreed to a meeting. (This narrative is based on interviews Vandemoer gave at the time of his sentencing, as well as conversations with sources close to him.)

The next day, Singer went to Stanford and sat down with the coach to talk in more detail. During the meeting, he played the part of the earnest and curious ingenue. There was nothing threatening or sinister about him as he told Vandemoer that he wanted to learn more about sailing and how recruiting for the sport worked. He'd connected student athletes with coaches in several other sports, but never in sailing. Would Vandemoer teach him more? He put the coach at ease, flattering him by making him feel like a valued expert. How could he not be charmed? As for money or payments, Singer never brought any of that up, but toward the end of the conversation he said he had a student he wanted Vandemoer to meet. (Vandemoer pled guilty to charges against him. He was sentenced to one day in prison, but it was deemed already served.)

The student in question was Yusi Zhao, the daughter of a Beijing-based billionaire in the pharmaceuticals industry whom Singer had been introduced to through Michael Wu, a financial advisor at a Los Angeles–area branch of Morgan Stanley. Singer had been working with the family on Yusi's applications to US universities. Wu has not been implicated in the scandal.

Although Yusi had no sailing experience, according to the prosecution in the Varsity Blues case, Singer asked Vandemoer if he would designate her as a recruit to his team. This wouldn't be hard, seeing as many sailing walk-ons had little to no experience. "The average walk-on you'll get is someone who sailed a Sunfish at camp one summer," said one college sailing coach. Vandemoer generally had six or seven recruitment slots on a team of about twenty-two each year, which meant he'd try to recruit closer to ten, seeing as not everyone would accept the offer. Singer said that in exchange for labeling Yusi as a recruit, her family would "endow" Vandemoer's team, specifically sailing coach salaries.

Singer added that he would be the "guarantor" to make sure the funds were paid. The offer was incredibly attractive, seeing as sailing wasn't overseen by the NCAA, meaning there was no central body through which high school sailors could connect with coaches, and no scholarships. Vandemoer accepted the offer. Neither Yusi nor her parents have been charged in the scandal.

The pitch was also appealing for another reason. Vandemoer was struggling to pay for basic necessities for his team, such as uniforms and boats, which can each cost between $8,000 and $10,000. Although Stanford's was a very well endowed collegiate sailing program, with an annual budget of over $200,000, according to a source, most of the regattas and events the school participated in were on the East Coast. Vandemoer spent $100,000 on plane tickets alone every year, leaving less funds for everything else. And Vandemoer had only one assistant coach, whereas Stanford's top competitors had two, crucial in order to participate in regattas that often took place in multiple locations over the course of a weekend.

The situation put the onus on Vandemoer to fundraise, something sources close to him say was not his strong suit. "All he ever wanted to do was coach his team," said one person. Stanford certainly had a deep bench of enthusiastic and generous alumni, and there were parents who would sometimes call Vandemoer up and say, "Hey, what do you need?" But in order to fund his team the way he wanted to, he needed more than just cold offers. He needed to hustle and work the phones, something he was loath to do.

When Vandemoer first arrived at Stanford in 2008, athletic fundraising for smaller sports like sailing was almost entirely overseen by the university's development office, according to this source. Officers there would sit down with Vandemoer, and he'd lay out his team's needs. Development folks would then connect him with donors and invite him to social events where he could mingle with alumni. Vandemoer himself wouldn't make the ask, but he would help the development office along with the process. The athletic director at the time was Bob Bowlsby, who was "adamant that coaches don't fundraise," said one former Stanford coach. "That was the deal. That was the understanding."

But in 2012, Bowlsby was replaced by Bernard Muir—the former Georgetown athletic director who'd hired Gordon Ernst—and things changed dramatically, according to the source close to Vandemoer. Now the development office put more priority on bigger sports, like football and basketball, and stopped bringing development opportunities to coaches of smaller sports.

The new protocol became clear from the very first meeting Vandemoer had with Muir.

"If you want that [extra] coach," Muir said to him, according to the source close to Vandemoer, "you have to fundraise for it."

In an email, Muir wrote: "I am not aware of any substantive fundraising policy changes that have occurred during my time as Director of Athletics at Stanford.

"Our coaches are the face of our athletics programs, and as an ancillary role to their coaching and recruiting duties, they are encouraged to participate in fundraising activities that support athletics," he went on. "When they do, they are expected to work closely with our development team.

"While I would not say more priority is placed on fundraising for football and basketball, it is fair to say there is generally more donor interest in those sports. Accordingly, our development team works with donors interested in those sports and, whenever possible, helps identify opportunities for their gifts to assist our other sports.

"When our department's operating budget is not able to cover something that is important to the success of a particular team, it is not uncommon for me to instruct our development team, in collaboration with the head coach, to assess and pursue opportunities to fundraise for it. That was the case for an extra sailing coach."

A former Stanford athletic department source agreed that Muir's policy wasn't that different from Bowlsby's. It's just that Muir was more permissive about coaches going out and raising money for things that went beyond their operational budget. "Under Bob, coaches' fundraising was frowned upon," this source said. With Muir, "coaches were still given a budget, but if they said, 'Hey, I want to hire an additional coach or buy an additional boat, stuff that wasn't in the budget, that's when Bernard would say, 'You need to fundraise.'" This person also disagreed with the notion that Muir favored football and basketball to the detriment of smaller "Olympic sports," as smaller sports like sailing are referred to in collegiate athletics. "Every AD realizes the importance of football and basketball. Football, especially, has to be successful in order for other sports to be successful. If football doesn't bring in money, all sports are screwed. So there's an unwritten pecking order." But that attitude "has never been at the expense of Olympic sports."

With new fundraising duties, Vandemoer was spending less time coaching and more time doing alumni outreach. And he still couldn't afford a third coach. He'd been able to hire one for short spells, thanks to donations from parents, but then lost them when the money ran out. So when Singer wrote a check for $500,000 in the name of Stanford sailing and gave it to Vandemoer after Yusi Zhao had been admitted to the university, the coach took it. In the end, it had been too late for Zhao to apply to Stanford as a sailor (though Singer had made a fake athletic profile for her), but she'd ended up getting in through regular admissions. Singer wanted to make it clear to Vandemoer that he was still good for his word—and to ensure that this pipeline would continue. So he asked Zhao's family to pay him $6.5 million anyway, once again taking advantage of cultural differences. Believing the money was a charitable gift to Stanford, the family—which has not been charged—paid Singer.

Vandemoer walked the $500,000 check over to Stanford's development office himself. And over the next year, he would walk over more checks from Singer's charity, bringing the total to $770,000 made out to the university. In the end, no kids were actually accepted to Stanford through the side door—the two subsequent fake recruits that the college counselor presented to Vandemoer wound up choosing to go to other schools—but Singer kept the money flowing, in order, he said, to "keep the relationship alive." For his part, Vandemoer put the funds toward his team, never using any of it for personal use.

As the money piled up, sources say, Vandemoer received praise from development officers, who couldn't help but notice the influx of cash. Stanford has said that its development officers asked the sailing coach about the gifts and that "their understanding of the nature of the gifts was based on information provided by the coach, which did not raise a concern at the time." Indeed, one source said Singer was a known entity at Stanford and was not looked upon with any suspicion. Once, when Vandemoer started telling Muir where the donations were coming from, the athletic director cut him off. "Oh, I know Rick," he said.

In his email, Muir wrote: "I became aware of Rick Singer and the Key Foundation through the gifts made to our sailing program, but I had no reason at that time to believe those gifts were being made for fraudulent purposes."

In the wake of the Varsity Blues case, Stanford announced new regulations to tighten internal controls, such as creating written fundraising policies while recruiting athletes, and more carefully scrutinizing donations. It also said it would redistribute the $770,000 it received from Singer's foundation to an entity or entities "supporting financially challenged high school students who are seeking financial support and enhanced preparation toward their college admission."

As he was writing checks to John Vandemoer, Rick Singer was still pushing ahead with his dream of building a business empire that went far beyond college counseling. As first reported in the *Los Angeles Times*, in 2017 he started sinking money he was making from rich parents into a constellation of digital start-ups that he hoped to eventually bundle together and sell, maybe even spin off in an IPO. Most of the companies were based around his eternal theme of helping kids get into college, but each of them had a unique twist. GettingIntoCollege.com would be built around an algorithm that could take a student's academic profile, personality, values, and cognitive abilities, and pair them with the ideal match. USA-UES was a computer-based training program that would teach Chinese high school students "soft skills," such as time management and how to work as a team, things that are not typically covered in Chinese schools. And Counting Stars would use an algorithm to evaluate student athletes and determine their ideal colleges.

Singer had wrangled impressive experts and gurus in their fields to help him pull it off, such as Donna Orender, a well-known sports executive who had run the WNBA for several years, and J. Galen Buckwalter, a noted research psychologist and former chief science officer at eHarmony. Bill Templeton, Singer's old Money Store buddy, was also in on the act. In late 2017, Templeton, who was now in the consulting business, ran into Singer in the Whole Foods market in Sacramento. Templeton said he noticed a new polish to Singer. Since he'd last seen him, his friend was dressing more fashionably and cruising around in a luxury SUV. Added to Singer's track-suit wardrobe were "four-hundred-dollar sweaters," Templeton said. After some initial chitchat, Singer asked Templeton if he'd be interested in working on a vertical for him that would help middle-aged Americans navigate work issues such as age discrimination. Templeton agreed and began doing research, but a few months in, Singer decided to change tack and build a mobile app for addicts who were in recovery.

"He said he met a lady in a swimming club who was in recovery, and he was very impressed by her," Templeton said. "She shared some of the obstacles of addiction and brought him into that world a little bit. He then came up with this concept of creating a mobile app. The idea was to create a platform for people to use once they'd gotten out of a treatment program. It would create content, such as meditation videos, articles, and exercise plans, to keep recovering addicts on a so-called continuum of care."

Singer sank a couple million into his start-up projects, burrowing deeply into the details. "He was very controlling," said one person involved with GettingIntoCollege.com. "Nothing was too small" for him to stick his nose into, the person said. "Sample size, analytic strategies, recruitment strategies. He just had very strong ideas about everything."

As ever, his dreams were "just so grandiose," said this person. "He was going to change the world overnight."

In July of 2017, it seemed like he might be able to pull it off, with the help of one of his new clients, Bill McGlashan. Always looking for ways to capitalize on parents' connections and businesses, Singer had sensed an opportunity in McGlashan, the founder of the Rise Fund, a socially minded investment fund in Silicon Valley whose backers included Bono and eBay billionaire Jeff Skoll. McGlashan was a player both in tech and Hollywood (he sat on the board of the company STX Entertainment, which he'd helped launch), who worked fast and hard. He was always on the phone, always on planes. On Los Angeles pit stops, he palled around with Ashton Kutcher and producer Guy Oseary. He also worked for a private-equity powerhouse; the Rise Fund was owned by the investment firm TPG. McGlashan hired Singer to help his son get into college, and the boy was working with him on test prep— ultimately, Singer would arrange to have McGlashan's son take the ACT at his Hollywood test center. He would also start discussing a USC side-door scheme with McGlashan. Eager to impress this VIP connection, Singer took his résumé exaggerating to new levels with McGlashan, telling him that he had a connection to the president of Harvard and that USC's president and board had hired him several years earlier to change the school's brand and image. (McGlashan has denied any wrongdoing and is fighting the charges against him. He claims he did not know that Singer arranged to have someone fix his son's ACT, and that he pulled out of the side-door scheme before his son applied to USC.)

But for now, he had other angles to work with McGlashan, and through him he was put in touch with John Rogers, a partner at Rise. The two men spoke on the phone and, according to Singer, the possibility of TPG investing $25 million in his companies was discussed. After the meeting, Singer was elated. He sent a group email to his team, reportedly writing: "The message was clear. Rise and especially John Rogers and Bill McGlashan want us as partners." He emphasized to one member of his group that Rise's interest mainly had to do with one person: Singer. "They really want *me*," he said. "They really want *me*." (TPG would later state:

"Mr. Singer misunderstood or mischaracterized a polite no. The investment never reached even the first meaningful milestone in TPG's investment process.")

Things with the start-ups chugged along. Singer had weekly calls with each of the companies, where he'd check in on their progress and offer support. He flew everyone down to Newport Beach and put them up in the Marriott for a daylong conference. He struck up partnerships with tech companies to help build the infrastructure for his investments.

But over the summer of 2018, something seemed to be off. Singer was suddenly curt and impatient on the weekly conference calls. "I noticed a radical difference in his personality, his attitude," Templeton said. "He was almost verbally abusive to some people. Very short. Totally different than the old Rick I remembered years ago. You know, the coach, the inspiration. 'Let's make this happen!' Now it was, 'Goddamn it! We're supposed to get this done!' . . . It got worse over time."

Some of the parents that he was working with also noticed a stark change in behavior. He wasn't returning texts or phone calls. He'd call and say, inexplicably, that he was in Boston, building playgrounds, starting up a business—it was never totally clear. Eventually, the weekly phone calls with his start-up group were eliminated. "I wouldn't hear things for weeks at a time," Templeton said. "And then I get a phone call, almost like a panicked phone call: *'What are we doing?'*"

Templeton assumed Singer was just feeling pressure from all of the other demands he had with his college counseling business and his nonstop travel. It would take months for him to find out what really was going on.

CHAPTER 12

Beantown Showdown

On July 26, 2018, Rick Singer was lost, driving around London, when he got a call from Rudy Meredith, the women's soccer coach at Yale.

"Rudy, commissioner," Singer said amicably, picking up his cell phone.

"What's up, man?" Meredith replied.

Singer said he was in London, where he was meeting with some of his employees for a training session, but would be back in the United States in a few days. At one point in the conversation he swore, "Frickin A, where the fuck is it?" He was still uncertain of where he was going. "Now I'm on the main street again. You know what? I'm glad I live in the US."

"Can you stay in one spot?" Meredith joked.

"I can't, because the posse will come after me," Singer replied. "I got people always chasing me, big boy. Everybody wants something from me."

"'Cause they know you the man, that's why," Meredith said.

"I don't know about that, but I'm getting tired of being the man."

A ruggedly built athlete with a shaved head and infectious laugh, Meredith was over a decade into his coaching stint at Yale by the time of this jovial call with Singer. Since arriving at the school he'd gone from a goofy, gleeful coach who led his team to the Ivy League championship in 2005 to someone notably upset over losses yet also seeming to phone the job in. "When I was there, we had a lot of frustrating seasons due to injuries," said Adele Jackson-Gibson, a soccer player who graduated from Yale in 2013. "We had a good beginning, but then it started petering out. I felt like by the end, my senior year, I was pretty done. I don't think a lot of people believed in the program anymore."

This portrait of Meredith is in stark contrast with the way players who were at Yale in the 1990s remember the coach. "He was this very young African American guy, which made him unique compared to the other coaches at Yale, who were old and white," said one former men's soccer player, who said Meredith often kicked around soccer balls with the men's team. "He was a breath of fresh air." Former women's soccer players say that during Meredith's early days at Yale—he arrived as an assistant women's soccer coach in 1992 and was promoted to head coach three years later—he was fun-loving and inspirational. He gave boisterous talks before games and insisted his players wear costumes to practice on Halloween. But even these players noticed signs of insecurity. Meredith admitted he had a learning disability and would joke about the irony. "I have trouble reading and I'm a coach at Yale," he said. He also seemed cowed by the entitlement that some of his players exuded. Meredith, who wasn't from privilege, grew up modestly in Maryland and was an All-American at Montgomery Junior College (which he nearly failed out of) before transferring to Southern Connecticut State University. The environment at Yale could throw him off, said Theryn Gibbons, a soccer player who graduated from Yale in 2000. "Everyone was really smart and their parents were powerful," she said.

"Sometimes kids could have an attitude. So when Rudy coached, he wasn't as confident."

Yet Gibbons occasionally practiced with Meredith's non-Yale club team, and she said there he was an entirely different person. "He was much more confident. He was like a magician. At Yale—you could tell he was intimidated by it."

In recent years, he seemed less intimidated by Yale than disillusioned with it. He remarked to friends and former players that he wasn't as close with his team anymore and that he didn't interact with his players as much off the field. There'd been a team scandal when he was accused of pressuring two of his players to edit and write passages of grad school papers he was submitting for a master's degree he was pursuing at Ohio University in coaching education and sports science. (The matter was brought to the attention of both Yale's president and its athletic director, and an investigation was opened, but in the end no action was reported, according to the *Yale Daily News*.) Meredith also seemed wearied by the increasing involvement and demands of parents who simultaneously "threw money at him all the time," said one former player. One family offered to fly him to Paris to see a World Cup soccer tournament. And in 2013, Meredith's best friend and longtime assistant coach, Fritz Rodriguez, had stepped down, leaving Meredith without his closest sounding board and confidant on the team. Rodriguez and Meredith had played soccer and roomed together at Southern Connecticut State, and they had been an inseparable presence at Yale. Meredith once described the pair as "an odd couple and he balanced me out." (Rodriguez would pass away suddenly in 2017, something that friends say shook Meredith terribly.)

As Meredith's zeal for his job waned, Yale meanwhile was putting more emphasis on sports performance. According to one source familiar with the Yale athletic department at the time, "The culture definitely changed and the expectation was, 'You have to win.'" This person said that coaches felt pressure from their athletic supervisors, who had started to become more emphatic about winning tournaments. Coaches had even started receiving bonuses if they took home a league championship. This attitude, combined with Meredith's lackluster record, seemed to make him anxious. In private conversations with friends, Meredith said that he thought his job was on the line.

How this played into his decision to start working with Singer is unclear, but in April of 2015 he began accepting payments from Singer in exchange for flagging kids as soccer recruits. That same year, he told the *Yale Daily News* that he hoped to be given more recruitment slots as Yale enlarged its undergraduate student body by 15 percent. He said that even one more slot would help him put together a stronger team and mean that he wouldn't have to say no to a kid who would then be "mad at you, because you didn't take them at your school, and when you play against them, they have the game of their life."

More slots, of course, would give Meredith more opportunity to work with Singer.

Meredith's longtime friend Chigozie Offor, who'd played soccer against him in college and is now an attorney in Florida, began noticing a change in Meredith when Meredith came down to Florida over the summer of 2016 to coach at a soccer camp that Offor ran. Offor had been asking Meredith to coach at the camp for years now, but Meredith and his wife—Eva Bergsten Meredith, the women's soccer coach at Wesleyan University—usually spent summers in Sweden, where Eva was from. Offor felt he'd scored when Meredith said he wasn't going to Europe that year and agreed to come down and coach.

Unsurprisingly, Meredith was a big hit at the camp. It wasn't every day that the Yale women's soccer coach was available to train your kid and chat on the sidelines afterward, and he was swarmed by parents during breaks each day. Wearing a gray Yale T-shirt, his muscular frame covered in a thin layer of sweat thanks to the sweltering heat, he looked every bit the Ivy League sports god. But off the field, he seemed beaten down and disillusioned. He told Offor that he was thinking of packing up and moving to Florida. It wasn't a totally nonsensical idea. Meredith came to the area often to play in pickleball tournaments (he was an avid player), which were taking up more of his time. But Offor was nonetheless taken aback.

"I said, 'Rudy, who leaves Yale University?'" Offor said. "People don't just leave Yale. They retire from Yale."

All Meredith would say was that he was "fatigued," Offor recalled. And that there was "'All the pressure. All the pressure.'"

After chitchatting with Singer on the call to London, Meredith got down to business. "Do you have a name or something for me?" he asked. He meant a student that he could list as a soccer recruit in exchange for money, as he had done with Sherry Guo for $400,000.

Singer said he had two families he was working with and that he was talking to them about both Yale and Stanford. He said he wanted to "see who's stepping up first" before he gave Meredith their names, in case one or both chose Stanford.

"Maybe I might have a spot for both of them," Meredith said.

"Really?" Singer sensed an even sweeter deal.

"Maybe," Meredith said. "Yeah. Give me the...Give me the names. I'm working on it."

Singer said he'd talk to the families when he got back home and would be in touch.

The conversation then veered into a bro-y brag session, with Singer cheerily spewing gossip and Singer-style fictions tailored to impress Meredith, who gamely prodded him along. He said that he'd gone on a date with a woman who made "about five mil a year" but had been horrified by the fact that she was ten to fifteen pounds overweight and ordered two glasses of wine at dinner plus dessert ("That ain't helping the fitness level"). He mentioned a call with the president of Brown University. He told Meredith that he'd gotten a PhD at Stanford and an MBA from Berkeley, and that he'd been president of a bank after knowing "nothing about banking, zero." He mentioned that he was fifty-eight, but he said, "I am looking like I'm forty." And when Meredith asked him how many side doors he'd pulled off this year, Singer replied: "Aw, shit. Probably, I don't know, between seven and eight hundred."

At one point, Meredith inquired about Jerome Allen, the long-time men's basketball coach at the University of Pennsylvania who'd recently been indicted for allegedly accepting $300,000 in payments and perks from a dad who had bribed Allen to get his son into Penn's business school, Wharton, as a basketball recruit. Meredith seemed worried that he and Singer might suffer the same fate. But Singer assured him—claiming that he knew the whole backstory on Allen and saying, "I'll give you the skivvy"—that he was operating a much cleaner scam and that he wasn't involved with Allen. "Oh, no, no, no," Singer said. "That's his gig. You know?...These people think they can do it their way." (Allen pled guilty to the charges and was sentenced to four years of probation.)

"So how you doing it different than them so that, so that we're all good?" Meredith asked.

"'Cause I'm doing it. I'm doing it through my business. I'm doing it through my foundation. Right?"

"Gotcha. Okay," Meredith said.

Singer joked about playing pickleball with Meredith and beating him. Then the two men hung up. Singer had no idea that Meredith was working with the Feds and that the call had been recorded.

❧

Rick Singer's grand conspiracy, as the government would label it, was based on the presumption that the people he ensnared in his web would always keep quiet. Why would anyone ever reveal that they'd swindled their kid into college by paying an exorbitant bribe? The public humiliation and ruin for the parent, not to mention the devastation that would be wrought upon the (usually) unsuspecting child, was simply too great. Singer knew this better than anyone. When he'd started talking to Gordon Caplan, cochair of the prestigious Manhattan law firm Willkie Farr & Gallagher, a month before the call with Rudy Meredith, he'd said to him: "The only one who can catch [the crime] is if you guys tell somebody."

"I am not going to tell anybody," Caplan replied.

"Well," Singer said, laughing.

Caplan laughed, too.

Sometimes, gossipy parents would snoop around, suspicious that one of their pals was similarly engaging in shady business with Singer. Agustin Huneeus Jr., a Northern California vintner, asked him if fellow Silicon Valley bigwig Bill McGlashan, who had a son at school with Huneeus's daughter, was "doing any of this shit." "Is he talking a clean game with me and helping his kid or not?" Huneeus said. "'Cause he makes me feel guilty."

Quick to play both sides of the street, Singer suggested that McGlashan was, indeed, side-door-ing it, saying that McGlashan had "asked for [his son] not knowing." But then he duly reported to McGlashan that Huneeus "is pushing hard on trying to find out your guys' approach with [your son]. He came to me, and I said I did not, I was not willing to talk to him about it."

Paranoia also sprang up via text. When a friend of another Bay Area parent, liquor distributor CEO Marci Palatella, texted her saying, "We did not pay your price [for Singer]. That was ridiculous," Palatella texted back: "You were sworn to secrecy!!! Do not tell a soul!!" She then confided that she didn't think most of the money she paid Singer went to the school, according to legal documents. "Between us only," she wrote. "Please never ever repeat anything." Both McGlashan and Palatella deny the charges against them and are scheduled to go to trial.

At times, the parents' spiritual wrestling was painfully palpable, as when Caplan said on a call to Singer: "It's just, to be honest, I'm not worried about the moral issue here. I'm worried about the, if [his daughter's] caught doing that, you know, she's finished."

"It's never happened before in twenty-some-odd years," Singer reassured him.

"Someone talks—" Caplan nervously mused on.

But Singer continued to snowplow him with promises of a closed-circuit system where silence was yet another one of Singer's signature "guarantees."

Indeed, gossip always stayed between parents, who, along with a very limited number of employees of the Key, and associates like Mark Riddell and Igor Dvorskiy, were the only ones aware of what Singer was up to. Some of his relatives were on his payroll, including his stepfather and his sister, but it's unclear if they knew the charity was a sham, and they have not been implicated in a crime. Indeed, the real beauty of the operation was how little information anyone involved with Singer actually had. Although there were college coaches who knew what was going on—and forged introductions to other coaches—some had no knowledge of the existence of any others. The tutors he'd hired to show up at families' homes had no clue they were inadvertently assisting in a scam and had limited, if any, contact with Singer. "I never met with him. We all worked remote," said Tenley Hardin, whom Singer hired to work with kids on their college essays. "I'd go to a house and edit an essay, but I only had short exchanges with Rick: 'Can you go see so-and so?'" Even old cronies of Singer's, the closest he had to any confidants or real friends, such as Bill Templeton, had no idea what he was doing behind the scenes. "It was a hub-and-spoke conspiracy," said one person who was indicted in the scandal, who did not wish to be named. "Rick was the hub with a very small group of people [connected to him]. Everybody else was a spoke on the outside. We never knew of each other. We never touched each other."

Singer's assumption that parents would stay mum proved correct. A careless text message would not, in fact, lead to his undoing. What did was an FBI investigation that couldn't have been farther removed from him—it had to do with a stock scheme—except for one small detail. It involved a parent who was hoping to get his kid into Yale as a soccer recruit.

Morrie Tobin was a former stockbroker whose gap-toothed smile and mysterious Brooklyn drawl (he's Canadian) made him seem more like a retired boxer than a millionaire financier. Tobin lived in LA, where his youngest daughter attended Marlborough. Two of his older daughters were at Yale, and one had graduated in 2015. Tobin himself had gone to Yale for two years before transferring to the University of Vermont. The reported reason for the switch was to play hockey (Tobin played at both schools and would go on to play semi-pro hockey in Europe), but Yale's hockey team was sending kids to the NHL at the time. As one

Yale alum put it: "Nobody leaves Yale to go to the University of Vermont."

Friends joked with Tobin about the fact that he didn't have a Yale degree and yet his kids would, perhaps stoking his determination to see all of them—he had six—attend the school as a way of over-correcting history. Tobin was one of those parents, not uncommon in LA, who obsess about where their children go to school from an early age. Although he was relatively new to the city—he'd uprooted his family and moved from Toronto—he quickly figured out the private-school lay of the land and would talk about schools like Marlborough, John Thomas Dye, and the Center for Early Education in terms of their status and how to game your way in.

Acquaintances describe Tobin as a hustler around whom there was always a strange air of mystery. The whole "not finishing Yale" thing. The "moving to LA so suddenly" thing. In *Unacceptable*, the authors quote a Montreal criminal lawyer, Lloyd Fischler, who was a high school friend of Tobin's, saying that Tobin had "burned a lot of bridges" in Toronto, perhaps prompting the move to California. Tobin disputed the account.

Tobin's obsession with prestigious schools was even more extreme when it came to college. There's no evidence that Tobin's older daughters got into Yale by illicit means, but when it came to his youngest daughter, Anne, things took a turn. (Her name has been changed.)

Over the summer of 2017, Anne was preparing to enter her junior year at Marlborough, the prestigious all-girls school. She played club soccer for an elite team, but according to sources, she was not a strong enough player to play for a Division 1 college team. Academically, Anne was a very good student, but at a school like Marlborough, there were dozens of girls like her, and her father wasn't going to take any chances.

That summer Tobin went to Yale, where his older daughters both played club soccer. During the visit, he met with Meredith, whom he has claimed was recruiting Anne and whom he'd met through his older daughters' soccer playing. But his actions imply he wasn't so confident about Anne's soccer chances. According to legal documents, during their exchange Meredith propositioned Tobin about getting Anne into Yale as a soccer recruit in exchange for money. No price was determined, but Tobin agreed. He said he'd pay Meredith "in the six-figure range," according to legal documents. Tobin then began making monthly payments to the coach. Around that time, Meredith and his wife reportedly purchased a vacation home in Florida for $125,000 and took out a construction loan for $359,250.

A few months later, in September, as Anne's classmates at Marlborough prepared to take standardized tests and were editing, and reediting, their lists of colleges to apply to, Anne stunned them all on Instagram. She'd posted a selfie of herself smiling and wearing a Yale sweatshirt. "So excited to say that I have been committed to play soccer at yale," she wrote.

The selfie, however, would soon come down. Unbeknownst to anyone, Tobin was covering up another, bigger scam by the time he'd engaged with Meredith. In 2013, he'd embarked on a massive pump-and-dump scheme, in which he and a group of business partners ran promotional campaigns to stoke interest in two public companies that he secretly controlled. After the companies' stock prices soared, Tobin sold millions of dollars' worth of his stock, though it was orchestrated to look like normal trades on the stock exchanges. When the federal government caught wind of the scam, it opened up an investigation in Massachusetts, where some of the investors were based.

The Feds searched Tobin's house, looking for incriminating

evidence, in March of 2018. A few weeks later, Tobin flew to Boston to meet with members of the prosecution and the FBI, in hopes of finding a way out of paying a seven-figure fine and spending years in prison. He knew he had a nugget that might do the trick. He told investigators that he was involved in a bribery scheme with the women's soccer coach at Yale. Ears perked up. (Tobin pled guilty to one count of securities fraud and one count of conspiracy to commit securities fraud in the pump-and-dump scheme. He was sentenced to a year in prison. He was not charged in the Varsity Blues case.)

Next, a plan worthy of a B crime movie was set up. Morrie Tobin arranged to fly to Boston to meet up with Rudy Meredith on April 12. He told the coach to meet him in a hotel room. Meredith had no idea that when he walked into the room his every move and word would be monitored by video cameras that had been set up by the FBI. It was an odd scene: the Ivy League coach and the slick LA businessman sequestered in a hotel room, meeting to talk about how much it would cost to get Tobin's kid into Yale. During the course of the conversation, a price was finally settled on: $450,000, or $50,000 more than Meredith had gotten for the Chinese student he'd falsely recruited. But he wasn't going to get all that dough now. Tobin handed him $2,000 (which the Feds had supplied him) in cash and said he'd send the rest to a bank account in Connecticut that Meredith provided him with the info for. The meeting was adjourned. Six days later, Tobin wired $4,000 to Meredith from a bank account in Boston that the Feds controlled. Meredith was caught. The government now had evidence of wire fraud.

But the government had inadvertently stumbled on much more than a criminal coach. During the meeting, Meredith brought up someone the agents had never heard of before: Rick Singer.

After that, Singer's fall happened in remarkably swift fashion. Only a few weeks after Morrie Tobin and Rudy Meredith met, in April of 2018, Meredith agreed to cooperate in an investigation of Singer and began making recorded calls to him—one of them was the London call. By June, the Feds had enough on Singer to tap his phone. Over the next few months, they gathered evidence not just on Singer and his fake charity, but on nine coaches, Donna Heinel, Mark Riddell, Igor Dvorskiy, and others.

On September 21, Meredith walked into another hotel room in Boston. He had set up a meeting with Singer at the Marriott Long Wharf, a barn-shaped redbrick building on the waterfront, not far from Faneuil Hall. In the midst of the meeting, three agents from the FBI and one from the IRS showed up and confronted Singer.

The Feds laid out their charges—racketeering conspiracy, money laundering, and fraud—and asked Singer if he would cooperate in their investigation and be interviewed. Singer agreed. But as he spoke with the officers, he became defensive, according to government reports. "He was, initially, a reluctant cooperator," stated one. "He did not fully accept responsibility for his crimes. He continued to use the word 'donation' to describe payments to university athletic programs in exchange for the coaches' agreement to recruit unqualified students based on fabricated credentials."

Things got more heated in an exchange with Elizabeth Keating, a special agent on the IRS criminal investigation team. Keating insisted to Singer that it didn't matter if a payment was *called* a "donation." If the payment was made to a university athletic program in exchange for getting a student who was not actually an athlete into a school, it was a crime. According to Singer, the discussion with Keating got "boisterous." Keating said that she did not raise her voice, but became more "animated" than usual. She said that it was her impression that Singer "was not being completely truthful and was minimizing his conduct."

The next day, Singer met with his lawyer and then agreed to make consensually recorded phone calls with the FBI. But he remained unhappy about it. He'd make a few calls for the Feds, and then not want to make any more. The calls were to new clients or to clients that he was in the midst of working with. The FBI agents instructed him to be specific in what he said to them, and to spell out that the payments to coaches would be bribes. The purpose, said Keating, was to make things so crystal clear to parents who had not yet committed a crime that "there would be no confusion about their intent." But Singer didn't like the government's wording. He said that that wasn't the way he typically talked to his clients—he normally said the money was for a donation to an athletic program. He said that saying otherwise would be a "fib."

The friction between Singer and the FBI came to a head on October 2. In notes that he took on his iPhone that day, he wrote: "Loud and abrasive call with agents. They continue to ask me to tell a fib and not restate what I told my clients as to where there [sic] money was going—to the program not the coach, and that it was a donation and they want it to be a payment.

"I asked for a script if they want me to ask questions and retrieve responses that are not accurate to the way I should be asking the questions. Essentially they are asking me to bend the truth..."

He also referred to Keating, writing: "Liz raised her voice to me like she did in the hotel room about agreeing with her that everyone Bribed the schools. This time about asking each person to agree to a lie I was telling them."

Keating recalled having "stern conversations" with Singer during this period, both about what he was saying to parents and about "his cooperation generally." Already, he had tried to warn some parents that the ruse was up. He secretly reached out to Bill McGlashan, saying he needed to meet with him at the Santa Monica airport because he was afraid his phone was "wired." (He told several other parents he was wired.) The meeting, alas, never happened. Another time, he entered a family's home and warned the father that he was wiretapped, telling him to not say anything that would get him in trouble.

In his iPhone notes, Singer said that the government wanted to "nail" certain individuals. After attorney and client Gordon Caplan texted him, saying that his daughter had not received extended time for standardized tests, Singer wrote of the government: "They still wanted me to ask him for a payment to take the SAT through [the West Hollywood test center] even when he was not approved just to nail him. I said that is ludicrous as he will not entertain because she was not approved."

Singer also wrote that the Feds had him tell John Vandemoer, the Stanford sailing coach, that his next payment to him, of between $100,000 and $200,000, would go to him directly, not to Stanford's sailing program.

Whether or not Rick Singer was a willing, cooperating witness, he was incredibly busy helping the Feds reel in dozens of clients and associates. According to his notes, on a single day, October 5: He went to Bank of America with two agents to get two $10,000 cashier checks made out to Mark Riddell and the West Hollywood test center c/o Igor Dvorskiy. He then walked the checks to the post office, where the agents took photographs of the checks and envelopes. He made a "series of successful phone calls," stating in all of them that he was in Boston "to set the stage." These included a voicemail for client Gregory Abbott, thanking him for his $75,000 donation and saying that "we will achieve 750+ on the [SAT] subject tests tomorrow in LA"; a call to Riddell, who informed him that "all is good," that he'd score over 750 on the tests for Abbott's daughter; a voicemail for Vandemoer saying to "call me to discuss his request for $160k to pay coaches"; a call to Donna Heinel, who told him that two students had been admitted to USC and agreed that the $50K payments could "come at a later date"; a call to Ali Khosroshahin for an update on a student; and calls to Bill McGlashan and Gordon Caplan. A few days later, Singer texted Martin Fox, the head of an elite tennis academy in Houston who has admitted to helping Singer facilitate bribes. He also got a text from Felicity Huffman. The actress's older daughter, Sophia, was gearing up to apply to college and Singer confirmed her meeting with him "to do applications." He added to his notes that agents would wire him for the meeting.

Starting in late September, Singer was instructed to call up past clients and tell them that his foundation was being audited and that he just wanted to give them a heads-up, should they receive any calls from the IRS about their donations to his charity. The purpose was to corroborate evidence, or to get parents to admit to crimes they'd committed. It was, according to the government, "the equivalent of a wired-up cooperator asking a drug dealer, to whom the cooperator has previously sold drugs: 'Do you remember when I sold you those drugs?'"

Some parents who'd been Singer clients were suspicious of the sudden incoming call from him, in some cases many years after they'd worked with him, and they declined to call Singer back after he left a message ("Hey, it's Rick. I just wanted to talk to you about something). Their instincts would save them from a federal investigation.

But those that did pick up or return the call were dutifully fed the IRS line by Singer. His inability to veil what was going on was almost painfully comic, yet most parents seemed to be only half listening and/or eager to swat away the annoying news.

In a call to Agustin Huneeus, Singer said: "So what I want to make sure is that you and I are both on the same page, because what I'm going to tell [the IRS] is that you made a fifty K donation to my foundation for underserved kids and not that Mark Riddell took the test for [your daughter] or she took the test at the [West Hollywood Test Center]."

"Dude, dude. What do you think, I'm a moron?" Huneeus shot back.

"I'm not saying you're a moron," Singer said. "The point is, is that—"

"I got it, Rick. I got it…I'm going to say that I've been inspired how you're helping underprivileged kids get into college. Totally got it."

In a call to Mossimo Giannulli—who informed him that "the girls are absolutely loving SC"—Singer mentioned the audit by the IRS. "So they're looking at all the payments," he said. "So they— they asked me about your two payments of two hundred thousand…And, of course, I'm not gonna say anything about your payments going to Donna Heinel at USC to get the girls into USC through crew."

"Sure," Giannulli replied.

"But what's funny," Singer said. "It's funny. Because Donna called me a couple weeks ago and says, 'Hey, uh, you know, going forward, can you use the same format you used for [Giannulli's daughters] and the regattas that you put in there for any girls going forward that don't row crew?' So it's funny how, I thought I was just makin' stuff up!"

"Uh, right, uh…," Giannulli responded.

"So I just want to make sure our stories are the same, because—"

"Yeah."

"And that your four hundred K was paid to our foundation to help underserved kids."

"Uh, perfect," Giannulli said.

In a call to Bill McGlashan, Singer said he was worried because Riddell was being audited by the IRS, who was questioning him about payments that Singer made to him as well as Singer's foundation.

"So when [Riddell] gets done speaking, I kinda freak out, right?" Singer said. "Because now I'm thinking, 'Oh, shit. I'm in a—I'm in a lot of trouble here,' and the IRS has me wired. They probably have me—you know, bugged my house, the whole thing, because he's talking all about my foundation, and, you know, he really wants to dive into this. So when I met with [my lawyer], he told me, 'Rick, hold on. Just relax. For them to get a wiretap on you, it takes a bunch of months to happen, and you just need to relax.'"

"Mm-hmm," McGlashan replied.

"You know, overnight I'm a lot less worried than I was a couple days ago"—Singer laughed—"when we talked. But I just, you know, I'm gonna use this [other] phone, which is my son's phone, and I did it...for us to talk so that there are, you know, no issues. Just in case."

"Yep, yep."

Meanwhile, back in LA, Jane Buckingham noticed that Singer had become increasingly erratic, according to a source. As Jack was entering his senior year at Brentwood with "his" new and improved ACT score, Singer was no longer a savior in her eyes. He was a flake—another man she'd grown to depend on who'd suddenly left her high and dry. He abruptly stopped returning texts or emails, even when she had burning questions, like: Should Jack apply early decision to Southern Methodist?

When he did finally respond, he told her to forget ED for SMU. "No. He'll get rejected," he said. "He needs to have good senior year grades. Don't ED."

"Ok," Buckingham wrote. "Well, then, should he EA?" she asked, meaning should he apply early action, which would show the school that it was one of his top choices but he wouldn't have to commit if he was accepted.

Singer failed to respond. He also failed to send in Jack's application to either SMU or Tulane.

Furious, Buckingham called him: "What happened?" she demanded.

"He wouldn't have gotten in," he said.

"What?" Buckingham was livid, as was Jack.

Trying to salvage something from the situation, she asked, "Well, what about the USC thing?" She was referring, the source said, to the idea Singer had mentioned about having Jack apply to USC with an eye toward becoming a team manager, which was why she'd sent him the photo of Jack in his soccer gear.

Singer brushed the question off; it was clear he hadn't done anything about it.

His start-ups were also being brushed aside. In November, just as Bill Templeton was about to test his recovery app in sober living homes in Sacramento, Singer called him up and said everything was off. "I gotta shut you down," he said.

"What are you talking about?" a flabbergasted Templeton replied. "We're about to beta test."

"Well, I had a board meeting last week, and they basically told me that my other businesses are burning too much cash right now," Singer said. "It's not what you're doing. It's what the foundation—I'm struggling right now with my other businesses, and I can't afford to capitalize you guys anymore. So I'm gonna have to shut you down."

Templeton laid off the handful of people who were working for him and closed up shop. Singer never followed up or checked in again.

He called another start-up founder in his group, who'd noticed that Singer had become increasingly "pissy" on calls, and said: "I'm being audited by the IRS, so our funding has been closed. You guys just continue what you're doing. But if you need more money, you've got to find it on your own."

☙

By early 2019, most of the parents Rick Singer had been reaching out to were going on about their lives in peaceful fashion. Stephen and Rita Semprevivo had a sunset dinner at Nobu in Malibu on March 1, an occasion that Rita commemorated on Facebook. On March 9, Jane Buckingham cohosted a fundraiser along with Will Ferrell and *Grey's Anatomy* and *Scandal* creator Shonda Rhimes for Democratic senator Kirsten Gillibrand. She had other reasons to feel festive—a few days earlier, Jack had gotten into Southern Methodist University. Buckingham had commemorated the occasion by going out and buying him balloons. Lori Loughlin was in Canada, filming *When Calls the Heart*, a Hallmark Channel show in which she played a widow in a coal-mining town in the Canadian West. The series, along with Netflix's *Fuller House* revival, was ushering in a major comeback for the eighties TV star. Morrie Tobin, who was refashioning himself as a social entrepreneur and do-gooder, was posting videos on Instagram to promote his career shift. "So this is a social purpose and a social impact that we all can contribute to," he said, standing in front of Los Angeles Mission, a homeless shelter where Tobin told his followers he volunteered every Saturday and Sunday.

Two days after Buckingham's fundraiser, on the afternoon of March 11, Bill McGlashan was sitting on the thirty-second floor of TPG's headquarters in San Francisco's financial district, mapping out the future of the Rise Fund with his executives and co-CEOs. Dressed in a charcoal-gray Zegna suit—his signature—he had a magnificent view of the Bay Bridge as he and his colleagues discussed a prosperous future for the fund, according to a source with knowledge of the meeting. Uber, which McGlashan had pushed TPG to invest $88 million in back in 2013, was gearing up for an IPO, and Rise's investments were seeing solid returns. The meeting lasted for four hours. McGlashan packed up and left the building at six o'clock.

The following dawn was typically serene in some of the country's most exclusive neighborhoods. In Bel-Air and Beverly Hills, the morning sprinklers hadn't yet kicked in with their rhythmic tick-tick-ticking. Up in Palo Alto and Atherton, a cool morning breeze was rolling in off the San Francisco Bay. And in Greenwich, Connecticut, where temperatures dipped below zero, the town was blanketed in a winter silence.

At six in the morning, these peaceful tableaux were interrupted.

A team of armed FBI agents stormed homes across the country, targeting parents that the government had gathered enough evidence on to arrest. It was an orchestrated mass operation, more akin to a drug raid than a roundup of affluent middle-aged parents, standing around, sleepy-eyed, in their pajamas.

Jane Buckingham thought there was a lunatic loose in the neighborhood and that someone was banging on her door to warn her and her kids. When she saw that it was the FBI and that they were demanding that she come with them, she fell to the floor and couldn't get up. The agents refused to say why they were there or where they were going to take her, but one agent graciously told one of her kids to get her a PowerBar for the ride.

Michelle Janavs thought it was an earthquake. She and her husband and kids stumbled out of bed and rushed to the foyer of their home as FBI agents flooded into the house, shouting orders. Two agents grabbed her two teenage daughters and another two grabbed her husband. Four latched on to her. They handcuffed their hands behind their backs and then led the family outside. Janavs's daughters stood there shivering and terrified in their bare feet.

In Menlo Park, Marjorie Klapper—a jewelry business owner who used Singer to cheat on the ACT for her son, and who falsely passed off her son as a first-generation minority student—was awoken by the screams. The FBI was banging on her front door and yelling out her name. As her children watched, she was handcuffed by agents who continued to shout commands and questions at her. Before carting her off to the Federal Building in downtown San Francisco, they allowed her to quickly go change her clothes.

At Felicity Huffman and William H. Macy's home, agents went straight into their daughters' room and woke them up at gunpoint—a moment that would give Sophia nightmares and make her fear sleeping alone from then on. A few miles away, Mossimo Giannulli, alone in his house—his wife was still filming, and their daughters were on spring break—was marched out of his home in handcuffs.

In San Francisco, agents entered Agustin Huneeus's home and ordered his daughters out of their beds. They stood in horror as agents handcuffed their father in front of them, a scene that would lead them to suffer from panic attacks.

As parents were rounded up like drug lords, Andrew Lelling, the US attorney for the District of Massachusetts, who'd led the government's sting, was going over his notes. Dressed in a charcoal suit and a red striped tie, he was about to address dozens of reporters who'd been tipped off about a major criminal announcement.

At ten o'clock, Lelling, a towering prosecutor with a bullet-shaped shaved head, walked stone-faced up to the podium and looked straight into the cameras. The world was about to be introduced to Rick Singer.

Author's Note

The immediate aftermath of the press conference on March 12, 2019, announcing the "biggest college admissions scam" ever prosecuted in this country was nothing short of a media earthquake. I first heard about the story that morning at my home in Los Angeles while I was on a work call. My husband texted me a link to a breaking news story, which I then read on my computer as I distractedly continued my conversation. Minutes later, I scrolled through Facebook and Twitter—there was little talk of anything else. The story was salacious and juicy—photographs of celebrities under the words "cheating" and "scandal" plastered the news—but it also hit on issues that touched so many Americans.

Varsity Blues, as the case was dubbed, is about the inequities of class, and how that plays out in college admissions, i.e., more ammunition against the premise that higher education in this country is the meritocracy it claims to be. It is a story about the power and entitlement of the (mostly white) rich in a country where the wealth divide is strained to the breaking point. It is about the quest for status and the desperate need for it in a nation that prides itself on not bestowing those things by title at birth. But it is also a human story about the fierce protection and love that parents feel toward their children and the lengths they will go to protect them, however wrongheaded or, even, illegal. It is about the confusion, anger, and frustration that families feel over a rite of passage, getting into college, that has become an obstacle course riddled with impossible-seeming challenges. And then there is Rick Singer himself, who pulled the $25 million crime off almost singlehandedly. Here was no brilliant mastermind in the vein of Bernie Madoff, but simply a maniacally driven, and tireless, hustler who happened to know a lot about college admissions. His operation, once the veil was pulled back, was remarkably rudimentary and unsophisticated, made possible by the staggering lack of checks and balances in athletic admissions at colleges.

Here in LA, the story was personal. The morning the news broke, the cell phones of parents in the private school world began blowing up with texts. So many of them, after all, knew who Singer was. More than a few had used him. There were those who were disgusted and outraged by the news. Others were sympathetic to the parents who'd been charged, some of whom they knew. Many, though, feared being sucked in. Lawyers' phones began ringing off the hook.

Meanwhile, the Instagram accounts of actresses Lori Loughlin and Felicity Huffman, as well as LA entrepreneur and socialite Jane Buckingham, began piling up with livid comments. Because all of the charged parents had their phones taken away upon their arrest, the insults remained visible for several hours, leaving a trail of public outrage.

Private high schools in the city went into defense mode, as they were asked by the Department of Justice to hand over student records. Rick Commons, president and head of Harvard-Westlake, sent out a letter to the school community clarifying that "Harvard-Westlake has never had any relationship with William Singer" and that "we discourage families from hiring independent college counselors." The letter did say that the government had requested records from two Harvard-Westlake alumni and that the school would "cooperate fully and readily with this investigation."

When Priscilla Sands, head of the Marlborough School, heard the news, she said she felt "a punch in the gut.

"Everybody was sort of in the same place," she said. "No one knew anything more than anyone else. At the time I didn't know if anyone would be involved from the school."

Sands's first thought was, *How did we get here?* "Yet, I could understand how it happened," she said. She'd been in the elite world of private high schools for so long, she knew the players, the attitudes, and how even the best intentions could be sullied by external pressures and an overzealous desire to succeed. She understood, all too well, the entitled attitude of some parents that boiled down to "You deserve to be in (a certain college), because we're just the kind of people who do," as she put it.

Her mind reeling, Sands walked out of Marlborough and crossed the street to her home in Hancock Park (not far from where Morrie Tobin resided, the parent who would reel Marlborough into the scandal). She sat down in her kitchen. "I thought, 'I have to write something.'"

The result was a thoughtful, elegant—and very honest—letter to the school community, in which she characterized the scandal as "the loss of dignity, humanity and morality that has undermined what we stand for and what we hold dear."

❧

Almost instantly, Loughlin and Huffman became the public faces of the scandal. The image of a forlorn-looking Huffman making her way somberly to the courthouse in Boston would be forever juxtaposed with that of a blissfully serene Loughlin, who stopped to sign autographs for fans on the same perp walk. The good girl–bad girl narrative became more pronounced as Huffman admitted her guilt and read a tearful apology in court six months later. Meanwhile Loughlin and her husband, Mossimo Giannulli, brashly fought the charges, and the paparazzi captured photos of Loughlin toting her yoga mat around town.

The public and media fascination lived on steadily as coaches and parents were sentenced one by one beginning that June. There was surprise when the Stanford sailing coach, John Vandemoer, who was the first to be sentenced, received a jail term of just one day, the reasoning being that he never personally pocketed the money he received from Singer, but put it toward his team. The most severe sentence thus far has gone to Douglas Hodge, the former PIMCO CEO. He received a sentence of nine months in prison for his decade-long collaboration with Singer. At his sentencing hearing, Judge Nathaniel M. Gorton was unsparing of Hodge's actions. "There is no term in the English language that describes your conduct as well as the Yiddish term of chutzpah," he said.

The world, of course, has turned upside down since that proc-lamation, and since the Varsity Blues scandal first became known. Almost exactly a year later, as a global community, we became fixated on something far more grave and frightening: COVID-19, a virus that has upended our lives in unimaginable ways. COVID has wreaked havoc on the world of higher education as well, with the onset of virtual learning and $50,000 college tuition bills suddenly seeming more outrageous than ever. Universities have suffered financial setbacks, and even heavily endowed schools like Stanford have been forced to slash programs—including its sailing team, ironically, which former coach John Vandemoer said he was trying to keep afloat with help from payments from Singer. Academic programs have been targeted, too. Ohio Wesleyan eliminated eighteen majors due to budget cuts alongside rising costs affiliated with COVID, and UC Berkeley put a brake on admissions to some of its PhD programs.

More than anything, though, COVID has simply made the divide between the haves and the have-nots in this country even more extreme, as many would-be college students from lower-income brackets have opted to forgo college in the midst of the pandemic. There has been a drop overall in college admissions—freshman enrollment was down 16 percent in 2020 from the previous year—but kids whose families simply can't financially justify tens of thousands of dollars for a Zoom education are opting out more dramatically. There is often more onus on these students to go out and make an income to help support their families, given the economic disruption wrought by COVID. According to a survey of 292 private, nonprofit schools released last fall by the Association of Independent Colleges and Universities, there was a nearly 8 percent decrease in enrollment among students who receive federal Pell Grants. As Suzanne Ortega, president of the Council of Graduate Schools, told the *New York Times*: "A couple years off is not necessarily the end of the world and may even be a wise thing. But if our universities don't remain in touch with those students, and connect with them, and encourage them to keep thinking about grad school, we could have our own lost generation of students who get busy with other things and then don't fulfill their dreams." This applies to undergraduate students even more so, as they have yet to even taste what a college education can mean in terms of expanding their perspective and opportunities.

As of this writing, twenty-two parents and two coaches have

been sentenced to jail. There are still seven more parents who have pled guilty and who are awaiting sentencing hearings that have been delayed due to the coronavirus pandemic. Ten other parents are fighting the charges against them and are scheduled to go to trial in February of 2021. (Due to the pandemic, the trial date has been repeatedly pushed back.) Among them are Amy and Gregory Colburn; Gamal Abdelaziz; I-Hsin "Joey" Chen; Elisabeth Kimmel; Bill McGlashan; Marci Palatella; John B. Wilson; Homayoun Zadeh; and Robert Zangrillo. Amin Khoury has also said he will fight the charges against him, though he has yet to make his plea.

Other individuals headed for trial at the time of this writing are former Georgetown tennis coach Gordon Ernst; former Wake Forest volleyball coach William Ferguson; former USC senior associate athletic director Donna Heinel; and USC former water polo coach Jovan Vavic.

The tone of the hearings, and of the media coverage overall, has been a diatribe against the entitlements of the privileged class and the charged parents' shameless desire to procure yet another upgrade in life. As Judge Indira Talwani, who has been a sober voice in the proceedings, said when she sentenced Stephen Semprevivo to four months in prison: "I keep coming back to the excuse for what happened here that people are using, and I'd like to quote one of the letters that one of the parents wrote, because I think this is something to reflect on.

"The parent wrote, 'As anybody who has had a high schooler navigating the chaotic, arbitrary, and, frankly, terrifying college admissions process knows, the importance of relying on academic tutors and consultants with expertise to help your kids is crucial.'

"Think about how terrifying that college admissions process

is for the applicant whose parents didn't even go to college. Think how terrifying that process is for the students and parents who don't have the resources to hire tutors and consultants with expertise no matter how crucial that might be.

"I don't criticize you for being taken into a crime by someone with skills of masterful deception," Talwani went on. "That's how crimes happen all the time...I do understand, from what I'm hearing in these papers, that Mr. Singer was open to parents in rooms, in lecture halls, parents with lots of money to whom he pitched the side door. And I think the question that all of these parents need to ask is not, 'Well, of course we all hired an expert.' I think the question that people need to ask is: 'What makes your children entitled to a side door?'"

The prosecution, of course, has been more scathing, both during lively hearings—at one that I attended, I pictured blood dripping from federal prosecutor Eric Rosen's mouth as he leaned into the podium—and in its detailed sentencing memos, which are heavy on lifestyle details of the rich. The government argued that Huffman, for example, should serve actual prison time, seeing as probation or home confinement "in a large home in the Hollywood Hills with an infinity pool" would not "constitute meaningful punishment or deter others from committing similar crimes." In the end, Huffman served eleven days in a minimum-security federal prison near San Francisco.

Because the case is ongoing, a federal criminal investigation with significant repercussions for those involved, reporting this story had its share of challenges. Many of the charged individuals were under orders from lawyers to not speak lest it affect the outcome of their case. People who had not been charged but who had insight into the story were often fearful of tarnishing their name by speaking aloud and inviting any association with

Singer. For this reason, I relied on many anonymous sources to help me piece aspects of the story together, and I am incredibly grateful for their guidance. I am equally grateful to the people—there are too many to name here—who were willing to speak openly about Singer, feeling it important to tell the truth about a man who, they now realize, was not at all what he seemed. Then there are those who saw the warning signs years ago, most notably Margie Amott, who so methodically kept records on Singer over the years, sensing that he was more than just a shady self-promoter.

The vast majority of people I spoke to about Singer had no association with his criminal acts. That includes childhood and college friends; the majority of parents and students who used him as a college counselor; former associates at his companies Future Stars and the CollegeSource; and individuals who worked with him more recently at the Key. Even Singer's family members, including his ex-wife, Allison, who ran his early businesses with him, have no connection to the scandal. As one charged individual told me, Singer ran a "hub and spoke conspiracy" in which information was fiercely guarded by Singer himself. On top of that, he was an intensely private person who rarely shared information or details that veered beyond his braggart schtick.

All of the text messages, emails, and phone calls that are cited in the book are from court records that have been filed in connection with the scandal, including the two-hundred-plus-page affidavit in support of the criminal complaint.

The schools I name in this book, both the private high schools and the colleges and universities, have also not been charged with any wrongdoing. The universities that employed coaches and administrators that Singer relied on for his scheme, and that admitted his students under false pretenses—including USC, Georgetown, UCLA, Stanford, and Yale—have undergone internal investigations in the wake of the scandal and adopted new policies and safeguarding mechanisms to prevent this kind of fraud from, hopefully, ever happening again. At USC there is now a three-tiered system, whereby student athletes being considered for admission are reviewed by a head coach, the senior sports administrator overseeing the team, and the USC Office of Athletics Compliance. Athletic rosters are now audited every year and cross-checked with admissions lists, and head coaches have to "certify in writing that the student is being recruited for their athletic abilities," USC said in a statement.

Harvard-Westlake and the Buckley School, high schools that I devote space to in the book, both declined to comment despite repeated requests for interviews. In some cases I have changed the names of students and former students at those schools who did not wish to be identified for fear of negative repercussions from the schools.

But perhaps most important to clarify is that very few of the children whose parents were charged in this case had any idea that their applications and/or standardized test scores contained false information, or that Singer was presenting them as embellished versions of themselves to colleges. (And no children have been charged.) Even those students who sat with Singer week after week, month after month, and in some cases were asked by a parent to perform strange acts—such as posing in a swimming pool wearing water polo gear—were unaware of any behind-the-scenes scheming. A day after the scandal broke, Jack Buckingham—who took the ACT in his home, where his mother, Jane, "proctored" him—released a statement to the *Hollywood Reporter* saying: "I know there are millions of kids out there both wealthy and less fortunate who grind their asses off just to have a shot at the college of their dreams. I am upset that I was unknowingly involved in a large scheme that helps give kids who may not work as hard as others an advantage over those who truly deserve those spots."

As for Singer, he's pled guilty to four felony counts of conspiracy to commit money laundering; racketeering conspiracy; conspiracy to defraud the United States; and obstruction of justice for alerting a number of subjects to the investigation after he began cooperating with the government. He could face up to sixty-five years behind bars. He is a cooperating witness for the government and remains on the go, usually at a gym, working out at 5:30 in the morning (where I saw him once, in Sacramento), or paddleboarding in the Newport Beach harbor in a Speedo to the delight of TMZ photographers.

There is yet to be a grand finale to the story, but one momentous turning point came in May of 2020, when Loughlin and Giannulli dramatically reversed course and made a plea agreement with the government. Since her initial court appearance in Boston, Loughlin had seemed more anxious about the case and the impending trial. Gossip magazines reported that the drama was taking a toll on her and her family. Olivia Jade Giannulli, who dropped out of social media and withdrew from USC, as did her sister, following the scandal, said in a video she posted in December of 2019: "I want to move on with my life."

The Giannullis' reversal came two weeks after Judge Gorton rejected a bid to throw out charges against them and other parents in the case. The defense had argued that Singer had been coerced by the FBI to lie during phone calls he made to clients during the wiretap period in order to get them to admit to crimes, based on Singer's iPhone notes he took at the time. But after reviewing denials submitted by FBI agents and the prosecution, Gorton tossed the bid out, dealing the defense a major blow.

Under their plea deal, Loughlin pled guilty to conspiracy to commit wire and mail fraud, and Giannulli pled guilty to conspiracy to commit wire and mail fraud, and honest services wire and mail fraud. Prosecutors agreed to drop charges of money laundering and federal programs bribery that were added after their case was filed. In exchange, prosecutors recommended two months behind bars for Loughlin and five months for Giannulli.

During their sentencing hearing, which took place on Zoom because of the coronavirus, the couple appeared somber as they answered questions from Judge Gorton, who at times struggled to hear them because of technical difficulties. "Mrs. Loughlin, could you please unmute?" became a refrain during the forty-minute proceeding. Loughlin and Giannulli appeared to be in separate rooms, and were accompanied by their lawyers. Loughlin was dressed in a high-necked black shirt. At times she frowned, but she responded with crisp, polite answers. When she finally uttered the word that the world had been desperately waiting for her to say— "guilty"—she closed her eyes and sighed.

Acknowledgments

There are many people to thank for getting this book from conception to actual book, far too many to name here. But I would foremost like to thank those who were willing to share their stories and insights with me about Rick Singer, the current state of college admissions, the culture within elite private schools, and their own journeys through it all. It has been an incredible education for me, most of all, one that wouldn't have been possible without the time, patience, and generosity of these individuals.

I would also like to acknowledge the stellar reporting on the scandal that helped make my own storytelling possible. Reporters such as Jennifer Levitz and Melissa Korn at the *Wall Street Journal*; Joel Rubin and Matthew Ormseth at the *Los Angeles Times*; and Kate Taylor, Jennifer Medina, David W. Chen, Billy Witz, and others at the *New York Times*; all made groundbreaking revelations as the scandal unfolded, adding context and important details to the narrative. The journalism team at Granite Bay High School, which quickly mobilized and started breaking news once the scandal broke, also deserves a shout-out. And Daniel Golden's reporting on Singer for the most recent edition of *The Price of Admission* is peak journalism.

The idea for this book came on the day the college admissions scandal broke: March 12, 2019. Thanks to my agent, Daniel Greenberg, who within days turned a conversation about the crazy college admissions story that was blowing up all over the media into a deal to write a book about it. Sean Desmond, my editor at Twelve, has been a calm and steadfast force throughout this project. When we first met—fittingly, in USC's student village over the summer of 2019—he helped me sketch out an outline for the book, and from that moment on, his thoughts on the story have been dead-on.

At *Fast Company*, editor-in-chief Stephanie Mehta couldn't have said the words "What do you need?" faster once this project was under way. And I was lucky enough to have David Lidsky, *Fast Company*'s deputy editor, with me for the writing process as an exacting eye and sounding board. David also helped me find the story within the story that I felt I could best tell: namely, the culture of elite education in Los Angeles.

Another gift, via Ruth Barrett, came in the form of Samantha Shapiro, my research assistant, whom I only wish I could have held on to longer. Sadly for me, a fall semester at Princeton beckoned. Sam was an amazing asset and has a star-filled journalism career ahead.

My tour guides in Sacramento were my sister and brother-in-law, Michelle and John Scharf, who not only introduced me to the locals but to the city's (and perhaps world's) best coffee. Note to anyone looking for Rick Singer stories: Situate yourself at Temple Coffee and chat up anyone around you.

Elizabeth Johnson whipped this manuscript into publishable form with her meticulous copyediting, and Carolyn Levin was an essential legal eye. Beth Johnson checked facts and was a great reader whom I relied on for feedback and appraisal. And Rachel Kambury at Twelve was both thoughtful and expedient in getting this book into its final form.

And innumerable thank-yous to a number of friends. Becky Rimbach, for moral support, always. Katy Erskine for helping me see less foggily into the world of criminal legal proceedings. Claire Martin for savant-level insight into the nuances of the LA parenting scene. And for batting around ideas that often turned into chapter ideas, I am grateful to Allison Woods, Chin-Chin Beckett, Vanessa Karubian, and Angela Homler.

My children, Alexei and Katrina, were my lights throughout the reporting and writing of this book, even as my work put a strain on our household, which suddenly doubled as school due to the onset of the coronavirus. They will always be my biggest reset button. And thank you to the Rushfields: Len, Karen, and Ali, for encouragement and helping us out so much with those lights.

Most importantly, thank you to my husband, Richard Rushfield, for love, wisdom, and cheerleading, and for holding down the fort in so many ways (he has all the Zoom passwords). As a fellow journalist, he is also an invaluable editor who nitpicked and massaged my manuscript in a way that only someone who is bound to you for life is willing to do.

Finally, thank you to my parents, Justin and Renée LaPorte, for a lot of things, including supporting my own education.

Notes

1. COLLEGE NIGHT TERROR

Quotes from Frank Bruni, Caitlin Flanagan, Julie Lythcott-Haims, Jeff Schiffman, Priscilla Sands, Luisa Donati, Jen Kaifesh, Sara Harberson, Mark Sklarow, and Alexandra Dumas Rhodes are taken from interviews conducted by the author. Samantha Shapiro spoke with Ned Johnson. Historical information about Harvard-Westlake was taken from *Harvard-Westlake: A History*, by Susan Wels. Bruni's book *Where You Go Is Not Who You'll Be* informed this chapter, as did Loren Pope's *Colleges That Change Lives: 40 Schools That Will Change the Way You Think About Colleges*. The sense of fear and anxiety that many parents at elite high schools in Los Angeles feel is based on dozens of mostly off-the-record interviews I had with parents, as well as conversations I had with school administrators and students. How fundraising works at these schools was also a subject of discussion with these sources. The figures for Harvard-Westlake's giving circles and matriculation statistics are taken from its website. The quote "the biggest college admissions scam" was said by United States attorney for the Massachusetts district Andrew Lelling at a press conference on March 12, 2019. Stanford announced on August 30, 2018, in a news release that it would no longer "announce undergraduate application numbers." Data about the reality of diversity in higher education was cited in "What College Admissions Offices Really Want," by Paul Tough, *New York Times Magazine*, September 10, 2019. Statistics about the percent of high-income students at Ivy League universities came from "Some Colleges Have More Students from the Top 1 Percent Than the Bottom 60," the *New York Times*, January 18, 2017. Information on Tulane's "VIP email" is in "Tulane University Gets Record 44,000 Applications This Year," by John Pope, the *Times-Picayune*, October 3, 2010. More information on Tulane's marketing tactics is in: "For Sale: SAT-Takers' Names. Colleges Buy Student Data and Boost Exclusivity," by Douglas Belkin, the *Wall Street Journal*, November 5, 2019. Details about Harvard-Westlake's Senior College Night were shared with me by parents who attended the event.

2. THE GUY

Quotes from Dan Larson, Bill Templeton, Arnie Bernstein, Mike Wolfe, Ross Benjoya, Marv Klebba, Paul Hensley, and Grant Scheiner are taken from interviews conducted by the author. Details about Singer's talk at the Hotel Bel-Air are from sources who attended, as well as the article "Holy Sh—t, He Was Telling Me He Could Rig It: Inside Admissions Scammer Rick Singer's Pitch to L.A.'s Elite Parents," by Nicole Sperling, *Vanity Fair–HWD*, March 14, 2019. Information about the event was also in Devin Sloane's sentencing memo (*United States of America v. Devin Sloane, case no. 19-CR-10117-IT*). Information on Brian Werdesheim and his connection to Singer is based on off-the-record interviews with sources as well as the articles "To Cheat and Lie in L.A.: How the College Admissions Scandal Ensnared the Richest Families in Southern California," by Evgenia Peretz, *Vanity Fair*, September 2019; and "Oppenheimer Financial Adviser Connected to College Admissions Cheating Scandal," by Jennifer Levitz and Melissa Korn, the *Wall Street Journal*, April 30, 2019. Details about Rick Singer's pitch to Devin Sloane are from Sloane's sentencing memo. Information about the Key's various projects is from a press release on Marketwire on April, 6, 2011. Information about Singer's childhood in Lincolnwood, Illinois, in the 1970s and Niles West High School is based on conversations with Arnie Bernstein, Mike Wolfe, Ross Benjoya, and other classmates. Anecdotes were also taken from the C13 Originals podcast *Gangster Capitalism: The College Admissions Scandal*, presented by Andrew Jenks. Information on the Skokie March was drawn from the documentary *Skokie: Invaded but Not Conquered*, produced by the Illinois Holocaust Museum. The deposition cited in which Singer discusses his educational background is *Dayo Adetu, et al. vs. Sidwell Friends School*, desposition transcript, October 14, 2016. Information on Singer's time at Trinity University is drawn from interviews with Hensley, Scheiner, and other classmates; *The Price of Admission: How American's Ruling Class Buys Its Way into Elite Colleges—And Who Gets Left Outside the Gates*, by Daniel Golden (2019 edition); and "Multi-Talented Singer Rises to Challenge, by Shannon Cameron, the *Trinitonian*, January 18, 1985.

3. BREAKING GLASS

Quotes from Bill Templeton, Margie Amott, Patricia Fels, Saddiq Abdul-Alim, John Meckfessel, Pete LeBlanc, John Rankin, Jeff Caraska, Ron McKenna, Kim Perry, Scott Kingston, Dorothy Missler, Mark Sklarow, Bill Rubin, Jill Newman, Gwen Meyer, Jen Kaifesh, Andy Lockwood, and Priscilla Sands are taken from interviews conducted by the author. Information on the early days of Future Stars is from interviews with sources familiar with the company as well as Daniel Golden's 2019 edition of *The Price of Admission*, which also discusses Singer's basketball coaching career in Sacramento. Details about Allison Singer are from Sacramento sources. Singer's quote about Future Stars appeared in "Counselor Helps Students Reach College," by Janet Motenko, the

Sacramento Bee, June 19, 1994. Singer's firing from Encina High School, and the verbal abuse of Corey Taylor, was reported in "Stepping over That Fine Line," by Pete LeBlanc, the *Sacramento Bee*, March 10, 1988. The article about Singer's coaching style is "Former Encina Hoops Coach Singer Finds Life in Rocklin," by Pete LeBlanc, the *Sacramento Bee*, December 15, 1988. Singer's fabrications about his college background appeared in "Double Duty Twice as Fun for Encina Coach," by Pete LeBlanc, the *Sacramento Bee*, January 21, 1988. Jeff Caraska's article, "Just Look Who's Undefeated in the CVC," appeared on January 17, 1988, in the *Auburn Journal*. The quote from Allen Koh appeared in "The Legitimate World of High-End College Admissions," by Douglas Belkin, the *Wall Street Journal*, March 13, 2019. Singer said he was better at coaching than running a business in the article "Thousands Turn to College-Prep Coach," by Kathy Robertson, *Sacramento Business Journal*, February 6, 2005.

4. TODDLER ADMISSIONS MANIA

Quotes from Michele Gathrid, Luisa Donati, Christina Simon, Anne Simon, Rita Cornyn, Betsy Brown Braun, Meredith Alexander, Julie Lythcott-Haims, and Sophie Robertson are taken from interviews conducted by the author. Insights into the culture of elite preschools in LA are based on conversations with dozens of former and current parents at the schools mentioned. Details about the Sunshine gala fundraiser are from an email sent to parents at the school that was shared with me. Sunshine did not respond to multiple emails and phone messages requesting an interview. Information about the legal dispute at Cassidy, as well as the cozy relationship between parents and the school's former director, was chronicled in "Inside the Cutthroat Rivalry Between Two of L.A.'s Elite Preschools," by Claire Martin, *Los Angeles* magazine, September 1, 2016. More details about Kinder Ready's program are included in "7 of Hollywood's Favorite Summer Camps," by Lindsay Weinberg, the *Hollywood Reporter*, August 4, 2018.

5. WELCOME TO THE GOLD COAST

Quotes from Jill Newman, Karl Grubaugh, Margie Amott, Patricia Fels, Luis Robles, Jon Reider, Steve Repsher, Brent Goldman, and Andy Lockwood are taken from interviews conducted by the author. Singer's stint as a youth basketball coach in Omaha, Nebraska, was reported in "The Mastermind Behind the College Admission Scandal Used to Be a Crazy Middle School Basketball Coach," by Jahd Khalil, *Deadspin*, May 16, 2019. His time in Nebraska was reported in a Business People announcement in the *Omaha World Herald* ("Stangle Takes Post at West") published on November 5, 2000. Singer's job at FirstRing was reported in "Uncle Sam, Come and Talk to 'Em," by Vipin V. Nair, the *Hindu BusinessLine*, March 21, 2002. The anecdote about Singer meeting a client on an airplane was reported in "Thousands Turn to College-Prep Coach," by Kathy Robertson, *Sacramento Business Journal*, February 6, 2005. The email exchanges prompted by Jon Reider regarding Rick Singer and his advisory board were shared with me. Singer's relationship with IMG Academy was reported in "A Core of the College Admissions Scandal Was Built at Elite Florida Sports Academy," by Jennifer Levitz, the *Wall Street Journal*, July 1, 2019. Singer's use of the term "master coach" is in *Dayo Adetu, et al. v. Sidwell Friends School*, desposition transcript, October 14, 2016. Singer's quote saying that "Harvard's asking for $45 million…" is from defendant John Wilson's supplemental motion to compel production of exculpatory evidence (*United States of America v. David Sidoo et al., case no. 1:19-cr-10080-NMG*). Singer's connection to PIMCO was reported in "Pimco's Ties to Architect of College-Admissions Scam Ran Deep," by Justin Baer, Melissa Korn, and Gregory Zuckerman, the *Wall Street Journal*, May 20, 2019. Details on Douglas Hodge's background and his dealings with Singer are from Hodge's sentencing memo (*United States of America v. Douglas Hodge, case no. 19-10080-NMG*), and the government's consolidated sentencing memo for Hodge (*United States of America v. Elizabeth Henriquez, Manuel Henriquez, Douglas Hodge and Michelle Janavs, case no. 19-10080-NMG*). Hodge's comments about Singer are from the op-ed "I Wish I'd Never Met Rick Singer," by Doug Hodge, the *Wall Street Journal*, February 9, 2020.

6. THE SPORTS CONNECTION

Quotes from Travis Dorsch, Matt Butler, Richard Odell, Greg Breunich, Casey Marx, and Fred Stroock are from interviews conducted by the author. Ryan Downes is featured in an IMG Academy promotional video available on YouTube ("IMG 7th Grader Obtains D1 Offers"). The description of the IMG campus and program are from IMG Academy promotional materials. The quote about Julie Riddell's society outings is from "The Social Detective" column in *Sarasota Magazine*, July 1, 2006. Background on Mark Riddell was taken from "Road Trip Home: Former Sailor Riddell Back in Area with Harvard Tennis Team," by Mic Huber, *Sarasota Herald-Tribune*, March 1, 2004, and interviews with former classmates from Sarasota High School. Singer splitting his fees is from "A Core of the College Admissions Scandal Was Built at Elite Florida Sports Academy," by Jennifer Levitz, the *Wall Street Journal*, July 1, 2019. Information about the petition that Georgetown's field hockey team started is from "Homefield Disadvantage: Why Hasn't Georgetown's Field Hockey Team Had a Winning Season in Over a Decade?," by Chris Castano, the *Georgetown Voice*, January 23, 2014; as well as a conversation with a former member of Georgetown's athletics staff. Information on Georgetown's tennis facilities is based on conversation with people with knowledge of the situation and "Break Point: The Murky Future of Tennis on Georgetown's Campus," by Chris Almeida and Joe Pollicino, the *Georgetown Voice*, October 8, 2015. The comment Gordon Ernst made ("Well, a coach has to eat.") is from "'Nope, You're Not Special.' How the College Scam Mastermind Recruited Families," by Jennifer Levitz and Melissa Korn, the *Wall Street Journal*, September 6, 2019. Singer's quote ("They want this thing done.") is from the affidavit in support of the Varsity Blues criminal complaint. Michelle Janavs's quote ("They're not stupid") is from the government's consolidated sentencing memo (*United States of America v. Elizabeth Henriquez, Manuel Henriquez, Douglas Hodge and Michelle Janavs, case no. 19-10080-NMG*). Information on the athletic vetting process at Georgetown is from Daniel Golden's most recent edition of *The Price of Admission*. Details about the 2013 recruitment of a nonplaying tennis player to UCLA's tennis team in 2013 are from the Student-Athlete Admissions Compliance Investigation Report by Director William H. Cormier, Administrative Policies & Compliance Office, UCLA, July 1, 2014.

7. THE FALL OF TROY

Quotes from Samantha Johnson, Mary Ellen Olcese, John Bransfield, Myron Dembo, and Tom Walsh are from interviews conducted by the author. Ali Khosroshahin's emails and the sequence of events describing how Douglas Hodge's daughter was presented to USC as an applicant, as well as the payments that Hodge made, are from the affidavit in support of the Varsity Blues criminal complaint. Janke as "the glue that keeps this program running" is from the 2013 USC Soccer Media Guide. Khosroshahin is described as "one of women's soccer's hottest coaches" in "Soccer: The Rookie vs. the Mentor," by Scott Reid, *Orange County Register*, February 21, 2008. Khosroshahin is quoted in "Unfamiliar Territory," by Nick Burton, *Daily Trojan*, November 9, 2011; and "Women of Troy Gearing Up for Title Run," by Nick Burton, *Daily Trojan*, August 14, 2011. The detail about Khosroshahin throwing away his USC gear was reported in *Unacceptable: Privilege, Deceit & the Making of the College Admissions Scandal*, by Melissa Korn and Jennifer Levitz, Porfolio/Penguin, 2020. Khosroshahin's and Janke's salary figures are taken from the government's consolidated sentencing memo against Hodge. Details about Toby MacFarlane's interactions with Singer are from MacFarlane's sentencing memo (*United States of America v. Toby MacFarlane, case no. 1:19-CR-10131 NMG*). USC as a symbol of "affluent mediocrity" and other information about the school's rise, including its fundraising efforts, are from "How USC Became the Most Scandal-Plagued Campus in America," by Jason McGahan, *Los Angeles* magazine, April 24, 2019. The interview with Pat Haden is a video on YouTube, "A Conversation on Athletics Fundraising with Al Checcio and Pat Haden," August 5, 2011. The emails between USC admissions and athletics staff are taken from Varsity Blues Defendant Robert Zangrillo's Response in Opposition to Nonparty University of Southern California's Motion to Quash (*United States of America v. David Sidoo, et al., case no. 19-10080*). Information about Heinel's Clear the Clearinghouse business is in "USC Athletic Administrator Arrested for Bribery 'Knew Her Stuff,'" by J. Brady McCollough, the *Los Angeles Times*, March 13, 2019; and "Indicted USC Administrator Involved Colleagues in Her Private Dealings," by Kaidi Yuan and Ashley Zhang, *LAist*, December 5, 2019. Information on Jovan Vavic's reign as a water polo coach is in "How a USC Water Polo Dynasty Doubled as a Perfect Entryway for the Admissions Bribery Scandal," by Tim Rohan, *Sports Illustrated*, March

20, 2019. Information on Wilson's son's application to USC is taken from the affidavit in support of the Varsity Blues criminal complaint. The quote from Stephen Larson ("It should not be any surprise...") appeared in "Admissions Scandal: Charged Parents Try to Drag USC into the Fray," by Joel Rubin and Matthew Ormseth, the *Los Angeles Times*, January 13, 2020. Singer's quotes ("Let's say, if it's USC...") are taken from the Government's Consolidated Response in Opposition to Defendants' Motion to Compel *(United States of America v. David Sidoo, et al, case no: 19-10080-NMG)*. The anecdotes about Pat Haden's interactions with Singer were reported in "How Rick Singer Tried to Rope in USC Legend Pat Haden amid Admissions Scandal," by Joel Rubin, the *Los Angeles Times*, August 30, 2019. (This article was used with the permission of the *Los Angeles Times*.)

8. BUCKLEY BLUES

Characterizations about the Buckley School are based on more than a dozen interviews with current and former students; parents; and former administrators. Buckley did not respond to interview requests. Names of students have been changed in order to protect them from possible repercussions from the school. Information about Adam Semprevivo and his father, Stephen Semprevivo, and the family's interactions (including emails) with Rick Singer are taken from Stephen Semprevivo's sentencing memo *(United States of America v. Stephen Semprevivo, case no. 1:19-CR-10117-IT-10)*. Forensic psychologist Richard Romanoff's psychological assessment is also included in the sentencing memo. Information about Devin Sloane and his interactions with Singer are taken from his sentencing memo *(United States of America v. Devin Sloane, case no. 19-CR-10117-IT)*. Matteo Sloane's comment that Singer "would kiss up to my dad" is from "Why Didn't You Believe in Me?: The Family Reckoning After the College Admissions Scandal," by Jennifer Levitz and Melissa Korn, the *Wall Street Journal*, January 17, 2020. Details about Brian Werdesheim and the Buckley board are from conversations with Buckley sources. The lunch between Werdesheim, Singer, and Valeria Balfour was reported in "The 'A List': Under Pressure from Parents to Deliver Students to Top Colleges, Elite Prep Schools in L.A. and Across the U.S. Are Brazenly Inflating Grades," by Max Kutner, *Los Angeles Magazine*, October 2020. That Qiuxue Yang introduced a Chinese family to Singer was reported in "Oppenheimer Financial Adviser Connected to College Admissions Cheating Scandal," by Jennifer Levitz and Melissa Korn, the *Wall Street Journal*, April 30, 2019. Exchanges between Sloane and Singer and Sloane's photographing his son in a pool are taken from the affidavit in support of the Varsity Blues criminal complaint. Details about Eliza Bass's college applications are based on conversations with a source close to the Bass family and a Buckley source, as well as the article "To Cheat and Lie in L.A.: How the College Admissions Scandal Ensnared the Richest Families in Southern California," by Evgenia Peretz, *Vanity Fair*, September 2019.

9. DON'T CHEAT

Quotes from Camilo Estrada are taken from an interview conducted by the author. Jane Buckingham's interactions with Singer are based on Buckingham's sentencing memo (*United States of America v. Jane Buckingham, case no. 1:119-CR-10117-IT*); the government's sentencing memo (*United States v. Jane Buckingham, case no. 19-10117-IT-3*); and sources close to Buckingham. The racial slur involving Brentwood School students was reported in "White Students Rapping a Racial Slur Stirs Posh Brentwood School," by Sonali Kohli, the *Los Angeles Times*, May 18, 2016. Buckingham's talk ("It's not their fault...") was reported in "Inside Jane Buckingham's Stunning Fall from Parenting Guru to Alleged College Admissions Cheater," by Gary Baum and Seth Abramovich, the *Hollywood Reporter*, March 19, 2019. Information about Felicity Huffman's interactions with Singer as well as information on Sophia Grace Macy and Georgia Macy are taken from Huffman's sentencing memo (*United States of America v. Felicity Huffman, criminal case no. 1:19-CR-10117-IT*); and the government's sentencing memo (*United States of America v. Felicity Huffman, case no. 19-10117-IT-6*). Background information on Huffman was taken from a video interview with Huffman by the Television Academy in 2016; as well as "Felicity Huffman: Desperate Housewife, Devoted Parent and Now a Defendant," by Cara Buckley and Adam Popescu, the *New York Times*, March 23, 2019.

10. NAILING A SCORE

Quotes from Dylan Gygax, Jen Kaifesh, Oren Boxer, Kathy Pelzer, and Gina Kornfeind are taken from interviews with the author. That Mark Riddell had entertained the idea of starting his own test prep company was reported in "College Admissions Scandal: Who's Mark Riddell, the Florida Man and 'Really Smart Guy' Who Took Tests for Kids?," by Susan Taylor Martin, *Tampa Bay Times*, May 31, 2019. Singer's quotes about Riddell being able to "bubble in all the answers" is from Singer's plea hearing on March 12, 2019 (*United States of America v. William Rick Singer, case no. 1:19-CR-10078-RWZ*); as is the quote: "Mark would get that score exactly." Details about Niki Williams, Igor Dvorskiy, David Sidoo, Manuel Henriquez, Elizabeth Henriquez, and Robert Flaxman are from the affidavit in support of the Varsity Blues criminal complaint. Singer's quotes to Gordon Caplan are also from the affidavit. The rise in 504 plans, as well as the rise in the number of requests for SAT accommodations, was reported in "Many More Students, Especially the Affluent, Get Extra Time to Take the SAT" by Douglas Belkin, Jennifer Levitz, and Melissa Korn, the *Wall Street Journal*, March 18, 2019. The quote from the ACT ("There are exceptions...") appeared in "Abuse of 'Extended Time' on SAT and ACT Outrages Learning Disability Community," by Nick Anderson, the *Washington Post*, March 29, 2019. The College Board's decision to stop making its own accommodations assessment is from the College Board press release, "College Board Simplifies Request Process for

Test Accommodations," which was published on December 5, 2016. The comparison between Pali and El Monte High Schools and the data regarding students' 504 plans was reported in "Why Students at LA's Richest Schools Are Far More Likely to Get Extra Time on the SAT," by Austin Peay and Sam Kmack, *LAist*, August 29, 2019.

11. MOSS BABY

Quotes from Gabby Johnson, Ross Johnson, Eric Webb, Montana Butsch, Abby Falik, and Bill Templeton are taken from interviews conducted by the author. The phone call between PJ Petrone and USC, as well as the meeting between Mossimo Giannulli and Petrone, is based on notes that Petrone took, detailing those interactions. They are included in the "Government's Response in Opposition to Dismiss Indictment..." Other details about Singer's interactions with the Giannullis are included in the "Government's Consolidated Response in Opposition to Defendants' Motions to Compel." Both are filed under the case *United States of America v. David Sidoo, et al., case no. 19-10080-NMG*. Information is also laid out in the affidavit in support of the Varsity Blues criminal complaint. Information on women's rowing numbers at colleges is available in the NCAA Sports Sponsorship and Participation Rates Report, by Erin Irick, October 2018. Loughlin's text ("a flag for the weasel to meddle") was stated at Loughlin and Giannulli's plea hearing on May 22, 2020, by federal prosecutor Eric S. Rosen. Information about the charges against Jovan Vavic and Donna Heinel are in the Superseding Indictment *United States of America v. Gordon Ernst, Donna Heinel, Mikaela Sanford, Niki Williams, William Ferguson, Jorge Salcedo and Jovan Vavic, case no. 19-10081-IT*. Information about Toby MacFarlane, Bruce and Davina Isackson, and Gamal Abdelaziz is from the affidavit in support of the Varsity Blues criminal complaint. Details about Sherry Guo's application to Yale is found in Rudy Meredith's plea hearing (*United States of America v. Rudolph "Rudy" Meredith, case no. 19-10075-MLW*) as well as in "In College Admissions Scandal, Families from China Paid the Most," by Melissa Korn and Jennifer Levitz, the *Wall Street Journal*, April 26, 2019; and "A Mystery Solved in the College Admissions Scandal: The Family Who Paid $1.2 Million," by Kate Taylor and Jennifer Medina, the *New York Times*, April 26, 2019. Singer's attempts to make inroads with Stanford coaches was revealed in a letter to the Stanford community by President Marc Tessier-Lavigne, "External Review of Athletic Admissions Reaches Conclusions, Recommends Reforms," published on December 3, 2019. Details about John Vandemoer are based on Vandemoer's sentencing memo (*United States of America v. John Vandemoer, case no. 1:19-CR-10079-RWZ*) and conversations with sources close to him. Singer's digital start-up project was first reported in "Rick Singer Had Grand Plans Beyond College Admissions. Then Scandal Brought Him Down," by Joel Rubin and Matthew Ormseth, the *Los Angeles Times*, April 29, 2019. Additional information and details are from interviews with Templeton and others involved in the companies.

12. BEANTOWN SHOWDOWN

Quotes from Adele Jackson-Gibson, Theryn Gibbons, Chigozie Offor, and Tenley Hardin are from interviews conducted by the author. The phone exchange between Rick Singer and Rudy Meredith is taken from "Defendant John Wilson's Supplemental Motion to Compel Production of Exculpatory Evidence" (*United States of America v. David Sidoo et al., case no. 1:19-CR-10080-NMG*). Meredith allegedly pressuring players to help him with grad school work was reported in "Meredith Allegedly Used Players to Write His Grad School Papers," by Bill Gallagher and Skakel McCooey, *Yale Daily News*, March 16, 2019. Meredith talking about recruiting slots appear in "With Expansion, Changes to Recruitment Policy Unclear," by Greg Cameron and Rachel Siegel, *Yale Daily News*, March 4, 2015. Conversations between Singer and Gordon Caplan, Agustin Huneeus Jr., and Bill McGlashan are from the affidavit in support of the Varsity Blues criminal complaint. Marci Palatella's text messages are included in the "Government's Response in Opposition to Defendants' Motion to Dismiss Indictment, or, in the Alternative, for Suppressing of Evidence and for Discovery and an Evidentiary Hearing" (*United States of America v. David Sidoo et al., case no. 19-10080-NMG*). Information on Morrie Tobin and "Kate" Tobin are based on interviews with sources as well as "The Bizarre Story of the L.A. Dad Who Exposed the College Admissions Scandal," by Joel Rubin, Matthew Ormseth, Suhauna Hussain, and Richard Winton, the *Los Angeles Times*, March 31, 2019; "To Cheat and Lie in L.A.: How the College Admissions Scandal Ensnared the Richest Families in Southern California," by Evgenia Peretz, *Vanity Fair*, September 2019. Tobin and Meredith's discussions about a bribe, both at Yale and in Boston, are documented in Meredith's plea hearing (*United States of America v. Rudolph "Rudy" Meredith, case no. 19-10075-MLW*). Details about Meredith's purchase of a vacation home and taking out a construction loan are in "At Yale, a Once Respected Soccer Coach Becomes an Enigma," by David W. Chen and Marc Tracy, the *New York Times*, March 15, 2019. The FBI's confrontation with Singer in Boston is detailed in the "Government's Sur-Reply in Opposition to Defendants' Motion to Dismiss Indictment..."; and Singer's iPhone notes are included in the "Government's Response in Opposition to Dismiss Indictment..." (*United States of America v. David Sidoo et al., case no. 19-10080-NMG*). Details about the FBI's raid on defendants' homes on the morning of March 12, 2019, are detailed in each defendant's sentencing memo.

About the Author

Nicole LaPorte is a senior writer for *Fast Company* magazine and the author of *The Men Who Would Be King: Movies, Moguls and a Company Called DreamWorks*. She previously wrote a column for the *New York Times* Sunday Business section and was a senior writer at *Newsweek*/the *Daily Beast*. She lives in Los Angeles.